THE SHAAR PRESS

THE JUDAICA IMPRINT
FOR THOUGHTFUL PEOPLE

Dear Rabbi, Dear Doctor
Volume 2

Rabbi Abraham J. Twerski, M.D.

*The renowned rabbi-psychiatrist
gives straight answers to tough questions*

A SHAAR PRESS PUBLICATION

Published by **SHAAR PRESS**
Distributed by MESORAH PUBLICATIONS, LTD.
4401 Second Avenue / Brooklyn, N.Y 11232 / (718) 921-9000 / www.artscroll.com

Distributed in Israel by SIFRIATI / A. GITLER
6 Hayarkon Street / Bnei Brak 51127

Distributed in Europe by LEHMANNS
Unit E, Viking Business Park, Rolling Mill Road / Jarrow, Tyne and Wear, NE32 3DP/ England

Distributed in Australia and New Zealand by GOLDS WORLD OF JUDAICA
3-13 William Street / Balaclava, Melbourne 3183 / Victoria Australia

Distributed in South Africa by KOLLEL BOOKSHOP
Ivy Common / 105 William Road / Norwood 2192, Johannesburg, South Africa

ISBN 10: 1-42260-545-0 / ISBN 13: 978-1-4226-0545-5 (h/c)
ISBN 10: 1-42260-548-5 / ISBN 13: 978- 1-4226-0548-6 (p/b)

Printed in the United States of America by Noble Book Press
Custom bound by Sefercraft, Inc. / 4401 Second Avenue / Brooklyn N.Y. 11232

Contents

PARENTS AND CHILDREN

ADDICTION

MIDDOS

INTERPERSONAL RELATIONSHIPS

ANXIETY

SHIDDUCHIM

SELF-ESTEEM

EMOTIONAL DISORDERS

FAMILY

PARENTS-IN-LAW

SHALOM BAYIS

INTRODUCTION

In our complex society, problems involving feelings and behavior are quite common. Problems that involve religious issues can be taken to a *rav* for a ruling. Problems that are of a psychological nature can be taken to a mental-health therapist for clarification and, it is hoped, for a solution.

Some problems straddle the fence, involving both religious and psychological issues. These may require the attention of both a *rav* and a therapist.

Several years ago, the *Hamodia* newspaper initiated a column to try to address some of these problems. The column is entitled "Seeking Solutions," because it would be naïve to assume that one could provide solutions to complex problems in the format of a newspaper column. However, some direction may be given to help people look in the right places for solutions. Many of the published queries and responses were assembled in a book, *Dear Rabbi, Dear Doctor*. Since publication of that book, many new queries have been received, and they are presented, with expanded responses, in *Dear Rabbi, Dear Doctor, Volume 2*.

Although I have *semichah* (rabbinic ordination), which authorizes me to rule on certain halachic issues, many questions are not specifically addressed by halachah, and require an approach based on Torah principles that can be found in the vast Torah literature, particularly in the works of *mussar* and *chassidus*. Proper application of these principles is often a challenge. They must be addressed with the truth of Torah, and as Rabbi Dessler points out in his classic essay on the "Perspective of Truth" (*Michtav M'Eliahu*, Vol. 1, pp. 52-69), truth is often elusive. Many factors may influence our thinking, so that we may think we have the truth, whereas we may actually be missing it.

This is why I often direct the reader to consult *daas Torah*, which I define as an authoritative *posek* whose thinking is not influenced by any principles other than Torah. *Daas Torah* must be taken literally; i.e., *daas* (wisdom and understanding) that emanates from a comprehensive knowledge of Torah, without the influence of ethical and behavioral concepts from sources other than Torah.

In seeking a solution, the first and most important point is to clarify the problem. This often suffices to enable one to arrive at a solution. However, as Albert Einstein said, "We can't solve problems by using the same kind of thinking we used when we created them." The responses to queries are generally geared toward helping a person look at the problem from a different perspective.

Many problems are not unique, yet people may think that they are the only ones who have ever encountered a particular issue. Many readers of *Hamodia* have reported that the column has been helpful to them, as they have been able to identify with the correspondent. Sometimes just the knowledge that one is not alone in dealing with a particular problem is helpful, and sometimes the response indicates a way to find a solution.

I am pleased that people found *Dear Rabbi, Dear Doctor* to be helpful. I hope that Volume 2 will similarly facilitate finding solutions to a variety of problems.

CHINUCH

LACK OF RECOGNITION LESSENS MOTIVATION

My 15-year-old son is B"H a fine yeshivah bachur. He is never late for minyan. He is a prince in middos, and a father's delight. He is a real masmid [diligent student]. However, the fact is that he is not as gifted as some of the other bachurim who are exceedingly bright.

The problem is that he sees that these very bright bachurim, who are excellent Torah scholars, get the recognition and admiration of the maggidei shiur, while he does not. He has mentioned this several times. I see signs that he may be losing some of his enthusiasm for Torah study. I am so afraid that he might lose interest and chas veshalom drift away. Let's face it — we all want recognition. What can I do to keep him enthused about learning Torah?

It is true that Torah knowledge has been (and should be) respected throughout the ages. We require Torah leadership, and our leaders must, therefore, be great Torah scholars. However, this does not mean that a person who is diligent in Torah study is any less worthy if he does not have the brilliance of a great Torah scholar.

The *berachah* we say every morning is *"la'asok bedivrei Torah."* Hashem commanded us to engage ourselves in Torah study. How much we end up knowing is not the standard by which we are judged. A student who learns only two hours a day and grasps what another student does in ten hours, but who does not use the other hours appropriately, may be guilty of *bittul Torah*, although he may "know" more than the diligent student.

The Chofetz Chaim pointed out that in the words we say when making a *siyum* we acknowledge that we receive reward for the study of Torah, whereas others do not receive reward for their work. He asks redtorically, "Are not other people rewarded for their work?" and he answers, "People are rewarded only for work that results in a product. If a tailor stitches for several days and his work does not result in a garment, he is not paid. Torah study is different. We are rewarded for the action, for the process of Torah study."

You should convey this information to your son and let him know how proud you are of him and how happy you are with his Torah study, and tell him that every minute he spends in Torah study is precious.

I'm sure that the *maggidei shiur* are aware of your son's *hasmadah*. You might alert them to your son's observation regarding recognition and admiration, so that they will direct more attention to him and others like him.

BEST FRIEND ENDS FRIENDSHIP

My 10-year-old daughter came home from school after the Pesach break, crying. Her best friend wants nothing to do with her, and has taken up with another girl instead. My daughter did nothing to provoke this. They parted as the best of friends before Pesach and she can't figure out what happened. She tried to ask her friend what went wrong, but the girl just said "Don't bother me," and walked away. I feel terrible for my child. What can I do to help her?

This is not unusual in children of that age, who can act capriciously. Although it was more than sixty years ago, I remember this happening then, and apparently things have not changed.

Some think it is a kind of "power-play," wherein kids want to show that they can make or break friendships as they wish.

You should tell your daughter that this occurred through no fault of hers, and that this is the way some children who do not know better may act. Although it hurts to lose a friendship, she should realize that it is due to the other girl's juvenile behavior, and your daughter should not be critical of herself. You can help her realize that eventually her former friend will probably jettison this new friend and go on to someone else or maybe even try to come back to her.

I would suggest to all our readers that we really have no way of knowing how our children behave toward the other children in school. It would devastate us to think that our child might be a bully. Yet bullying is very common, and most often, parents are totally unaware of their child's inappropriate behavior.

Young children may not understand that their actions may hurt someone, and it is important that we teach them proper *middos*, even at a young age. Sensitivity to others is not always an inborn trait, and needs to be cultivated. We can tell children stories about good *middos*. They may be able to understand that just as they do not want to be hurt by others, that they must be careful not to hurt or embarrass others in any way.

ABUSIVE REBBE

*I have a real dilemma. My sons attend a
chassidic cheder in the New York area.
Most of the rebbeim and the principals use
corporal punishment (potching) as a frequent
disciplinary tool. I very much disapprove,
as we rarely hit our children at home,
and if they do "need" an occasional potch
(slap), I believe that it is the parent's
job, not the teacher's, to administer it.
In any case, I've never made much of a fuss
about it, because if I choose to send my
children to this mosad, I realize that I
have to put up with their policies.*

*However, the rebbe who is scheduled to
teach my 7½-year-old son next year goes far
beyond the occasional potch. He is very
moody; the boys never know what to expect
from him, and he has been observed to use
real violence at times. He has also been
verbally and emotionally abusive. I have two
children who went through his class already.
They both say that was their worst year of
cheder. When my second boy came home with
stories of what he was experiencing in this
rebbe's class, my first son opened up and
began telling us of his experiences that he
had never mentioned before.*

*My third son, who is about to enter this
rebbe's class, is very sensitive. He also
has slight delays in language processing,
which make it difficult for him to follow
directions, and even more difficult to
express himself verbally. Despite this, he
has a good head, ka"h, and has always been
at the top of his class academically, B"H.*

*I am very worried about putting him into
this rebbe's class. I have the option of*

switching chadarim, but the two grades following in this cheder have excellent rebbeim, much better than in the second cheder we are considering, and I don't like the idea of bouncing a child from one school to the next.

We did try to speak to the hanhalah about this rebbe, but found them totally unresponsive. We also tried to get the parents together, but not enough parents were willing to become involved. As things stand now, unless we switch this child to another cheder, he will spend a year with a rebbe who is physically and verbally abusive.

Which is the better of the two options, in your opinion?

The problem you have mentioned is not as rare as we would hope.

Child abuse is unfortunately not an uncommon problem. The instances of child abuse by parents exceeds that of episodes in school, and few effective measures have been taken about the problem. In the past, when emergency rooms have reported cases of parental child abuse to the authorities, not much was resolved.

The problem of abuse, whether it is spousal abuse, child abuse, or elder abuse, is always the result of poor management of relationships. The Satmar Rebbe, *z"l*, said, "If a *shochet* had allowed an improperly *shechted* chicken to be sold in the market, there would be an uproar and the *shochet* would be dismissed. *Neveilah* is indeed a terrible *issur*, but for that there can be *teshuvah*. But if a teacher humiliates or abuses a child, leaving an emotional scar that may remain with him for life, for that there is no *teshuvah*. We would never accept a *shochet* unless he had certification that he underwent adequate training. Why do we allow teachers to interact with our children if they have not been trained in teaching methods and how to manage a class? Isn't a Jewish child as important as a chicken?"

These are holy words from a holy person. They should also be extrapolated to spouses and parents. Not everyone is a natural-born husband, wife, or parent. Years ago, life in the shtetl was far less turbulent, complicated, and stressful than life is today. Young people should be educated in preparation for marriage and parenting far more extensively than with *kallah* and *choson* classes that deal mainly with halachos.

This is, of course, true for teachers as well. Fortunately, there are courses for teachers. I recently visited a class where chassidic young men were being trained by experts to be *melamdim* and *mechanchim*. Untrained teachers may have a negative impact on children.

In your case, the most advisable step is to transfer your child to another school.

If meeting with the *hanhalah* was not productive, perhaps a number of parents could get together to meet with the Rebbe of the chassidic *kehillah* to express their concern. We should realize that if we know that children are being harmed and we do not do whatever is within our means to prevent it, we are in violation of *lo taamod al dam re'achah* (do not stand idly by while your brother's blood is being shed).

TEENAGE SON DRIFTING AWAY FROM FAMILY VALUES

The oldest of my seven children is a boy, 15. He was never really a difficult child, but did require discipline. He is an average student in the yeshivah, not one of their "bright stars." Recently, he has been taking some liberties with Yiddishkeit, by which I mean the level of Yiddishkeit in our family. He cut off his long peyos. His beard is not growing in yet, so shaving hasn't become an issue. Instead of a traditional black yarmulke, he wears one of those small ones. I see him drifting away from Yiddishkeit.

This is something which you should discuss with *daas Torah*. I can only give you an opinion.

The Baal Shem Tov was asked the same question by someone whose son seemed to be slipping from Yiddishkeit, and he said, "Give him even more love. He needs it most."

Rabbi Meir of Premishlan said that his rebbe, Rabbi Chaim of Chernovitz (Be'er Mayim Chaim) had a son who was not behaving properly. He showed him much love and said, "*Ribbono shel Olam!* I am giving much love to my child even though he is misbehaving. You are an even more merciful Father, so You should show love to Your children even if they are misbehaving."

A study of young people who have gone off-the-*derech* indicated that many of them felt that they were not being loved and respected, either at home or in the yeshivah, or both. Because they felt rejected in their immediate circle, the expressed their anger at Yiddishkeit and started to reach out to a different group where they felt they would be accepted.

If you take a very firm stand, you may reinforce your son's feelings that he is not being loved unconditionally, because he will feel that he will be accepted only if he complies with certain standards. I think this is why the Baal Shem Tov said to show him even more love.

Nevertheless, your concern that he may set a bad example for his younger siblings cannot be ignored. However, they may see your very firm stand as meaning that they, too, may be rejected if they deviate from the family tradition.

The situation may be best handled by being open with everyone, telling this son something like, "You know that we love you and will always love you. However, I don't approve of what you're doing, and I think it is wrong. I think it is my duty to let your brothers and sisters know how I feel about this."

You then should meet with the other children and say, "You know that as much as I love him, I disapprove of your brother's behavior. I believe that Yiddishkeit is the right thing, and that he must have an emotional reason for doing this. If he were physically sick, we would still love him very much. We would love him, not his sickness. Drifting away from the Yiddishkeit that we observe is no different. We love *him*, not what he is doing. He should feel that although we disapprove of what he is doing, we love him and we want him to belong with us."

It is important to try to understand how he feels about himself in the yeshivah. Some students may feel that if they do not excel in learning, they are not valued. He should know that the mitzvah is to *learn* Torah. A student who learns diligently but does not excel has as great and perhaps even a greater mitzvah than one who is very bright and absorbs learning quickly, but who, although he may know more, is less diligent. The mitzvah is in the effort.

Every child has positive traits. You should look for these and commend him for the good things he does.

Your son should know that you are discussing this with the siblings, rather than just ignoring him and pretending that nothing is happening.

This is not a one-time thing. The love for him and the message to the siblings needs to be reinforced. It is to be hoped that this will prevent his breaking away.

It is extremely painful for parents when a child seems to reject the level of Yiddishkeit they hold so dear. The parents often see this as an affront to their value system and take their child's behavior personally. It is important for you to ascertain just what your son's behavior is trying to tell you. Is he still a firm believer in Hashem and His Torah but merely wants to serve Him in a slightly different manner or are his actions indicative of a firm disassociation from all the values you cherish? Although the answer is the same — love him, love him, love him — if he is not openly rebellious to the essence of Torah it may be in your best interests to go easy on him — he may just be flexing his wings, trying to determine if he can make his own decisions, and in truth is not rebelling at all. If it is only the outward manifestation of Yiddishkeit that he has changed and he is keeping all the mitzvos, it may be best to allow him to experiment — as long as he does not really go "off-the-*derech*."

As I said at the outset, you should discuss this with *daas Torah*, specifically with someone who has had experience in *chinuch*.

HUSBAND'S SLOVENLINESS IS AFFECTING CHILDREN

I have an issue that I am hoping you can address in your column. I have learned so much from your responses. I know that to be a successful parent, one needs tremendous Siyatta Dishmaya and that parents must speak with one voice. My spouse is the most wonderful husband and parent. However, the one area my spouse struggles with is tidiness of belongings. He does not put away his hat, jacket, and briefcase when he comes home. He does not clear away his dishes after he eats and does not keep our room neat. We have spoken of this issue often and I have followed through on his requests that everything have its place. However, he admits that he just can't change. I have accepted this behavior on his part because we all have our weaknesses. The problem is with our children. My husband does not enforce the rules of the house and our children therefore are following in his ways, despite years of clear expectations and incentives on my part. What do you suggest?

Orderliness and neatness are important *middos*, and if indeed, your children are not learning them because your husband is not orderly and neat, then this constitutes a lack of proper *chinuch*. *Chinuch* means "training," and it is the parents' role to train children so that they are prepared for successful lives as adults. If your children do not learn orderliness and neatness, that will be a drawback when they grow up, and that is not fair to them. Children cannot learn many things on their own, and it is the parents' obligation to teach them. As we know, teaching is best done by example.

You must take every precaution not to criticize your husband in the children's presence. Although overcoming a habit may be difficult and require much effort, your husband must make that effort for the children's sake. I suggest that you sit down quietly with your husband and reiterate how the priority in your home is proper *chinuch* of the children. You hear what he is saying and you know it is hard to change and you would like to know how you can help him to improve in regard to this *middah*. By speaking softly but firmly, you will impress upon your husband the seriousness of the problem and together you can brainstorm to come up with a solution. As you stated, he is the most wonderful husband and parent, and he will surely do everything he can to ensure the proper *chinuch* for the children.

SMALL CHILD *DAVENING* WITHOUT ENTHUSIASM

My 5-year-old used to love davening. When I bought him his own siddur, he was thrilled and spent many hours reading from it. The first few Shabbosim he did not have to be reminded to daven and did it with much enthusiasm. Lately, however, it seems as if his excitement and "cheshek" have died down I have to remind him again and again to daven and when he does, it is without the feeling he once had. This week I told him an emotional story about a king and a servant as a "moshol" [parable] and he seemed very touched by it. But when it came time to daven, there was no change at all. Do you have any ideas on how I could get him to enjoy davening once again?

I f I had the formula for enjoying *davening*, I would recommend it to many adults. Let's face it. We dutifully *daven*, but many of us would be less than truthful if we claimed to enjoy *davening*. In many morning *minyanim*, the *davening* is very hurried, with people hastening leave for work. If *davening* were really enjoyed, it would take longer than 28 minutes!

Your son's initial enthusiasm was probably because *davening* was a novelty to him, and all novelties eventually wear off. The most effective way to train a child to enjoy *davening* is for him to see that the grown-ups enjoy *davening*. First and foremost, you must bear in mind that your child is only 5 years old and that a 5-year-old can have little or no understanding of the meaning of the words he is mindlessly mouthing. Do not turn *davening* in a burden. As he gets older, he will learn the meaning of his *tefillos* and this will help.

It is important not to nag him about *davening*, because nagging tends to produce resistance. Be lavish with your praise when you see him *daven* — even if his *davening* is without much enthusiasm — and curtail your admonishments when he does not. Telling inspiring stories about *tefillah* can help. It is also helpful to relate some comments by the *gedolim* on *tefillah*, especially at the Shabbos table. All of us can benefit from stories of the effectiveness of sincere prayer and of how much Hashem loves the *davening* of young children.

MUST A PRINCIPAL ALWAYS BACK HIS TEACHERS?

A principal of a yeshivah said, "I must support the authority of my teachers under all circumstances. Even if the teacher is wrong, I must support him, because otherwise I will be undermining his authority."

What kind of chinuch can it be if wrong is considered right? Where is mishpat tzedek?

Your point is well taken. The principles that apply to *beis din* apply to individuals as well. "Do not pervert a judgment .... I shall not exonerate the wicked" (*Shemos*, 23:6-7). Just as a *beis din* is not permitted, under any circumstances, to say that a wrong is right, neither is an individual.

We can understand the concern of a principal to preserve the authority of a teacher. Inasmuch as I am not an educator, I cannot suggest just how this should be handled. I'm sure that other principals can suggest how this situation can be handled to avoid perverting justice yet maintaining the teacher's authority.

When I served as the medical director of a hospital with a large staff, there were some complaints about the actions of various staff members. If the investigation of an incident revealed that the complaint was legitimate and that the staff member was wrong, I would discuss this with the staff member and tell him that he must admit to the complainant that he was in error. He may be able to explain the circumstances that caused him to be in error. Although this confrontation was not pleasant, the staff member invariably felt good about it after meeting with the complainant.

In the twenty years that I served as medical director, there was not a single suit of malpractice. People understand that doctors, nurses, and other health providers are human and can make mistakes. It is when we try to cover up a mistake that we get into trouble. The only president of the United States who had to resign was the one who tried to cover up a wrong.

Parents have asked, "Should we ever apologize to a child? Won't this undermine our authority as parents?" My answer is, "If you do not own up to a mistake and apologize, how is the child supposed to learn to admit he or she was in error and to apologize?"

Harav Chaim Shmuelevitz cites the incident in which Aharon Hakohen questioned a directive issued by Moshe *Rabbeinu*. Moshe admitted that Aharon was right, and that he was in error. Moshe said, "You are right. Hashem's instructions were indeed as you said, but I forgot" (*Vayikra*, 10:19-20, *Midrash*).

Harav Shmuelevitz says that Moshe *Rabbeinu* had to consider the possibility that if he admitted that he was mistaken and had forgotten what Hashem said, he was putting the authority of the Torah in jeopardy for eternity, because if Moshe was in error in this incident, perhaps he was in error at other times, too. Moshe was the sole conduit of Hashem's word to us. How could he allow it to be thought that he could be in error?

Harav Shmuelevitz says that Moshe *Rabbeinu* decided, "My obligation is to be truthful. What will happen with the Torah throughout eternity is Hashem's responsibility, not mine."

In the end, Moshe's admission that he was in error did not undermine the authority of Torah nor his own authority.

It is most likely that a conflict in opinion or approach between a teacher and a parent will be resolved to the satisfaction of both if it is not blown out of proportion and does not become grist for the gossip mills. Any problem should be discussed with the teacher in a non-confrontational manner ("I would like to ask your advice on how we can help Chaim overcome his problem"). If the parents feel that the teacher is not receptive to their overtures of working together, they should then approach the principal, again in an unbelligerent manner ("I am sure the teacher has Chaim's best interests at heart, but we don't seem to be on the same wavelength. Perhaps you can see a way that we can resolve this. Chaim's success is obviously a top priority to all of us, so we are coming to you for help in this matter"). This gives everyone leeway to express their honest opinions without feeling defensive or disrespected. As long as the problem does not erupt into a public campaign involving the entire parent body, the chances of success are high.

I believe that being truthful will not undermine a teacher's authority. As for the exact way it should be handled, perhaps experienced principals and experts in *chinuch* can offer suggestions.

NEEDY STUDY PARTNER

I am a 19-year-old bachur in beis midrash. Several months ago, the Rosh Yeshivah asked me to learn an hour a day with a 15-year-old boy who was "shvach" in learning. I was glad to do so. The hour gradually extended, because he is very needy, and we now study together nearly two hours each day.

The extended learning does not pose a problem, but the boy is clinging to me beyond our learning time. He comes over to me at any time to ask something. I can see that some of his questions are not real, but he is using them simply to get close to me. This is an intrusion on my time. I also don't think it is good for him to become so dependent on me. But I don't know how to tell him this without hurting him. What should I do?

The first thing is to discuss it with the *Rosh Yeshivah*. He has probably seen instances similar to this and can advise you what to do.

I defer to your *Rosh Yeshivah's* advice. My approach would be to be gently frank with the boy. Tell him that you enjoy learning with him and that you wish to continue this, but that he must understand that you must have time for yourself and cannot be interrupted or distracted. Any questions he has for you should be saved until the allotted time that you learn together.

You should set an appropriate limit on the time you spend with him. If you don't, his neediness may result in his taking progressively more time from you to the point that you will have to put a stop to it. At that time his dependence on you may have increased and your attempt to contain it will be harder for him to take.

Do discuss with the *Rosh Yeshivah* what limits to set. It is important for him to be aware of this boy's needs.

HEALTH

PASSIONATE PLEA — MAKE SMOKING AN *AVEIRAH*

I realize I may be out of order, but I am in such great anguish.

A year ago my husband, a fine talmid chacham, was operated on for lung cancer cased by cigarette smoking. Recently it recurred, and the doctors are not giving him much time. Only a miracle can save him, and I pray for him every day at the Kotel.

I had pleaded with him for years to stop smoking, but to no avail. Now, unless Hashem grants us a miracle, I must face the bitter reality that I will be left with nine children to care for, without a source of parnassah.

What do I have to look forward to? A full-page ad signed by the gedolim, "Rachmanim bnei rachmanim. Come to the rescue of the widow of a talmid chacham and his nine yesomim, whose father died an untimely death"? Am I to send out letters soliciting help? Why should they expect others to be rachmanim on nine yesomim when their father was not a rachman on them? If he didn't have enough rachmonus on them to give up smoking, why should strangers care? I love my husband dearly, but as much as I love him, that's how angry I am at him for what he did to us.

The gedolim who will sign the appeal for me — why didn't they use their authority to make him stop smoking? What could they have done? They could have said, "Because you are committing the terrible sin of suicide and leaving your family destitute, you will not have an aliyah, you will not be permitted to daven for the amud, you will not get a hakafah, and you will be pasul as a witness unless you stop smoking." I think he would have listened. They might even say that anyone who dies from a self-inflicted disease will be treated according to the halachah of suicide.

I appeal to the gedolim. You be the rachmanim. You can prevent women from becoming widows and children from becoming yesomim. Your signing an urgent appeal for me and my children will be too little and too late. I need a husband and my children need a father.

To other wives whose husbands are smoking, don't just sit there. You have a responsibility to protect your children. Protest to your rabbonim that they should do everything in their power to prevent such tragedies, and they should know that if they are lax in doing so they must share the responsibility for the tragedy that befalls wives and children.

cannot add anything to your poignant letter. We have previously published letters about the disaster of smoking. I hope that your expression of anguish will motivate people to eliminate this lethal habit, but I must remind you that smoking is addictive. Addictions are extremely difficult to break. It is entirely possible that had your husband been shunned publicly, it would have had little or no effect, so strong is the grip of this killer addiction. The most we can do is hope and pray is that this heartfelt plea will discourage others from ever tasting the first cigarette.

MOTHER REFUSES HEARING-AID FOR SON

Two of my sister-in-law's children, a girl, 9, and a boy, 7, have hearing impairments.

The girl wears a hearing aid and hears well, but my sister-in-law refuses to get a hearing aid for the boy. I have talked to him and he doesn't hear at all. He is having trouble in school because he can't hear. She says that she agreed to obtain a hearing-aid for her daughter since her hair can cover the device, but she finds that with her son it would be visible and he would be thought of as being "different." Also, when he gets older, his deafness will spoil his chances for a good shidduch. How can I make her see that this is a mistake?

This is about as distorted as reasoning can get. His inability to hear will be a far greater obstacle to socialization than wearing a hearing aid will be and his education is in jeopardy. If, because of poor hearing, he will miss out on his learning, that will be a great drawback to a *shidduch*, in addition to the more obvious problems that will arise.

Parents have a great responsibility to see that their children are given the best possible chance to be successful. This requires careful attention to their health and to anything that may be a hindrance to their development.

You did not indicate whether your sister-in-law is a single mother. If the child's father is in the picture, he should be made aware of the mistake in denying the child the ability to hear well. Perhaps the rabbi, the pediatrician, and the school principal together can help your sister-in-law correct her thinking about this.

Thankfully, there are many fine organizations that are available to offer help, counseling, and even hearing aids to assist hearing-impaired individuals achieve their highest potential. No child should be made to suffer unnecessarily when help is available. The Appendix has a list of agencies that may be helpful.

ONE MUST CARE FOR HIS HEALTH

My husband is 50, and I have been urging him to undergo the various examinations that can detect early heart disease or cancer, but he refuses. He says that he has bitachon that he will be healthy. I'm worried, because we have had friends who have died from diseases that could have been cured if they had been detected earlier. Is there any way I can convince him?

Health issues are not a matter of *bitachon* alone. A person is required by halachah to do everything reasonable to treat an illness, and by the same token, to preserve one's health in every way possible. Inasmuch as there are noninvasive tests to detect cancer in its early stages, it is probably a halachic requirement to do so. Your husband should check this with a *posek*.

The Torah requirement to protect one's health should control much of our behavior. *Poskim* have now declared an unequivocal *issur* on smoking. Inasmuch as excessive weight contributes materially to high blood pressure, heart disease and diabetes, it is really a mitzvah to maintain a healthy weight. Inasmuch as judicious exercise is recommended by most health experts, this, too, is a mitzvah.

There is a story about the Tzaddik of Sanz, who, in his later years, wanted to use a large amount of *marror* at the Pesach Seder. His children tried to discourage him, because it was dangerous to his health, but to no avail. It is related that he took the *marror*, began making the *berachah*, paused and ended the *berachah* with "*vtzivanu ... ushmartem meod l'nafshosechem.*" (I cannot vouch for the authenticity of this story, but the principle is valid. Preserving one's health *is* a mitzvah.)

CHILDHOOD OBESITY

My 10-year-old son is chubby, about 20 pounds above normal weight for his age and height. My mother says I shouldn't worry, because his weight will normalize as he grows. Is this correct? I hear so much about obesity that I'm concerned.

Although I respect the advice of the older generation, I don't think it is wise to assume that his weight will normalize. Many children who are overweight carry this over into adolescence and adulthood, and the longer the overweight persists, the more difficult it is to control. In just two decades, the prevalence of overweight in children ages 6-11 has doubled, and tripled for teen-agers! Obesity can lead to many health complications.

While there may be genetic and hormonal causes in some cases, most excess weight in kids is due to eating too much and exercising too little. In addition to physical complications such as diabetes and high blood pressure, overweight children are often teased or bullied, with resultant loss of self-esteem. They may have poor social skills, and their anxiety may impair their scholastic performance. All these factors may contribute to childhood depression.

To prevent obesity, the entire family should adopt a healthy diet and raise their activity level. If the parents set a good example, the children are more likely to follow. Discourage, by example, high-calorie fast-foods. If parents calm their nerves by nibbling, children may do likewise. Food should be eaten for nutrition only, not used as a tranquilizer.

Encourage exercise and activity, and keep fresh fruit available as a snack. Never use sweets as a reward or bribe. To build their self-esteem, look for opportunities to praise your children for their efforts, and help them focus on positive goals, such exercising for 20 minutes without becoming tired.

However, be careful to ensure that your child does not interpret your concern negatively and suffers low self-esteem because of his weight. You must also be alert to inappropriate extremes in the oppo-site direction. Some children become so obsessed with losing weight that they become anorexic or bulimic.

Consult your pediatrician. The risks of obesity are too great to rely on the hope that the child will outgrow it.

RISKS POSED BY NECESSARY MEDICATION

We need guidance. We have been married for six happy years. Our only problem is that we have no children. My wife has a medical condition that has been brought

under control with a new medication, and
she must stay on this medication. The doctor
says that there is not enough experience
with this medication to know if it is
safe during gestation. He says that there
are medications similar to this that pose
minimal risks for the baby.

The doctor said that she can be
monitored if she becomes pregnant. How
can we decide whether the minimal risk is
worth taking?

I cannot think of a question that is more serious than this. The responsibility of exposing a fetus to a "minimal risk" is awesome. When a child is born with a defect, everything possible is done to give him/her the best opportunity to lead a normal life. However, to deliberately bring a child into the world with a defect that may be lifelong and of unknown severity is assuming an awesome responsibility.

In halachah, there is indeed a principle of "going according to the *rov*," which means that when in doubt, one may rely on a majority percentage. Thus, a 1% incidence may be overlooked. This is not the case where health is concerned. We know that one may violate Shabbos in the event of *pikuach nefesh*, where there is a life-threatening situation. If there is only 1% chance of danger to life, one may violate Shabbos, even though there is 99% likelihood that it is not a life-threatening situation. If statistics state that there is only a small possibility of a birth defect, one still must ask for a ruling by a *posek*.

The doctor said that she can be monitored; this statement must be clarified. He may mean that if tests show that there are abnormalities, the pregnancy can be terminated. He may not be aware that for Torah-observant people this may not be an option.

You should gather as much information as possible about the nature of the risk, then consult a *gadol* for a ruling. When you follow halachah, you will be doing the right thing.

RETIREMENT WOES

I am not an observant Jew, but I happened to pick up Hamodia while waiting in the beauty parlor and I was impressed by your column. Perhaps you can help me.

My husband is 52 and was a successful businessman. He lived for his business and worked at it 24/7/365. Almost two years ago, he suffered a massive heart attack, and after a month, the doctor allowed him to go to the office only two hours a day, three times a week. This drove him crazy. He received an attractive offer from someone who wanted to buy his business, which he sold at a good profit. He decided to sell our large home, and we bought a condo in Florida, to which we moved.

This did not work out well. All the other people in our complex are in their 70's and 80's, and he has little in common with them. At home, we would visit our children and friends and that was at least some distraction. Here we have nothing. I do some gardening and have joined the sisterhood of a nearby synagogue, but my husband has no outlets. He is not a golfer. He cannot watch television and sit by the computer 16 hours a day. He is way too young for "senior citizen's" activities.

What can you suggest for us?

You might begin by consulting your local rabbi, who may be able to get your husband interested in some Judaica studies courses. The rabbi might also introduce him to other people in the community who are in his age bracket, and with whom he may have things in common.

Some retired business people have put their "know-how" to work as consultants, especially to younger people starting off in business who would benefit from your husband's experience. Since this would not put any responsibility on him, it would not constitute a stress on his heart. Your rabbi might be able to direct him, or you may call your local Chamber of Commerce for leads. He might volunteer his time to a charitable organization that could benefit from his business acumen.

I would like to take this opportunity to point out the advantage enjoyed by people who observe Shabbos properly. Not only do they not work on Saturday, but they also do not go shopping, take trips, or watch television. In fact, they do not even think about business. In addition to being an extraordinary mitzvah, observing Shabbos forces a person to learn how to relax without resorting to *chillul Shabbos.*

Let's hope we will all reach an age at which we will not be actively engaged in work. Shabbos helps us prepare for this, to make this phase of our lives enjoyable.

SHOULD FAMILY PSYCHIATRIC PROBLEMS IMPACT *SHIDDUCHIM?*

What are the facts about inheriting psychiatric problems, and how much weight should be given to the presence of a psychiatric condition in the family of a man or woman when considering a shidduch?

In many instances, what is transmitted genetically is the degree of vulnerability to a psychiatric condition. A person with high vulnerability may develop the condition with less external stress, whereas a person with low vulnerability may not develop a problem unless there is great stress.

In any case, what one should do is to try and get accurate information. Just what was the nature of the psychiatric problem? Who had it — a parent, sibling, or other relative? Was there more than one instance of this problem in the family? When one has all the information, one should submit it to an expert in genetics for an opinion on its significance as far as the young man or woman is concerned. When one has this information, one should then present it to *daas Torah* for an opinion as to whether this should affect the decision on the particular *shidduch*.

If all the qualifications of the young man or woman are favorable, I personally, would hesitate to discourage a *shidduch* because of the incidence of a psychiatric problem in a family member. The reason for this is because there is wide prevalence of conditions such as depression, OCD, or panic disorder, and it is not easy to find a family that is absolutely free of any such problem. Most of these cases are not made public, so that no one knows that there is or was such a case within the family.

One father of a young woman who was *redt* a *shidduch* with an outstanding young man consulted me because it was discovered that the young man's mother had once been treated for depression. I gave him the guidelines suggested above, and then I told him why I did not think this should be an obstacle, because his choice was whether to do a *shidduch* with a family where there was a known case, or with a family where the case was covered up, and that it is difficult to find a family that is absolutely free of a problem.

The man said, "That's not true! I know that in our family there has never been a case of psychiatric illness." Because I am bound by strict doctor-patient confidentiality, I could not tell him, "I treated your wife for a rather severe psychiatric condition when she was seventeen!"

DROWSINESS AND LOW BLOOD SUGAR

I'm in the third year of high school and I have a problem. Every morning in class, between 9:30 and 10, I can't keep my eyes open. The girls who sit near me poke me to keep me awake, and I was embarrassed when the teacher scolded me for sleeping in class. It's not that the subject is boring, because I am interested in it. It sometimes happens in the afternoon too, but not as regularly. I get a good night's sleep. I don't know what's wrong. Do you have any suggestions?

This sounds like a classic case of low blood sugar (hypoglycemia).

The sugar we ingest (or foods we eat that are converted to glucose) is metabolized by insulin, a hormone produced by the pancreas. As you know, a deficiency of insulin results in high blood sugar, but the reverse is also possible.

The body has a delicate regulatory system, so that when there is glucose in the blood, the pancreas puts out just enough insulin to metabolize the glucose, keeping the blood sugar at a steady level, between 70-110 mgm %. (This may vary slightly with different laboratories). If the regulatory mechanism is just a bit off, the pancreas may produce a little more insulin than is necessary for the amount of glucose in the blood, so that more of the glucose is metabolized, causing the blood-sugar level to drop below normal. When this happens, the brain does not have enough glucose, resulting in drowsiness. A drink of orange juice may correct this, but you can't drink orange juice in class (unless the teacher approves).

Not all doctors ascribe to this, but I am a believer. There is a test that can indicate if the insulin regulation is accurate. It is a "5-hour glucose tolerance" test. You take a fasting blood sample in the morning to establish what your fasting level is. Then you drink a heavily sugared drink, and have a blood sample taken once every hour for five hours. Normally, there is a rise in the blood's glucose level, which gradually returns to normal and may even dip slightly below the fasting level. If any of the samples in the five hours shows a drop of more than 10 mgm % below the fasting level, this may indicate hypoglycemia. If it drops more than 20 mgm %, it confirms the condition.

But you don't have to take a blood test. A simple test is to go on a hypoglycemic diet, which usually solves the problem. You may consult a dietitian, or read the book by Carlton Fredericks, *The New Low Blood Sugar and You*. It is not a difficult diet to follow.

If this does not solve the problem, you should consult your physician about being tested.

HASHKAFAH

IS IT POSSIBLE TO FORGIVE AND FORGET?

We would greatly appreciate your advice on this matter. Although we thought about it, trying to resolve the issue before Rosh Hashanah – Yom Kippur, at the time of year when we ask forgiveness from each other, this is still as relevant and disturbing as it was at that time.

When someone hurts another with words, money, or other hurtful actions:

1. Are we obligated to "forgive and forget" just because someone asks forgiveness before Rosh Hashanah without real regret?

2. Is it possible to truly forgive if the hurt feelings are still felt, especially if the hurt caused further aggravation?

3. I was told that we are obligated to forgive anyone who hurts us, whether or not they ask forgiveness. A. Is this halachah? B. Is this possible?

4. An acquaintance of ours who had spoken lashon hara about us (although we overlooked it and are still quite friendly) will phone before Rosh Hashanah (as they've done other years) or another time during the year to ask forgiveness, saying "If I said or did something that hurt …" They know what they said, so we wonder, what is the best answer to this?

5. Before saying the bedtime "Krias Shema" and also on Yom Kippur (tefillas zaka) we say that we forgive anyone who hurt us. Are we to say it if it's not 100% true — if someone knowingly stole money or hurt us in some other way?

6. A while ago, I was told of someone (who is well-known and held in high esteem in the community) who said some very hurtful untruths about my family. We were melamed zechus on them, thinking that if that person really said those words, they would obviously have been regretted later. However, a while later, I met the one who said it and in the course of conversation, I mentioned that I could not understand how this person could have said such a thing. This was an opportunity for the person to ask mechillah (forgiveness) and to explain. Instead, the person only confirmed what had been said, not expressing charatah (regret), saying, "Yes, I said it and I'll say it again." The person then went on to repeat what was said earlier.

A. What is the halachah about forgiving this?

B. Is it possible to truly "forgive and forget"?

We've been told that not to forgive brings to sinas chinam, unwarranted hatred. We say that we feel hurt, not hatred.

As much as I've tried, I find it difficult to forget those words. Is it possible to forget things that we want to forget? I've been told not to be so sensitive, not to take things so to heart. My reply to that is that I might be sensitive personally but am also sensitive to others' feelings and try not to hurt others.

These are all straight halachah *sh'eilos*, and I do not give decisions on these. However, I can address some of the issues.

The *sefarim* stress that Hashem relates to us *middah keneged middah*. Therefore, if we forgive someone even though he has not asked for forgiveness or has not sincerely regretted his actions, then Hashem will forgive us even if we have not done adequate *teshuvah*, and who can say that one's *teshuvah* is adequate? In other words, it is to our own advantage that we forgive.

A person asked *mechillah* from one of the *gedolim* for having said unkind things about him, and was told to return in three days. When the person returned, the *godol* said, "At the time you asked for *mechillah*, I did not feel that my forgiveness would be sincere. It took me three days to work on myself to erase any trace of resentment toward you. Now I can tell you that I forgive you wholeheartedly."

If we realize that it is *we* who stand to gain by forgiving and that it is to *our* advantage, we can forgive sincerely. However, it may take some time to come to that realization.

We should learn from our *gedolim*, and even if we cannot reach their level of *middos*, that should not stop us from trying.

Reb Yisroel of Salant was en route to Vilna, when a young man in the train was very *chutzpadik* toward him. When they arrived in Vilna and he realized whom he had insulted, he asked for *mechillah*. On inquiring, Reb Yisroel learned that the young man had come to be certified as a *shochet*, but Reb Yisrael found that he was not well-versed in the laws of *shechitah*. Reb Yisrael spent much time teaching him and preparing him for certification.

Reb Yisrael said that just forgiving may not be enough. The thought of forgiving may not eliminate the feeling of resentment. Therefore, he felt that he had to take action to rid himself of the resentment, because action is strong enough to overcome feeling.

When Reb Levi Yitzchok of Berditchev's opponents put his wife and children on a trash wagon and sent them out of town, his comrades asked Reb Wolf of Zhitomir to bring down the wrath of Hashem on them. Reb Wolf said, "I cannot, because Levi Yitzchok is standing with a *Tehillim* before the *aron kodesh* praying that no harm come to them."

Our *gedolim* may appear to us as superhuman, but the fact is that they were *very great* humans, but humans nevertheless. It is asking much of ourselves, but we should at least try to emulate them.

AHAVAH VS. YIRAH

I am a 16-year-old yeshivah bachur, and before Rosh Hashanah I attend special mussar shiurim that focus on increasing our yiras Shamayim. What has bothered for me for a long time is how can we have ahavas Hashem when we are supposed to fear Him? It's difficult to love someone whom you fear. I raised this question with my rebbe, and although he tried to answer it, it still bothers me. I wonder, is there is any psychological way of explaining how you can have both ahavah and yirah at the same time?

There are several ways to understand this. In *Yesodei Hatorah* (2:2), Rambam says that the way to have *ahavas Hashem* and *yiras Hashem* is to contemplate the great wonders of creation, which will give a person a feeling of the grandeur of

Hashem, and this will lead to both *ahavah* and *yirah*. The *peirush* on the Rambam explains that the Rambam is using the term *ahavah* to refer to a feeling of adoration rather than what is usually translated as love. Furthermore, *yirah*, rather than meaning *fear*, can be defined as a sensation of awe and reverence for Hashem. In this way, *yirah* and *ahavah* are perfectly compatible.

Nevertheless, there likewise should be *yirah* as fear as well. If a two-year-old child runs into the street, it will not help if his father explains to him the danger of traffic. He cannot understand it. To protect him from the danger, the father pulls him back, shouts 'NO! NO! NO!" and gives him a *potch*. This is not punishment, but is the only way a two-year-old can be taught not to run into the street. The child might *fear* the immediate reaction of the parent. Similarly, we may not be able to understand why the things the Torah forbids are dangerous to us, and so we need the threat of a *potch* to protect us from harming ourselves.

If we understand this, we can understand that we should fear to disobey Hashem because it is harmful to *us*. We should have a love for Him because He is protecting us. This way, we can have both *ahavah* and *yirah*. There are numerous additional sources that address this issue. In time you will learn them. But in the present it is sufficient to know that there is never a *stirah* (dichotomy) in the words of Torah and that Hashem does not ask the impossible of his beloved nation.

HASHEM'S *RACHAMIM* AND NATURAL DISASTERS

I have a chavrusah who left the yeshivah, but still comes to night seder three times a week and we learn together. He raised the question about how we repeatedly say the 13 Middos of Hashem in selichos, stating that Hashem is "Rachum" and "Rav Chessed." How can we explain natural disasters like a tsunami that killed a hundred thousand people, and earthquakes and hurricanes and the like that cause so much human suffering? I don't know what to answer him.

The intent of this column is primarily to deal with psychological problems, some of which may touch upon Yiddishkeit. Pure halachic and *hashkafah* questions should be addressed to *talmidei chachamim* who are qualified to give a *psak*.

Nevertheless, I will share my approach with you, which is simply that these are things we cannot understand or explain, and we must have *emunah* that Hashem has His reasons for making things happen.

Natural disasters are not recent occurances. They occurred in the time of the *Neviim*, the *Chachmei HaTalmud,* and in more recent generations. These questions certainly occurred to *gedolim* throughout history, and their *emunah* was strong enough to withstand these challenges.

It is of interest that the Talmud said that because Yirmiyah saw the destruction of the *Beis Hamikdash*, he did not want to refer to Hashem as "awesome." Daniel, because he saw Jews enslaved, did not want to refer to Hashem as "mighty." Although they knew that Hashem was awesome and mighty, they did not want to say something that they had not seen with their own eyes. The *Anshei Knesses Hagedolah* said that if a tiny people like Israel can survive among a hostile world, that alone shows Hashem's awesomeness and might (*Yoma*, 69b).

Our *gedolim*, throughout the ages, could see Hashem as *Rachum* and *Rav Chessed*, even though they were well aware of natural disasters. We should accept their leadership in *hashkafah*.

In Judaism, questions are always welcomed. Most often they are addressed to the inquirer's satisfactions. In the event that one does not feel that he has been given adequate answers, it is imperative to realize that this is due to his lack of understanding and not, *chas v'shalom*, in a lack in Hashem. We must realize that we, with our limited understanding, are here on this earth for a limited time. It is much as if we came in for 10 minutes right in the middle of a 4-hour movie. The script is incomprehensible. *Moshe Rabbeinu* similarly asked "*tzaddik v'ra lo*" — Why do bad things happen to good people? And Hashem told Moshe that on this earth it is not possible for mortal man to recognize the truth in all He does.

As much as I don't like to do this, I feel I must alert you to beware of where your friend is getting his ideas. Sometimes questions such as these may indicate a problem in *emunah*, and you may be able to help your friend. Since he has left the yeshivah, it is important to know whether he is now exposed to non-Torah ideas, and if so, to distance yourself from his possibly destructive attitude. On the other hand, he may be questioning sincerely, without an anti-Torah agenda. You may wish to speak to your *Rosh Yeshivah* about this.

HISHTADLUS AND BITACHON

As a working mother who supports my family, I was wondering: how far does my hishtadlus have to go? If I work at a regular job with a decent salary, may I take on a small side job to increase my income and maybe help us live more comfortably? Or is my working in the office the utmost hishtadlus for me to do? Should I leave the rest to Hashem, trusting that somehow more money will just flow in somehow?

I recently heard from other people who tried to increase their income by working more than before that somehow there was not the extra money at the end of the month that they expected to have from working longer hours. In fact, they realized that with the increase in money came the increase in expenses.

I nsofar as the question of *hishtadlus* is concerned, this subject is widely discussed in *sifrei mussar*. How much should one have *hishtadlus* as compared to *bitachon*? This requires the opinion of *daas Torah*.

However, there is another consideration. Our children certainly have material needs that parents must try to provide. However, they desperately need the emotional care and interest that parents can give them.

I know of people who put in extra time at work because they want to give their children more than just the basic needs. However, if this takes away from the time that they could be personally involved with the children, it constitutes the statement, "I can give you *things*, but I can't give you myself," as if things are more important. This may also be a reflection of how a parent feels about himself/herself. One mother said, "I give myself over completely to my children. So what do they have from that? Nothing!" This was a clear expression of how little self-esteem she had, believing that giving herself to them was giving nothing.

If the children have their basic material needs met, your relating to them will provide them with optimal emotional stability, which can be worth more than living "more comfortably."

SHOULD A THERAPIST IMPOSE HIS STANDARDS?

I have been seeing a frum therapist for several months, and he is helping me with some of my problems. However, he is more to the right than I am, and he is subtly and not-so-subtly trying to influence me to become more frum. Is that proper for a psychotherapist?

Clearly, the role of a psychotherapist is to address the client's psychological problems.

However, every Jew is obligated with the mitzvah of *hoche'ach toche'ach*, and if a person sees that another Jew's behavior is not compliant with Torah, there is an obligation to correct him. There are halachos governing when one should or should not give *tochachah*.

The mitzvos were not given for Hashem's benefit, but for our betterment. A therapist may think that what he sees as laxity in observance of mitzvos is disadvantageous to you.

People may have different ideas about how *frum* one should be. For example, some people keep Shabbos until 50 minutes after sunset, while others wait 72 minutes. Some people rely on the *hetter* for *chalav stam*, others do not. When a person is observing Yiddishkeit according to the halachic guidance of a reliable *rav*, I doubt that there is mitzvah of *tochachah* to urge him to be more *machmir*.

There are reliable *poskim* whom you may consult. If your therapist brings up an issue of Yiddishkeit, you may tell him that you will consult a *posek* about this, and indeed do so.

MISPLACED EMPATHY

I possess a very sensitive nature and ever since childhood I have always been affected by my environment. I find that anything sad or upsetting will "set me off." If I hear or read about present day tzaros or even about past ones (e.g., Holocaust books) I am consumed by heavy feelings of sadness and cannot focus for days. I sometimes experience physical reactions such as insomnia and loss of appetite. I have been advised by a well-meaning relative that I should train myself to mentally shut off my reactions to other people's pain and focus on myself.

I wonder if the proper Torah-oriented psychological approach would concur.

Further, how is it even possible to distance oneself from the many tragedies and mind-numbing events that occur daily in our complex world?

S hutting oneself away from other people's pain and focusing only on oneself would result in absolute selfishness. Obviously, we must feel for others, but if we do not regulate our feelings, we can be overwhelmed by them, as you describe.

The Talmud says that if a person prays for the impossible, it is a futile prayer. Of course, there is nothing that is impossible for Hashem, but one should not expect a prayer to split the sea for him to be answered. "One should not rely on a miracle" (*Pesachim*, 64b). Therefore, although there are many things in life that are unpleasant, and it would take a miracle to change them, we do not pray for that miracle. For example, if someone has lost a loved one, it is futile to pray the he/she be resurrected. Rather, one should pray to Hashem for the strength to survive the ordeal.

There are many things in life that we can change, particularly ourselves. We can always improve ourselves, but we may sometimes give up doing constructive things because we are preoccupied with things that we cannot change. Sometimes, if we are reluctant to exert the energy to bring about positive change, our minds may re-direct our attention to things we cannot change.

There are things that we can realistically do for people who need help. Of course we feel sad when hearing about anyone's distress, and we must empathize with them and feel their distress so that we are properly motivated to help them.

Make a list of the things you need to do or should be doing. Consult this list frequently, and when a task or project has been completed, check it off. Writing things down clarifies them. Make another list of things that bother you but that you cannot alter in any way. Look at this "can't-do" list and compare it to the "can-do" list, and determine that you are going to put your energies where they can do some good. Practicing this will eventually put the *tzaros* that are beyond your help into proper perspective. You can pray that Hashem should help those people, but consult your "can-do" list, and pray that Hashem give you the ability to do the things within your means.

If you are uncertain about in which category to place an issue, consult a rav, one of your teachers, or a counselor to clarify it for you.

WHEN *KIRUV* CONFLICTS WITH CHIDREN'S *CHINUCH*

I'm in a bit of a dilemma. I like to do kiruv. I invite young people to my home on Shabbos, and it is very enjoyable and rewarding. We sing zemiros and discuss the parashah of the week and other topics.

Every once in a while, one of the young people will bring up questions in emunah or discuss the age of the universe. I try to deal with these issues as best I can. My problem is that my young children are at the table and they listen to these discussions. I don't think it is good for them, at this young age, to hear concepts that conflict with emunah. Yet I don't want to stop inviting these young people for Shabbos, because I think it makes a good impression on them. What should I do?

Bringing these young people closer to Yiddishkeit is not too likely to be accomplished by intellectual discussions. If they walk into a *Shabbosdige* home and see the beauty of it, this will impress them more than anything else.

In a home where there is true *shalom bayis,* with mutual respect and consideration between husband and wife, there is a feeling of *menuchah* and *kedushah* that permeates the home. When they see how children respect their parents, and how parents relate lovingly to their children, in an era when families in the secular world are torn apart by strife and disrespect, they gain respect for the Torah and Yiddishkeit.

The *Midrash* says that with the onset of Shabbos, a person should feel that all his work has been done and is completed. He owes no one any money and no one owes him any money. All the merchandise has arrived and all orders have been shipped. Nothing from the weekdays carries over to Shabbos. A ringing telephone is simply ignored. Shabbos is an oasis of peace in a frenetic world. Nothing like a truly observed, spiritual Shabbos exists in the secular world.

Hashem said to Moshe *Rabbeinu,* "I have a special gift in my treasury that I wish to give to the Children of Israel." The greatest attraction to Yiddishkeit is to see how we cherish Shabbos as a precious gift.

Insofar as debating issues that conflict with Yiddishkeit, I don't think that one should get into these discussions unless one is fully competent to do so. When such issues come up, it is better to suggest that your guests discuss them with a person who has the necessary knowledge of the conflicting issues and how to resolve them. When I was computer illiterate, and someone wanted to discuss the operation of a computer with me, I had no problem in telling him that this was not within my range of knowledge. When the Sages said, "Accustom your tongue to say 'I don't know,'" it is for situations such as this.

In any case, your guests can be told that you wish to limit the discussions at the table to topics the children can understand. The Shabbos table-talk should be about Torah, about *middos,* and about stories of our great *tzaddikim.*

Words are not the most effective vehicle. The atmosphere of a truly spiritual Shabbos in a home that is truly peaceful is a much more potent tool for *kiruv.*

CAN INTERNET RESTRICTIONS BE EFFECTIVE?

Do you think that the restrictions on having internet can be effective? It sounds to me like the attempt to control alcohol consumption by outlawing production of alcohol during the Prohibition Era, which was a failure.

Contrary to popular belief, Prohibition was not the failure it has been made out to be. Statistics show that there was, in fact, a lower incidence of alcoholism during this period.

While no method of control is foolproof, restrictions have eliminated internet in some homes, and saving even one person from internet addiction is worthwhile. Furthermore, the restrictions have emphasized the severity of the problem, and this may help discourage those people who were sitting on the fence.

What is, of course, necessary is an intensification of *kedushah* in our lives. Eating glatt kosher, *yashan,* and *pas Yisrael* are certainly praiseworthy, but not enough. We must work diligently on improvement of *middos.* A person who *really* wants to avoid this problem but feels himself pulled by temptation should make a serious effort at daily learning of *sifrei mussar* and *chassidus,* preferably with a *chaver,* and implement the teachings of these *sefarim* in daily life. *Repeated* learning of the first three parts of *Mesillas Yesharim (zehirus, zerizus, nekiyus)* is a must. Children who see their parents' serious dedication to *kedushah* will be impressed. But, for example, if a person loses his temper, this is a failure in *middos,* and undermines *kedushah.*

The last *mishnah* in *Sotah* accurately predicted the moral climate that will exist before the coming of Moshiach, and we have arrived there. An intensification of methods to resist the wiles of the *yetzer hara* is necessary.

CAN NON-JEWISH SELF-HELP BOOKS PROVIDE SUCCESS IN *AVODAS HASHEM?*

Looking back at my upbringing, I can honestly say that I have B"H had a very secure childhood. I grew up in a home where Torah ideals and middos tovos were embedded in us with constant love and care.

In recent years I have picked up some psychology self-help books (mostly from non-Jewish sources) which have strongly helped me become calm, confident, and happy. I've found that these traits have not only made day-to-day life easier but have also helped me improve my avodas Hashem.

Now, the questions that plague me are:

1. Why is it that the only way I could attain this level of happiness is through non-Jewish sources, despite my very fine upbringing? Shouldn't a Torah-observant Yid naturally acquire this state of serenity just by keeping Hashem's Torah and mitzvos?

2. How can I b'ezras Hashem bring up my children to attaining such a calm state of mind, without exposing them to secular material?

The kind of advice one finds in secular self-help books may indeed guide a person to be calm and happy, because this is as far as the secular aspiration can go. Being content appears to be the secular goal in life. I am reminded of the slogan of Carnation milk: "Milk from contented cows." Contentment may be the sign of excellence in a cow, but that should be beneath human dignity.

The Torah concept is one of *simchah,* which, according to our *sefarim,* has several meanings other than "happiness." The Talmud says that when a person suffers a tragedy (*r"l*), he must recite the *berachah* "*baruch dayan emes*" with *simchah*. Rashi explains that in this case, *simchah* does not mean "joy," because that is impossible. Rather, Rashi says, *simchah* here means *lev shalem*, the acceptance with *emunah* in Hashem that His wisdom is just. *Simchah* is not simply the feeling of joy felt when one achieves one's desires or participates in a happy occasion. "*Ivdu es Hashem b'simchah*" means that we must work — *ivdu* — to attain *simchah*.

Hagaon Harav Samson Rafael Hirsh says that the similarity of the words *some'ach* (joy) and *tzome'ach* (growth) indicates that they are related, because spiritual growth is true *simchah*. As *Tanya* and other *sefarim* say, a person should always realize that he has not yet achieved adequate *avodas Hashem*, and this should spur him on to additional growth in Torah and mitzvos.

Our *sifrei mussar and chassidus* teach us to be confident in the knowledge that we have the ability to do all that Hashem asks of us. An awareness of one's abilities is self-esteem, but that just adds to a person's responsibilities. Reb Yisrael Salant said, "I know that my mind equals that of a thousand others, but that means that my obligations are a thousand times as great."

I have referred people to books on relaxation, because it is important to know how to relax, but relaxation should be with the intent of increasing one's abilities in *avodas Hashem*.

Our *sefarim* speak of *menuchas hanefesh*, a feeling which can come from true *bitachon* in Hashem. Secular books generally try to teach people how to be satisfied with themselves, whereas our *sefarim* teach us **not** to be satisfied with what we have achieved in *avodas Hashem*. Many of the secular books are essentially tranquilizers, a kind of Valium. Certainly, there may be times when a tranquilizer is needed, but tranquility is not the goal of Torah. If you have not found help in our Jewish sources, you may not have been guided to the correct areas of *mussar*.

So, show your children that you have confidence in them. Build up their self-esteem by giving them much love and care, taking great interest in them, encouraging them, and showing appreciation of their efforts. However, don't set up calmness as the goal in life. Yiddishkeit's goal in life is *avodas Hashem*, and *avodah* means work. Show them how to work at increasing the quality of Torah and mitzvos.

PESACH NEUROSIS

I am about to become a wreck. I have a "Pesach neurosis." Regardless of how much cleaning and scrubbing I do, I still don't feel that it's enough, and there still may be a trace of chametz around, especially in the kitchen. Is there anything I can do to get rid of this anxiety? Someone said that I have OCD [Obsessive Compulsive Disorder], but I don't think so. Will medication be of help?

OCD is indeed a condition in which one does not feel certain about something, and is always in doubt: "But maybe ..." However, OCD usually manifests itself in multiple ways. If your only uncertainty is on Pesach, it is probably not OCD.

Nowhere do we find as many *chumros* as on Pesach. Some keep the *minhag* of not eating *gebroks,* because of the remote possibility that a speck of flour might not have been saturated with water and hence did not bake, and if it comes in contact with liquid, it can turn into *chametz.* The Chasam Sofer dismissed this as an unnecessary *chumrah* and ate *kneidlach.* However, we do not consider not eating *gebroks* to be a neurosis.

The Brisker Rav was extremely *machmir* on Pesach. One of the contemporary *gedolim* asked him, "How can you fulfill the mitzvah of eating matzah with *simchah,* when you are trembling with the fear that the matzah might not have been properly baked and you are *chas v'shalom* eating *chametz?*" But the Brisker Rav did not have a "Pesach neurosis."

We have a *Shulchan Aruch,* and when we abide by the halachah, there is no reason to worry. If there are any *minhagim* of *chumros* in your family, you may keep them, but then stop worrying.

I saw in a *sefer* that it may be humanly impossible to avoid a *mashe-hu* of *chametz,* but if a person does everything that the *Shulchan*

Aruch requires, Hashem will see to it that every *mashehu* of *chametz* is eliminated. So, we must do what the *Shulchan Aruch* requires, and be *mispallel* for *Siyatta Dishmaya* to protect us from anything that is beyond our means. That is what you should do, and enjoy Pesach with *menuchas hadaas*.

HOW GOOD IS TOO GOOD?

I am concerned about my friend. She is a middle-aged woman who incessantly does mitzvos to the point that she harms her own well-being. She cooks for various people in the community and loves doing it, but she does it at the expense of her health. She cooks at night and then just keeps going to the point where she falls apart and gets sick. She does daycare every morning, and one of the children is a special-needs child. Nobody can do for her, only she can do for others. I'm afraid for her health. What can I say to her to make her realize that she is overdoing her chessed?

I think it would be more effective if this intervention came from a *rav*.

Tzedakah is the greatest mitzvah, yet the halachah states that a person should not give more than twenty percent of his earnings to *tzedakah* lest he impoverish himself and become dependent on others (*Yoreh Deah*, 249). One must be guided by halachah, because if doing to excess exhausts a person, either physically or economically, one will not be able to continue doing mitzvos. Your friend should accept guidance from a *rav*.

Before an airplane takes off, the flight attendant makes the announcement on using the oxygen in the event of a drop in cabin pressure. She says, "If you are traveling with a child, put your own mask on first, then assist the child." If a mother is so devoted that she wishes to attend to the child first, she may be deprived of oxygen and may be so confused that she will put the oxygen mask over the child's ear rather than over the nose and mouth. If you want to help someone else, you must be sure that you are in a condition to do so.

If your friend reduces her activities so that she can care for her own health, she may feel guilty. That is why she should be counseled by a *rav* so that she knows that she is doing the right thing.

AYIN HARA VS. LASHON HARA

I once had an acquaintance of whom I was extremely jealous. This led to mixed feelings of hatred, and, on a couple of occasions I even spoke lashon hara about him. Unfortunately, he passed away suddenly, and at a young age.

I once heard a story told about a Tanna who walked past a cemetery with one of his talmidim and exclaimed "Do you know that ninety-nine percent of the people buried here died from ayin hara?" (I don't know if I am quoting the story correctly, but this is the gist of it).

Very often, this story comes into my mind, and I'm consumed with guilt, feeling that I am at fault for this fellow's death.

What is the proper way to think about this matter? Is there any way I can repent for my terrible misdeed?

Although they may seem similar, *ayin hara* and *lashon hara* are different. Begrudging someone for what he has and not *farginning* one's possessions or *mazal* is *ayin hara* even though one did not speak a single word.

Concepts such as these from the Talmud require the interpretation of a *gadol* in Torah.

There are differences of opinion about asking for *mechilah* for having spoken *lashon hara* about a person, because apprising one of this misdeed may cause the subject anguish. However, this does not apply if the person has died. It is appropriate to ask a *sheilah* from a *posek* as to what one should do if the person about whom one spoke *lashon hara* has died.

Legitimate guilt can be a constructive feeling if it leads one to make amends and to avoid repeating the act. However, we must be cautious not to allow guilt to destroy us. A Torah authority can instruct you what one must do to overcome legitimate guilt.

IS ONE ALWAYS RESPONSIBLE FOR HIS ACTIONS?

A few months ago, you wrote that people with behavior disorders, such as ADD, ODD, alcoholism, and kleptomania, are responsible for their actions. You did not clarify in any way. I suppose you meant either that people are responsible for fixing their behavior by getting treatment, or that they can forcibly restrain their improper behavior. If you meant something else, please let us interested readers know!

Assuming that you meant the two choices above, then I have a few questions.

1. At the outset of the treatment, before it has taken effect, is the person already responsible?

2. If responsibility lies in the obligation to restrain oneself, and the restraint has negative consequences, is the person responsible for the consequences?

Here's an example of negative consequences: I am compulsive in the sense that I have a terrible time stopping whatever I am in the middle of doing. I am not a perfectionist in any way, nor must I finish things. I just find it extremely hard to fight the momentum of whatever I am doing. As a result, it takes me a lot of effort and a very long time to stop in the middle of a job. Likewise, when in the middle of a job, I am usually too involved to give proper attention to whatever might interrupt me — including people.

Let's say someone wants my attention when I am doing something. I can pretend to listen to them while I work, but really not hear a word they are saying, or I can ask them to wait ten minutes until I can stop myself and concentrate. Or I can force myself to stop working, but the effort will take up so much of my attention that I won't hear the other person, anyway. All three choices are rude. My blank, distracted look doesn't fool anyone, and my keeping someone waiting for ten minutes while I wind down something (like sorting socks) that is clearly not very important is offensive.

What good choices do I have? Am I responsible for behaving rudely or not?

In sum, what are people supposed to do when their behavioral problems leave them with only bad choices?

Insofar as responsibility for one's behavior when one has a psychological problem is concerned, it must be considered from several aspects. Unless one meets the criteria of insanity, one must be held responsible for one's behavior. Accepting "irresistible impulse" as excusing one's actions would leave one open to committing crimes and saying, "I couldn't help it. I could not control my urge." From a practical aspect, a person must be held responsible.

Incidentally, it is not clear just what constitutes insanity, both legally and halachically. One may be considered a *shoteh* in regard to some things, although he is not considered a *shoteh* in regard to others.

Furthermore, suppose a person says that he could not resist the impulse to do a particular *aveirah*. Would he do it if someone were pointing a gun at him and threatening to kill him if he does it? Given such a threat, a person would restrain himself. True *yiras Shamayim* requires that one have a similar fear of doing an *aveirah*. Similarly, if a person has an "irresistible" compulsion to wash his hands repeatedly, would he do so if he were threatened as above?

A person with a compulsion *can* resist the act, but it may cause him great anxiety and distress to do so. Most often, the person feels that there is not sufficient reason to be forced to tolerate the discomfort of restraint. Although it would seem that only Hashem is capable of making such a judgment, there are times when a *beis din* must act in that capacity and determine whether expecting restraint was realistic.

The example you gave is really not one of compulsion. We are all confronted with making choices, and our decision depends on what we consider most important. If you ignore a person because you are preoccupied with something, that is because you consider your involvement with what you are doing to be more important than avoiding being rude. That is a value judgment you have made. If ethics indicate otherwise, then you have made an unethical judgment, and you are responsible for making that judgment.

We are often confronted by situations in which whatever we do will have some kind of negative effect. If we use Torah principles and consult Torah authorities whenever feasible, our decisions will be right. That it may result in discomfort does not make a choice a "bad" choice.

Incidentally, telling someone, "I want to give you my full attention, but I must finish what I'm doing" (assuming this is reasonable) is not being rude. If the person does not wish to wait, that is his choice.

As I pointed out, the diagnosis of any condition, unless it is of a psychotic nature that would classify a person as a *shoteh*, does not eliminate responsibility.

The force of a compulsion can be very intense, but it can be resisted. The problem is that resisting a compulsion results in anxiety, anywhere from mild to severe.

There are some compulsions that must be restrained with *mesiras nefesh*, as when one has a compulsion to kill or injure people. With less harmful compulsions, the individual has a choice of whether to submit to the compulsion or tolerate the anxiety of resisting it. For example, a person with a compulsion that he must cleanse himself of germs may stay under the shower for three hours, depriving everyone else in the house of the use of the shower. It can be legitimately argued that in order not to inconvenience everyone else in the household, he should bear the anxiety of getting out of the shower in 20 minutes.

The entire body of *mussar* is directed toward teaching people not to be pawns at the mercy of their emotions. True, it may take great effort to develop self-control, but unless one is a *shoteh* one has the ability to do it.

We read about how *tzaddikim* mastered their emotions. One may say, "What do you expect of me, to be a Chofetz Chaim?" Well, the Chofetz Chaim was not born a *tzaddik*. Hagaon Harav Hutner writes that the Chofetz Chaim struggled enormously to become who he was. No one is being asked to develop the extreme self-mastery that *tzaddikim* had, but on the other hand, to yield to internal drives or pressures because to resist them is uncomfortable is the other extreme.

Reb Zushe of Anipole was in a hurry to get somewhere when someone called to him, "Come here and help me lift this load." Reb Zushe responded, "I can't." The caller said, "Yes, you can. You just don't want to." Reb Zushe took this as *mussar*. There are times we say "We can't," when the truth is that we are not willing to make the necessary effort.

IS ONE HELD RESPONSIBLE? II

I read your column last week that discussed the age-old question of victim vs. responsibility. You stated clearly that no matter what, a person is responsible for his actions.

I could use a little more clarity on exactly what you are saying.

In every person's life there are actions, speech, and thought that are not in accordance with halachah but nevertheless the person has no bechirah on these issues. Why? Because, as R' Dessler explains in his famous treatise, "Kuntros Hebechirah," due to this person's nature and nurture it is impossible for him not to transgress. As R' Dessler clearly writes, an act that is beyond a person's level of bechirah has the same din as the tinok shenishba.

I agree the person has to take responsibility for where he is now and try to move himself slowly up the ladder of Avodas Hashem. As is well-known, the path of Avodas Hashem is a step-by-step process. It is hard to understand what exactly you mean by stating that unless one is a shoteh he is always responsible for his behavior. Could it not be that getting up for Shacharis is beyond this person's level of bechirah today?

Basically it boils down to this question: Do you believe that nature and nurture do not affect a person's present decisions and he therefore should be responsible if he transgresses any halachah? Or do you believe that nature and nurture do affect a person's decision-making process? If so, how can you day he is responsible for transgressions he has no bechirah on?

I suggest you re-read Rav Dessler's essay carefully. In regard to a person who is addicted to cigarettes, Rav Dessler says, "What causes him to choose to smoke rather than to protect his health? He himself is the cause. He could say, 'Why should I delude myself?' ... How foolish are those who think that it is weak willpower that causes a person to live in error .... A person has the ability to accept the truth, or to reject the truth and live with false ideas. The ability to choose either way, that is *bechirah*."

When Rav Dessler refers to things that are beyond *bechirah* he is saying this: I do not have to exercise *bechirah* to avoid going into McDonald's for a cheeseburger. For me that is an impossibility. But it is possible that I might overhear a piece of juicy *lashan hara*. My job is to make listening to *lashan hara* as impossible as going into McDonald's, to put it **beyond** *bechirah*.

Clearly a *tinok shenishba* is not responsible for things he does not know. But there are times when a person *should* know. Bilaam said to the angel "I have sinned, for I did not know that you were standing opposite me." The *Shelah* asks, "If he did not know, why is it a sin? Because," *Shelah* says, "he should have known." In civil law, ignorance of the law is no excuse. In a New Jersey case, the court held the entire medical staff liable for the mistakes of an alcoholic physician, stating, "If they did not know he was alcoholic, they should have known." In halachah, *omer muttar karov lemeizid,* a person who thinks that something forbidden is permissible is almost as culpable as an intentional transgressor.

A drunk does not have the ability to recognize that he is unable to drive. He is liable because **before** he became drunk he should have had the foresight to know that he would be driving and therefore to have refrained from drinking — or from driving.

If we would consider a person who cannot arouse himself to go to shul to daven *Shacharis* (assuming that he does not have an incapacitated brain) as having no *bechirah,* we would essentially be excusing many, if not most, inappropriate behaviors.

There is a distinction between a *tinok shenishba* and a person who has the capacity for *bechirah* but is influenced by some things, and it requires great competence and much thought to decide to which category a person belongs.

DOUBTS IN *EMUNAH*

> I am a yeshivah bachur, from a very frum
> family. I have been bothered by problems in
> emunah. I have read sefarim on emunah, but
> I still have sefeikos. I am afraid to ask
> the Rosh Yeshivah about this, because he may
> consider me an apikorus [heretic]. I want to
> believe. What can I do to put my mind at ease?

Looking for *chizuk* in *emunah* can hardly be considered *apikorsus* (heresy). The reason that there are so many *seforim* about *emunah* is precisely because it is a difficult concept. One *segulah* for *emunah* is to say the *Ani Maamins* every day, not as a statement of fact, but rather as a *tefillah*: "Help me believe." The Steipler Gaon would say *Ani Maamin*, and for greater emphasis, he translated every word into Yiddish. If the Steipler Gaon felt he needed *chizuk* in *emunah*, all of us certainly do. There are two different kinds of disturbing thoughts. One kind is the work of the *yetzer hara*, who does its job in trying to deter us from *avodas Hashem*. The *yetzer hara* causes one to have doubts because of the notion that if it can get a person to question the truth of Torah, then a person would be free to do anything he pleases and would be free from the various guidelines Torah imposes.

We must be particularly careful that we do not allow ourselves to be "bribed" by our desires. The Talmud says that the Israelites of Tanach never believed that the *avodah zarah* they "worshipped" had any substance. Rather, they wanted to be free to satisfy those desires that the Torah forbids (*Sanhedrin*, 63a). The *yetzer hara* is shrewd and wily, and will use every trick to lead a person away from Torah. These *yetzer hara*-induced thoughts should be combated by increased resolve to study Torah and *mussar* and to do mitzvos.

We entrust our lives into the hands of a physician. We have enough *emunah* in the diploma on the wall to allow the doctor to operate on us, even to perform open-heart surgery. The "diplomas" of our great Torah personages are superior to the testimony of the doctor's license, and we can trust them for the validity of *emunah*.

You should not hesitate to discuss this with your *rebbe* or another competent *talmid chacham*. Tell him that you are honestly seeking answers, not contradicting or questioning the *gedolei Yisrael*.

WOMEN'S POSITION IN TORAH

> I have a friend who is a frum girl in seminary. She asks why women are not permitted to make a minyan of their own and say all the tefillos for a tzibbur, and things like that. I think she has been bitten by the "equality" bug, and thinks that Torah holds women in an inferior position. How do I answer her?

This issue has been widely discussed and much has been written about it. If your friend is really interested in the truth rather than in just making a point, she can get authentic information in the two-volume work by Rabbi Menachem Brayer, *The Jewish Woman in Rabbinic Literature*.

I find that often people who raise this issue have an agenda, and they are not too likely to accept explanations.

Ultimately it comes down to this. The prophet Habbakuk summarized Torah in the phrase, "*tzaddik b'emunoso yichyeh*," a righteous person lives by faith. If one has *emunah* in the authenticity of *Torah shebaal peh*, one accepts the halachah of the *Shulchan Aruch*.

Suppose a right-fielder told the manager of the baseball team, "I don't want to play right field. Hardly anyone hits the ball out there. I want to play first base. That's where the action is." The manager would tell him that *he* assigns the players to their positions — a player cannot decide where he wants to play.

For reasons known only to Him, Hashem has assigned a certain position to *Kohanim*, another to *Leviim*, another to men, and another to women. Every person has a specific role. As a Yisroel, I cannot do the functions of a Kohen. That does not mean that I am less worthy than a Kohen. Indeed, a Torah scholar who happens to be of illegitimate birth takes precedence over a Kohen who is unlearned, but that does not allow the Yisroel to perform the functions of a Kohen.

Your conviction into the authenticity of the *Shulchan Aruch* for how we conduct ourselves should be unwavering. If your friend is seriously seeking information, she should be addressing her question to her teachers. If she is trying to make a point that is in opposition to the *Shulchan Aruch*, you would be best off telling her that you are interested in understanding *Shulchan Aruch*, not in questioning it.

LOSING INTEREST IN LEARNING

I am only 60, and I am very unhappy with my inability to retain what I've learned. I can much more easily remember what I learned 45 years ago in yeshivah than what I learned two days ago.

I can remember telephone numbers or other information, so I know it's not Alzheimer's Disease. But I am losing my interest in learning. What's the use of learning something if you can't remember it? I used to have cheshek in learning, but now, when the Gemara refers to something I learned two days ago and I can't remember it, I get so frustrated that I don't even want to learn any more.

This is not an uncommon problem. The Talmud cites the importance of *girsa d'yankusa,* things we learn when we're young. As we grow older, each day we register new information that is stored in the brain. By the time we reach middle age, our brains are cluttered with so much material (most of it useless), that we can't retain what we want to.

The only solution to this is *chazarah,* review. The Steipler Gaon said that unless one reviews a Gemara four times, one cannot begin to grasp it. At *Daf Yomi,* we may learn something once and not review it. There is no way we can retain that. We must find time to review each *daf* at least four times. Ideally, one should spend one hour prior to a *Daf Yomi shiur* to learn the new material and an additional hour after the *shiur* to review what has just been studied. I highly doubt that many individuals who listen to a *shiur* without *chazarah* have much more retention than that to which you are courageous enough to admit.

Insofar as *cheshek* is concerned, our pleasure should be from the mitzvah of learning Torah rather than from how much one remembers. We make the *berachah, la'asok b'divrei Torah*; the mitzvah is to engage ourselves in the study of Torah, and this mitzvah is fulfilled even if we don't remember it. There is no reason to stop learning because one may not remember well. Knowing that you are fulfilling the great mitzvah of Talmud Torah should give you pleasure rather than frustration.

ONGOING DILEMMA: IS THE MITZVAH TO *LEARN* OR TO *KNOW* TORAH?

I am a serious, twenty-year-old yeshivah bachur, learning in a prominent yeshivah. I am considered a top bachur because I have a deep understanding and I try very hard to be exact and truthful in learning. However, I think that there is something that does not allow me to reach my full potential.

*Throughout my years in yeshivah, any time
I learned a couple of lines of Gemara, or
a sugya, I immediately had an urge to learn
it over and over, and even after that I
felt that I didn't have clarity in it. I
now understand this as follows: Most people,
after they learn something, or a series of
things, basically have it "in their heads,"
ready to be dealt with or discussed. This
gives them the realization that they know
what they learned. On the other hand, after
I learn something, my mind is completely
blank. In order to deal with the knowledge
that I gained I have to "dig up" bits and
pieces, requiring intense concentration. I
find this is very strenuous. I am always
afraid to speak to others in learning
because as a result of the conversation, I
will understand something differently and
parts of the sugya have to be changed, I
can't just change them in my head, because
my head is blank. I have no choice but to
learn the whole sugya again, changing things
along the way.*

*I think that this affects other areas of
my life as well, mainly in being organized.
If someone has "in his head' everything
that has to be done in preparation for an
event (e.g., planning a vacation), it isn't
difficult to get it done. However, if, even
after thinking of everything, his mind is
blank and he must again think of one thing
at a time, it is very hard to be organized
and get it done quickly. Any suggestions?*

Insofar as your learning problem is concerned, you are in good company. The Talmud says that Moshe *Rabbeinu* learned Torah and forgot it until Hashem gave it to him as a gift (*Nedarim*, 38a).

A learning problem in Torah is best discussed with a *Rosh Yeshivah*. I suspect that you worry that you might not remember it, and the anxiety generated by this worry may cause your mind to go blank.

The mitzvah is to learn and study Torah (*la'asok b'divrei Torah*), and you are fully fulfilling the mitzvah by learning, even if you do not remember it. If you can be happy with the knowledge that you are fulfilling this mitzvah, the anxiety may actually lessen and then you will remember it more readily.

In regard to non-Torah aspects of life in which you find difficulty in getting organized, it is recommended that you write down what you are planning. Here, too, anxiety may be a factor, and if things are written down and you review them, you will eliminate much of the anxiety. You may eventually find that you can be organized even without writing things down. Nevertheless, jotting down what you plan to do is a good idea even for someone who has no difficulty organizing.

ONGOING DILEMMA: PART II

In Rabbi Twerski's column, there was a statement that could very well be understood to mean that nowhere is there a mitzvah to know Torah or to remember Torah but that the mitzvah is to learn and study Torah (la'asok b'divrei Torah).

If, for therapeutic purposes, the professor feels that he must convince a patient that this is so, perhaps he is permitted, but printing it in his column is megaleh panim baTorah shelo kehalacha. Besides which, someone might believe it.

There is a pasuk in the Torah, "Pen tishkach es hadevorim haeileh asher ra'u einecha." From here the Mishnah in Perek Gimel in Avos derives that if one forgets his learning (through negligence) the pasuk considers it as if he was mischayev b'nafsho.

*The pasuk states, "Veshinantam levanecha,"
from which the Gemara in Kiddushin Lamed
derives that the words of Torah shall
be fluent in one's mouth to be able to
immediately answer when asked.*

*See the halochos of Talmud Torah by the
Shulchan Aruch HaRav and see how the Torah
requires one to learn, to know, and to
remember.*

*In his Likutei Torah on Parashas
Kedoshim, the Rav writes that when the
Gemara says that Torah protects and saves
a person from spiritual and physical evils
even at the time that he is not learning,
this only applies to the Torah that he
remembers.*

*Of course, all the Talmidei Chachamim
reading this letter will have many many more
sources to show that besides the mitzvah of
learning Torah, there is an obligation to
know and remember.*

I appreciate your comments. However, you did not quote the entire *mishnah* in *Pirkei Avos* (3:10) that refers to the sin of forgetting Torah. The *mishnah* states, "Does this apply even if he forgot because his studies were too difficult for him? This is not so, because the Scripture says 'And lest they be removed from your heart all the days of your life.' Thus, one does not bear guilt for his soul unless he sits idly and [through lack of concentration and review] *removes them from his consciousness*." Clearly, a person is not culpable if he has a weak memory or if the studies are too difficult for him to retain. He is culpable only if he *intentionally* forgets by neglect of Torah study.

Etz Yosef (in *Otzar Hatefillos*) quotes the comment of *Chavas Yair* that the *berachah* of *la'asok b'divrei Torah* was formulated in that way because "not everyone has the *zechus* of understanding Torah." But even a person whose ability to comprehend is limited has the same obligation to learn Torah as does a person with the greatest ability to understand.

The reason for this is obvious. The obligation to perform mitzvos is equal for everyone. A person with little intelligence has the same obligation to eat matzah, hear *shofar*, and take the *esrog* and *lulav* (Four Species), as the greatest Torah scholar. Everyone is capable of performing the mitzvos, although, of course, their intensity and *kavannos* may differ sharply.

There could not be a mitzvah to sing high C or paint a portrait, because these are talents that only some individuals possess. Hashem does not ask of us anything that we are unable to do. Rather, we are required to fulfill whatever He commanded, to the best of our ability.

The ability to remember varies greatly. Some people have very strong memories and some even have photographic memories. A good memory is a gift from Hashem, as the *Midrash* says, Moshe forgot what he learned until Hashem gave him the gift of remembering. On the other hand, some people have weak memories. A mitzvah to "remember" Torah could then not be fulfilled by someone with a weak memory. But everyone, regardless of the strength of his memory and intellect, can *learn* Torah.

Of course, a person must make every effort to retain what he has learned, and this is what *la'asok b'divre Torah* means, to review and review.

The Talmud relates that R' Preida had a student whose capacity to understand was so weak that R' Preida taught everything to him four hundred times. Once, when he did not grasp it after four hundred times, R' Preida taught it to him another four hundred times (*Eruvin* 54b). Each of the first 399 times (or, on the one day, 799 times) the student learned it, he was fulfilling the mitzvah of *limud haTorah* even though he failed to grasp it.

A person who has a sharp mind and photographic memory who does not study Torah but may know a great deal from his earlier days is not fulfilling the mitzvah of *limud haTorah*, whereas Rebbe Preida's student did fulfill the mitzvah each time he studied.

ONGOING DILEMMA: PART III

*I read with great interest the exchange
between Rabbi Twerski and a reader who took
issue with the fact that Rabbi Twerski
wrote that nowhere is there a mitzvah to
know Torah and to remember Torah but that
the mitzvah is to learn and study Torah.
He pointed out that Rabbi Twerski's words
could be misunderstood.*

*Rabbi Twerski responded by saying that
the pasuk that prohibits forgetting Torah
refers only to deliberately removing Torah
from one's consciousness through lack of
concentration and review. Rabbi Twerski
then went on to explain that the Torah
surely does not demand that someone remember
or know something that is beyond his
capabilities.*

*Although I appreciate Rabbi Twerski's
response and agree with his general point
stating that a person is not culpable if he
has a weak memory or limited intellectual
abilities, I still do not see how he
answered the reader's point. Every person on
his own level has a mitzvah to understand
and know Torah. If a person's intellect
and abilities only make him capable of
understanding one pasuk, than it is his
mitzvah to remember and understand that
pasuk. The lack of intellectual ability,
etc., does not change the meaning of the
pasuk and the halachah remains that each
person, of course on his level, has an
obligation to know and remember Torah.*

*Although I am certain that Rabbi Twerski
did not mean to dispute this simple
understanding of the pasuk the fact is his
original words clearly do contradict the*

pasuk as it is explained in the mishnah in Avos. I feel that his important and relevant words of response and clarification should have been preceded by a retraction saying that he had made the wrong choice of words. I am sure that if he would have done this he would have received equal schar for his "drisha" as well as his "prisha."

I deeply regret if my words lent themselves to misinterpretation by being taken out of context and being misquoted. The question was about a person who tries to learn Torah but is frustrated that he does not grasp and retain it well. To this I responded that if he learns Torah to the best of his ability, he has the mitzvah of *limud Torah*. Certainly, a person with the capacity to grasp and retain Torah and who fulfills the mitzvah of *la'asok b'divrei Torah* will know and remember Torah. If one does not apply his faculties to Torah study, he is guilty of *bittul Torah* for those faculties that he did not utilize (*Shulchan Aruch Harav*).

But let us consider this. A bright young man with a phenomenal memory, who was once an *elui*, unfortunately drifted away from Torah and became so involved in other things that he did not open a *sefer* for the next twenty-five years. However, at age 40, he can still quote *dafim* of Gemara verbatim, and can easily repeat a discourse of R' Chaim on the Rambam. Although he "knows" and "remembers" much Torah, he has been transgressing the *aveirah* of *bittul Torah* for twenty-five years. When he was young and learned Torah, he had the mitzvah, but his neglect of Torah for twenty-five years is not compensated by his retention of what he had once learned. On the other hand, someone who devotes every minute of available time to study Torah and may not know a fraction of what the one-time *elui* remembers, does have the mitzvah of *limud Torah*.

The mitzvah of *ve'shinontam* is that one should learn Torah in a way that it will be fluent on his tongue, and one must utilize every mental faculty one has in the study of Torah. If one diligently fulfills *la'asok*, one will achieve this.

LACK OF FEELING IN *DAVENING*

When I was young and would say Tehillim, I never had any feeling for what I was doing. It left me numb — dry, to the extent that I can't open up a Tehillim unless there is something major happening in my life. This lack of feeling also impacts my davening and extends to other aspects of my day-to-day avodas Hashem.

Is there a reason for this and can I get out of this rut?

You did not indicate what may have caused your feelings about *davening* and saying *Tehillim*. Sometimes, if a child is forced, rather than properly encouraged, to *daven,* the association to being forced may cause a lasting distaste. It is much like being forced as a child to eat green beans, which can result in a dislike of green beans to age 95.

But *Tehillim* are not green beans. *Tehillim* can be very soothing and comforting. The *Midrash* relates that King David did not have a single good day in his seventy years. (I cite this in detail in *Let Us Make Man.*) He suffered one tragedy after another, and he expresses his exquisite pain many times in *Tehillim*; e.g., "For my loins were filled with burning, and there is no soundness in my flesh" (38:8). Yet, amid his intense anguish, David says, "You have put joy in my heart" (4:8). Learning about the life of David and studying *Tehillim* can overcome unpleasant associations. However, we must not be afraid of feeling. Sometimes we numb ourselves because we are afraid to feel.

Davening should be the expression of the heart, and we should know that Hashem hears our prayers. Once at the *Kosel HaMaaravi* (Western Wall) I heard a blind man talking to Hashem. Abruptly he paused, then said, "Oh, I told You about that yesterday," and continued his conversation. He knew that Hashem had heard him yesterday.

Reciting the words of *davening* is meritorious, but to have the feeling of being in a relationship with Hashem, we must study the prayers and savor the words. I try to convey some personal interpretations in *Living Each Day* and *Twerski on Prayer*.

Unfortunately, many people are in a hurry and rush through *davening*. This may leave one unimpressed. However, if we make the effort to understand the prayers, and say them slowly, perhaps with a melody, we will develop feelings. It is related that the Steipler Gaon had a *niggun* (tune) with which he recited the portion before the *Amidah* (*Shemoneh Esrei*).

Saying *Tehillim* and *davening* with an understanding of the words and some of the interpretations given by our Sages are totally different than the negative childhood experience, and can arouse very profound feelings as we make contact with Hashem.

DAAS FORMED SOLELY BY TORAH

On several occasions, you have recommended that the reader should consult daas Torah. What or who constitutes daas Torah? Furthermore, since you are a rabbi yourself, why can't you give the opinion as daas Torah?

In your column, you disqualify anyone as daas Torah who has attained knowledge from sources other than Torah. What about Rambam, who studied Greek philosophy? I recall Rabbi Gifter, zt"l, listing gedolim who had secular knowledge.

Although a rabbi may be authorized to issue rulings on questions that can be answered by halachah, that does not necessarily qualify him to render an opinion on matters for which there are no direct halachic guidelines. In such cases, one should be guided exclusively by Torah *hashkafah*.

There are principles of Torah *hashkfah* that can serve as guidelines to all situations in life. However, a person giving an opinion must be certain that his opinion is based on pure Torah concepts. This can be done only by someone whose entire thought processes are the result of Torah knowledge.

I have studied psychology, and it is possible that my thinking may have been influenced by my secular studies. Even if I had adequate Torah knowledge, I could not be considered *daas Torah* because I have been subject to concepts that did not derive from Torah. Therefore, *daas Torah* is a *talmid chacham* who was never influenced by anything other than Torah.

No one today can compare himself to Rambam or to any other *rishonim kimalachim*. Furthermore, even Rambam did not escape criticism from the Vilna Gaon (*Biur HaGra, Yoreh Deah,* 179).

I have had the opportunity to discuss issues with *gedolim*, and I could see how their thought processes were qualitatively different than mine. I have also had discussions with some *talmidei chachamim* who had secular education, and although I respect them highly, I could see where they might have been influenced by non-Torah ideas.

Therefore, I reiterate, *daas Torah* is a *daas* that is formed solely by Torah.

IS IT POSSIBLE FOR *DAAS* TO BE IN ERROR?

In response to a previous question, you suggested we consult daas Torah. We did, and we think the answer we got was not correct.

I t is one thing if you ask for *Siyatta Dishmaya* on your own decisions, which you are free to change. However, if you consult *daas Torah*, it is very unwise to ignore the response, and it may be impermissible, according to the commandment, "You shall not deviate from the word that they will tell you, right or left" (*Devarim*, 17:11), although this applies primarily to the Sanhedrin and *Chazal*. This requires a *psak halachah*.

As far as consulting another *daas Torah*, it is obvious that if one shops around until one gets the answer one wants, that is really not consulting *daas Torah*. If you have new information to present or if you think that you did not present your case clearly, you may go back to the *daas Torah* you consulted. It appears from the Talmud (*Avodah Zarah*, 7a) that if you consult another *daas Torah*, you must inform him that you previously consulted another *posek* and you must tell him the answer you received from the first one.

WHOM DO YOU THINK YOU ARE FOOLING?

We are taught in mussar shuir that we must do everything leshem shamyim, not only mitzvos. So that when we eat, we should not do so for the pleasant taste, but only because we need the nourishment to have the energy to do mitzvos.

That sounds good, but is it realistic? I see very fine bnei Torah enjoying delicacies, and it is really hard to believe that they are eating them for nourishment rather than for pleasure.

To eat for nourishment rather than for pleasure is a *madrega* (high spiritual level). It is something to strive for. Before we are there, we should at least have proper *kavannah*, thanking Hashem for giving us things we can enjoy. This concept is expressed by the *berachah* we say for fruit blossoms: "Blessed is Hashem, for nothing is lacking in His universe, and He created in it good creatures and good trees, to cause mankind pleasure with them." It is possible to achieve lofty spirituality, but we must prepare ourselves for this.

A peasant went to buy a suit, and the salesperson gave him a suit of the correct size. The peasant put on the suit atop his coarse garments and complained that it did not fit properly. "You fool!" the salesman said. "The fit is proper, but you must first take off your coarse garments. Of course the suit cannot fit on top of them."

Madregos are achievable only if we are spiritual people. They will not fit over coarse garments. To be truly spiritual, we must refine our *middos*. We must eliminate all envy, greed, hate, vanity, anger, and falsehood. Rabbi Chaim Vital says we must attend to rectification of *middos* even more than to observance of mitzvos (*Shaar HaKedushah*). If we study *Orchos Tzaddikim* and *Mesillas Yesharim* and live our lives according to their teachings, we can then become spiritual people and can work on achieving *madregos*. It then becomes realistic to eat for nourishment and not solely for physical pleasure.

You may recall the famous anecdote about R' Samson Rafael Hirsh who visited the Alps and admired the beauty of the mountains. When asked why he took time to do so, he replied, "After 120 years *Hakadosh Baruch Hu* will ask me if I saw His mountains. How can I answer him if I haven't seen them?" We can learn from this anecdote that Hashem wants us to enjoy the pleasure of this world, in accordance with Torah guidelines.

UNWANTED THOUGHTS DISTURB PRAYER

I am a merchant, and it is very annoying to me that when I start the Shemonah

Esrei, I start thinking about my business, about orders I need to fill, whether the merchandise I am expecting will arrive in time, and other such thoughts. I have read sefarim about machshavos zaros, but I still get these thoughts. Do you have any suggestions about how I can get rid of them?

That these thoughts are the work of the *yetzer hara* is evident from the fact that they generally do not occur when you are enjoying a meal, for example, but only when you are *davening*.

Before going to sleep at night, we say *beyadcha afkid ruchi,* entrusting our *neshamah* to Hashem. When we wake up in the morning, we thank Hashem for giving us another day of life. If we could truly believe that our lives are in the hands of Hashem, our *davening* would be different.

In the beautiful "prayer before *tefillah*" composed by Rebbe Elimelech of Lizhensk, he mentions how the *yetzer hara* tries to distract us even when we are pleading for our lives. Imagine a person pleading to a judge to spare his life and not execute him. Would he be thinking of business then? All his attention would be focused on his plea to save his life. If we would concentrate on the fact that this is our position in *davening*, distracting thoughts would not occur to us.

The marvelous book, *Praying With Fire*, has helped a number of individuals to improve the quality of their davening. One point that is emphasized is that every time one comes to the word *Atah*, You, especially in a *berachah*, one should pause and concentrate on just to whom the *Atah* is referring. If you come to the realization that when *davening* you are conducting a one-on-one conversation with Hashem, it will serve as a powerful deterrent to the *yetzer hara's* wiles.

SHOULD AN ADDICTED PERSON MAKE THE *BERACHAH*, "*SHELO ASANI AVED?*"

I read your Haggadah, From Bondage to Freedom, and I agree that we may be slaves to a habit just as we were slaves to Pharaoh.

I was a two-pack-a-day smoker. I knew it was harmful to me. I stopped a few times for several weeks, but always went back. A year ago I suffered a severe heart attack, and it is only by chasdei Hashem that I am alive today. I have not smoked since. I realize how enslaved I was.

My question to you is, when one is enslaved by a habit from which he cannot break free, like I was, may he recite the berachah, "shelo asani aved," thanking Hashem for not being a slave, when one is very much a slave? Is it not a berachah levatalah?

Personally, I would be thrilled if *poskim* made such a ruling. Perhaps it would help people realize that they have lost their freedom, and they would pursue the pride of living as free beings.

However, this *berachah* is giving thanks to Hashem for giving us the many mitzvos that a slave does not have. Although a slave must abstain from all things the Torah prohibits, he does not have the mitzvos of *tefillin, sukkah, shofar,* and the like. Even if a person is an addict, he does have these mitzvos, for which he must be thankful.

However, it would be good if a person thought about the words he is saying and would realize that if he has a destructive habit from which he cannot break free, he is, to a certain degree, not being fully truthful when he recites the *berachah*, and would seek the proper help to regain his freedom.

HEART PATIENT REFUSES TO EAT ON FASTDAY

My father, B"H 80 years old, has heart disease. B"H, he survived triple bypass surgery. He is very weak, and the doctor told him that he is not allowed to fast. He is accepting the doctor's opinion about Tisha B'Av, but says that on Yom Kippur he will fast regardless of what the doctor says. I asked the doctor, who said there was no way he could fast on Yom Kippur, because it would endanger his life.

I don't know what I can do to have my father accept the doctor's opinion. Although he respects our rav, I don't think he will listen in this case. What can I do to convince him that he must eat something on Yom Kippur?

Check with your *rav*, then consult with the doctor whether it will adequate if he takes small amounts of food and drink at 10-minute intervals. If this is *completely* safe, the *rav* may have an easier time convincing your father. If this is not sufficient to assure his health, the *rav* will have to point out to him that we are obligated to do what the Torah says is right rather than what we think is right. If this is *pikuach nefesh*, then halachah demands that he do whatever is necessary to protect his life, and he must obey halachah.

You may tell your father this story:

In the *beis midrash* of the *tzaddik* R' Motele of Hornostipol, there was a man with serious heart disease whom the doctor ordered to eat on Yom Kippur or his life would be endangered. Yom Kippur, after *Shacharis*, R' Motele sent the *shammes* to ask the man if he had eaten something. The man told the *shammes* that he felt fine, and that there was no reason for him to eat. R' Motele sent the *shammes* back to repeat his instruction, and again the man refused to eat.

R' Motele went to the man himself and said, "If you eat as you were ordered to, I assure you *Olam Haba*. But if you endanger your life in defiance of the halachah, then the *Malach Domeh* will never be able to extract you from *Gehinnom*."

(R' Motele was my great-grandfather, and I had an eyewitness account of this incident.)

Our emotions about Yom Kippur are profound, and I can fully understand your father's feelings. However, our actions must be guided by halachah, not by emotion.

LEAVING *KOLLEL* TO EARN A LIVING

I know you have dealt with this before and you may not want to rehash it, but this is very important to me, and I'm sure to other women as well.

One woman wrote that her husband had to leave kollel to work, and that this hurt her deeply. She had been able to tell her children, "Totti is going to learn Torah," and now, since she is not going to lie to them, she must say, "Totti is going to work." It is not only a question of how she feels, but also of chinuch. Children look up to and emulate their father. If they are told, "Totti is going to learn Torah," they will develop a love for Torah, but if they are told, "Totti is going to work," they will develop a love for work. Is that what we want?

I am in that position. When my husband was in kollel, I felt fulfilled by his learning, because by taking care of the house, I was enabling him to learn. Now, I feel "less than," and I'm afraid that my children will also feel "less than."

The other woman wrote that her husband made the change with the approval of daas Torah. So did my husband. It was not a spontaneous decision, and the daas Torah he consulted gave it much thought. But that does not appreciably change my feelings. Frankly, I am not the happy person I was previously.

I am not stupid. I know I must face reality. Is there any way I can regain my feelings of worthiness and happiness?

I don't know that I can add much to my earlier response, other than to expand it a bit.

Yaakov Avinu is referred to as *bechir haAvos*, the choicest of the three Patriarchs. Yaakov was an undisputed *daas Torah*. When he gave his children *berachos*, he assigned Issachar to study Torah full time and Zevulun to engage in commerce. Yaakov certainly had great *bitachon*. Why did he not assign Zevulun also to full-time Torah Study? He did not doubt that Hashem could give Zevulun *parnassah*. I know that Yaakov, as *daas Torah*, conveyed the will of Hashem.

I heard a story that is awe-inspiring. The great gaon, R' Avraham of Sochotchov (*Avnei Nezer*), completed a commentary on *Shulchan Aruch Choshen Mishpat*, and showed it to his father-in-law, the Rebbe of Kotzk. The Rebbe said, "It is beautiful, but it is so beautiful that if it is published, people will study your commentary and neglect the commentary of the *Shach*, which was written with *ruach hakodesh*. That dare not be allowed to happen! I want you to throw this into the fire."

The great *Avnei Nezer* did not hesitate. He made a *berachah* "lishmoa l'divrei chachamim" (to heed the instructions of Torah scholars) and threw the manuscript, over which he had labored so long, into the fire. That is an example of the *mesiras nefesh* in following *daas Torah*.

When we have a *sh'eilah*, even a very serious one, we consult *daas Torah* and act according to his ruling. We don't second-guess, and in many cases, it is not even permissible to be *machmir*. We must act according to *daas Torah* rather than according to our feelings. Indeed, our feelings should be determined by *daas Torah*.

You have reason to be happy because you have followed *daas Torah*. Your children will love Torah because there is love for Torah in the home. I am sure that your husband will still be *kovea itim l'Torah* (set aside specific time for Torah study). When your children see the *menuchas hanefesh* with which you both acquiesced to *daas Torah* they will have absorbed a valuable lesson that will enable them to live fruitful Torah lives. If they see that Totti works only to earn a living, but that his focus — and yours — is still *limud HaTorah*, they will develop the same love for Torah that you and your husband are experiencing.

GUILT FOR AN INADVERTENT SHABBOS-VIOLATION

My 16-year-old son is a wonderful young man, a fine yeshivah student, who has always been emotionally stable. But I'm now worried.

Two weeks ago, on Shabbos, he discovered that he had been walking around on Shabbos with a $5 bill in his pocket. Usually, he does not have money in his Shabbos suit. A few weeks ago on Motzei Shabbos, however, I sent him to the supermarket, and he forgot about the money that he left in his suit pocket.

For the past two weeks he has been depressed, because (1) he was carrying on Shabbos and (2) it was muktzah. I can't seem to put his mind at ease. I don't know how to get him out of this mood. Do you have any suggestions?

Although halachah-wise there are a number of mitigating factors — it was totally without his awareness and unintended — nevertheless, the severity of Shabbos is such that he clearly feels guilty. However, what he should understand is that once a person has done *teshuvah,* one must believe that a transgression has been erased, as the prophet says, "I have erased your sin like fog." When a fog clears, it does not leave the slightest trace. You might share the following story with your son:

A man told the tzaddik, R' Michel of Zlotchow, that he had inadvertently violated Shabbos and asked what he must do for *teshuvah.* R' Michele gave him a harsh penance, to fast a number of days. The man came to the Baal Shem Tov and related this to him, and the Baal Shem Tov said that there was no need to fast. Rather, he should donate a pound of candles to the shul:

The Baal Shem Tov sent a message to R' Michel, inviting him for Shabbos. R' Michel set out on Thursday, with more than enough time to get to Medzhiboz before Shabbos. However, everything that could go wrong went wrong. First, the axle of the wagon broke, then there was a severe thunderstorm, then the wagon sank into the mud — in short, R' Michel reached Medzhiboz shortly before sunset on Friday. When he entered the Baal Shem Tov's home, the Baal Shem Tov was making *kiddush.* Fearfully concluding that he had traveled on Shabbos, R' Michel fainted.

When R' Michel was revived, the Baal Shem Tov said, "You did not violate Shabbos. I just welcomed Shabbos much earlier than usual. But when you thought that you had violated Shabbos, you were so horrified that you fainted.

"The essence of *teshuvah* is to sincerely regret what one has done. The man who told you that he had inadvertently violated Shabbos was in agony over it. His deep regret was already the sincere *teshuvah* that Hashem desires. There was no need to make him fast for *teshuvah.* However, in order to have him feel that he has done something tangible, I suggested that he donate candles. He had already done sincere *teshuvah* in his heart."

Tell your son this story. Point out to him that his regret about the $5 bill is the *teshuvah.* He should consult *daas Torah* whether there is anything else he should do.

Tell your son that to continue to ruminate over this and be depressed will interfere with his study and *tefillah,* and that after getting an opinion from *daas Torah,* he should feel *simchah* in Torah and *tefillah.*

PARENTS AND CHILDREN

ELDERLY FATHER MOVED IN

My father is 82 (to 120). Since my mother's death six years ago he has been living alone and managing fairly well, but in the last year there has been a marked change. He is very forgetful, and it became clear that he cannot take care of himself. We suggested an assisted-living facility where he could still be his own baalabuss, but he absolutely refused. There was no other choice, and he moved in with us. My two oldest children are married and we had room for him.

We love him dearly, and we are trying our utmost to accommodate him, but it is not easy. He can be very demanding and sometimes unreasonable. He never was this way before, and we know this is due to the changes in his brain. He is on medication but it is not helping much. The children love their Zeide but often find it difficult when he criticizes them.

We will do our best for him, but it bothers me that I have feelings of resentment that I shouldn't have. He took care of us when we were young. Why should I feel this way toward him? Is there anything I can do to rid myself of these negative feelings?

I think you are making a mistake when you describe your feelings as resentment. I think a more correct term is that you feel he is an "imposition," but this does not mean that you "resent" him.

When your children were infants and woke you up three times during the night to be fed, that was an "imposition." Obviously, you would rather have slept. Dirty diapers are no fun, and handling them is an "imposition," but you did not think of these impositions as being resentments. You loved your children in spite of the various "impositions" that caring for them caused, and you felt good accepting those "impositions" with true love.

It is the same with your father. You love him, respect him, and wish to care for him. True, this may constitute an "imposition" for you and your children, and there is nothing wrong with feeling it as an imposition, but it is an imposition that you accept with love. Don't consider an imposition to be a source of resentment just because it may interfere with your comfort. You did not "resent" your infants' impositions.

I remember a man, Leibel, who cared for his elderly father in a way that my father considered a model of *kibud av*. One time, Leibel said to him jokingly, "Pa, I love you and would not give you away for a million dollars, but I would not give a nickel for another one of you." This was Leibel's way of acknowledging that caring for his father was an imposition, but it did not diminish Leibel's love and respect for him. Leibel did not resent his father.

Giving your father the maximum care and showing him respect is the greatest of mitzvos, equivalent to respecting Hashem, and you should be aware of the great *zechus* you have. But that does not mean that you have to deny that this an imposition, one that you accept willingly. Had your father accepted assisted living where all his needs could have been met, it would have been easier for you, but it would have robbed you of an opportunity to excel in *kibud horim*.

You should also be aware that in addition to the great spiritual reward for *kibud av*, caring for your father shows your children how much you value this mitzvah, and this impresses upon them the importance of *kibud av vo'em* much more than any didactic teaching could do.

It is advisable to consult the geriatric specialists at the Jewish Family Services. They may have suggestions that can help you accomplish this mitzvah with greater ease.

MUST WE TOLERATE SECOND-HAND SMOKE?

I don't know what to do with myself. Since I can recall, my father said we should never put him in a home for the aged when he grows old. He was 83, and had been living alone for years after my mother died. He suffered a mild stroke, and although it did not completely disable him, he was unable to care for himself. He wanted to move in with us, and we were glad to have him. The only problem was that he is a heavy smoker, having smoked two packs of cigarettes daily since age 15. My husband is extremely sensitive to cigarette smoke. In fact, if he must pass someone in the street who is smoking, he crosses the street. My father said he would smoke only in his room, but even with an air filter, there would be smoke in the house, which my husband could not tolerate. There was a year-long waiting list for an assisted-living apartment.

After living with us for just several days without smoking, in spite of the nicotine patches and medications, my father said he could not take it, and agreed to enter a home for the aged, where there was accommodation for smokers, although he hated the idea. We asked a posek, who said that my husband could not be expected to tolerate smoking. My father was unhappy at the home for the aged, deteriorated physically, and died just four months later.

I am ridden with guilt. My father was in fair health, and I think he could have lived longer if he had stayed with us. It seems that tolerating smoke is a small sacrifice to save a life. I can't help feeling resentment toward my husband for not tolerating my father's habit. How can I overcome this?

Although *kibbud av* is one of the most important mitzvos, there are halachos about what a child must do for *kibbud av*. If you received a ruling from a *posek* that your family was not required to be exposed to second-hand smoke, then it is not proper to have resentment toward your husband. Whenever we follow halachah, we are doing what is right.

Stopping smoking after 65 years of indulging a daily habit is indeed very difficult, but the medications that were prescribed could certainly have lessened the withdrawal symptoms. Your father had a choice between two options — stopping smoking or moving to a home for the aged. Obviously he felt that the latter was less unpleasant. It was he who made the choice, not you.

To some people, smoke is an annoyance. Others are more deeply affected. We know that secondary smoke can affect a person's health. No doubt, the *posek* felt that it was a matter of your husband's health — and the health of other family members in the home, including yourself — being affected, which is why the *rav* ruled that your husband was not required to expose himself to it.

We are living in an era where medical advances have resulted in many people living longer. However, many of the problems of aging have not been solved. There is still no cure for Alzheimer's disease. Problems of *kibbud av vo'em* may become more prevalent, but we should not make decisions based on our own judgment. It is important that a *posek* be consulted and his advice followed — without guilt.

KIBBUD AV AFTER VERBAL ABUSE

My father, who is 83, has been living alone for the past six years, since my mother's death. He has recently begun to be confused, and it is obvious that it is not safe for him to be on his own. The only realistic arrangement is for him to move in with us. We do have an empty room, since several of our children are married.

The problem is that my father was verbally abusive to me. He belittled and insulted me, and when I married and left home I felt I was being freed from a prison. I don't have good feelings toward him. As long as he lived by himself and I visited occasionally, it was tolerable. Now that he is going to be with me constantly, it may be more than I can handle. He hurt me too much. I think I am strong enough to control my actions, but I can't help feeling the way I do.

Is there any way I can overcome my harsh feelings toward him? How much kavod am I required to give him?

This is essentially a halachic question which should be addressed to a *posek*. The Shulchan Aruch prescribes how a person must act respectfully toward parents. I do not recall any halachah about how one feels. Precisely about how to relate to difficult parents should be discussed with a *posek*.

While being exposed to abusive or other harmful behavior can generate feelings of resentment, it is important to try to overcome such feelings. The mitzvah, "Do not carry hate for your fellow in your heart," includes one's parents. It is obviously difficult to rid oneself of resentments, but it is a mitzvah, and doing mitzvos requires effort. The *sifrei mussar* suggest ways to minimize resentment. For example, we do not know what circumstances may have caused a person to act inappropriately. While this does not justify such behavior, because a person should work on his/her middos and avoid improper acts — and one certainly need not be a victim of such behavior — nevertheless, considering the roots of the negative actions may lessen the negative feelings.

Many people are totally unaware that their behavior is inappropriate, even when it is blatantly so. We all have blind spots. We can easily see the faults of others but not our own. It is very likely that in spite of how he acted toward you, he thought he was being a good father. It may be that he was simply repeating the way his father acted toward him, and to him, this was normal.

I had a patient who suffered a great deal from an abusive mother. I was surprised when she told me that she wanted to visit her mother. She explained, "She is my mother, so I love her, but there is nothing about that woman that one can like." Evidently, there can be love even when one does not like a person. Similarly, anger and love can coexist. Parents can have much love for a child at whom they are very angry. True, the love of a parent for a child is a biologic instinct, while the reverse is not. Nevertheless, there can be genuine love that is not extinguished by anger. You may realize that while you may not like him, you may still love him as a father.

You wrote that your father was abusive to you. If this behavior is no longer manifest, it should be easier for you to come to terms with it. Since it is not ongoing you may assume that your father has done *teshuvah*. *Teshuvah* wipes the slate clean and there should be no resentment for what is over and done.

Obviously, you are torn between your resentment of his abuse and the mitzvah of *kibbud av*. Another person in your position might have simply arranged for placement in a facility, which would have been quite understandable. You are to be commended for your courage in having him move in with you. I must caution you that elderly people are often cantankerous and demanding. Should your father evidence such behavior, it is important that you differentiate between abuse and impatience. Your personal sacrifice for *kibbud av* is a great *zechus*. For details on how you should relate to him, you should consult a *posek*.

MOTHER-GRANDMOTHER FEUD — HONOR ONE'S MOTHER VS. HONOR ONE'S GRANDMOTHER

My mother and grandmother have not spoken to each other for 27 years because, among other things, my mother believes her mother contributed to my mother's failed marriage. She also has no contact with her mother's family, mainly to ensure that they do not provide her mother with information that will enable her mother to have her address, etc. Although I am in contact with my grandmother without my mother's knowledge, my mother has threatened to cease contact with me if she ever finds out that I am doing so.

My grandmother wants to make peace with her daughter, although I strongly doubt this is possible. Just the mention of my grandmother upsets my mother and she variously refers to her mother as "evil," "insane," and "witch." I was wondering what my obligations are under Jewish law and what recommendation you may have. What I have written is only the tip of the iceberg.

nasmuch as there are halachic issues involved, you should consult a *posek*. To the best of my knowledge, the halachic conclusion (*Yoreh Deah,* 240) is that a person is obligated to honor a grandparent. The halachah is also that if a parent tells you to violate halachah, you are not to obey. In this case, it would appear that your mother's forbidding you to be in contact with your grandmother is in violation of halachah. After consulting a *posek*, you may tell your mother that it is a Torah obligation to honor your grandmother and that you must do so.

From what you describe, your mother's reaction to attempts to make peace may be quite radical, and there is no need to provoke her. If there is a *rav* whom she respects, he may try to suggest this to her. Because he is not related, her response to the *rav* might not be as severe as her reactions to your suggestion.

SCAPEGOATING PARENTS

I want to thank you for referring me to a cognitive psychologist. My problem was that I was never able to finish anything I started, always dropping any project in the middle. The first psychologist I saw for several sessions tried to point out to me that it was the fault of my parents, who had ruined my self-confidence. That is not true. My parents are wonderful people.

The cognitive psychologist focused on what I was doing and how I was sabotaging myself without knowing it. He really helped me.

A friend of mine saw a psychologist who blamed her parents for her problems, and now she doesn't even talk to them. My question is, why do psychologists blame parents for everything? Is that really necessary to help a person?

In principle, I agree with you. One of the things we learn from Adam and Chavah is that there is no way one can blame what they did on their parents.

Because much of a person's personality is formed in early life, and the people a child is exposed to the most and who have the greatest impact on him/her are the parents, it is understandable that psychologists may implicate the parents as the cause of the child's problems. There are some parents who make serious mistakes in how they raise their children. However, even when mistakes are made, their overwhelming majority of parents sincerely try to do what they feel is best for the child. However, what they feel is best may not really be so. Even if the way the parents acted was the cause of a problem, that does not mean that they are at fault. They meant well.

When a patient would try to blame his problems on his parents, my response was, "Even if you are today what your parents made you, its up to you whether you remain that way or make positive changes in yourself." I believe that is the approach the cognitive psychologist took with you.

The fact that well-meaning parents may make mistakes in raising a child points up why it is so important for young people to learn about proper parenting before they become parents. I strongly advocate instruction in parenting at the senior high school level.

For generations, parents have been raising their children the way they themselves were raised. But today's world is not the world of previous generations. Life is much more complex, and the challenges from the environment that children face today are unprecedented. This is why learning the best parenting methods before one becomes a parent is so important.

MENDING FENCES

My relationship with my husband at the beginning of our marriage was not healthy. I was in denial, fooling myself that our relationship was good. I had low self-esteem, and often screamed at my children. B"H, after starting a twelve-step program and a lot of "Siyatta Dishmaya," I am really improving. I feel happier about myself and I am therefore automatically calmer and more positive with my kids. I have one child with whom my relationship is extremely shaky. He acted like a teenager even before he became one (which I am sure was a direct result of my considering him to be a difficult child, and he didn't feel accepted). This child is very "closed" (similar to me, but I am working on it) and super-sensitive, even to the regular instructions a parent usually uses to guide children the first time they learn a new skill. He takes everything as a criticism. The child also escapes reality through reading and procrastinating, always delaying what has to be done. He is obviously not interested in any advice I have to give. Is there any way to help him? I really wish he could go to a therapist to help him get rid of his resentment towards me, but I don't think he would open up to one or even be willing to go. I wish I could change the past, but since I can't, I wish I could at least help him have a better future, which might be hard since he is keeping so much inside.

P.S. I try spending quality time with him, but I know that it's barely enough. I *would love to do more, but my schedule is extremely tight and complicated.*

C hildren are less fixed in their personalities than adults, so change is always possible.

Many children find it difficult to open up to parents, and it is not necessarily the parents' fault. Although spending quality time with children is important, there are circumstances in which a parent may not have much time available. It is, therefore, important that whatever time is spent should be used to the greatest advantage.

Don't harp too much on the past. The last thing a child needs is a parent who feels guilty and tries to assuage that guilt by acting in a particular way toward the child. Acting out of guilt is counterproductive.

It is difficult to generalize. You may be familiar with the book, *How to Talk so Kids Will Listen and How to Listen so Kids Will Talk.* Although the specific suggestions in the book may not be universally applicable, the principle is valid. If we can find a way to talk to and listen to a particular child, the relationship can improve significantly, even though it may take some time.

If the suggestions in that book are not appropriate for your son, you could discuss with a child psychologist what approach is more likely to succeed.

Children do want a relationship with their parents. You may need some guidance on how to remove the barriers. It is never too late, so persevere. When you find the correct approach, you will have an excellent relationship with your son.

DAUGHTER IS *CHUTZPADIK*

We are desperately seeking your guidance in the following matter. Our daughter, aged 16, is a particularly sensitive, smart girl excelling in all school subjects. She has

good friends and is socially well-liked.
Already at a young age, her restless nature
became apparent, as she exhibited terrible
unease, worsening with each passing year.

As her parents, we are worried about
her extreme chutzpah and lack of respect.
Mostly, we are concerned about her
irritability that takes her out of control.
Terrible mood swings are a daily occurrence,
transporting her on a journey of extremes,
very high and low attitudes, never leaving
her on a balanced level. Especially now,
before entering into shidduchim, can we
continue letting her be so unhappy with
herself?

Knowing how much we provide for her and
what we endure when she attacks or mimics
us in return, we would like to know what
else can be done for her sake. Does she
need psychological help? If so, how in the
world will we convince her to agree to see
a professional?

I am hesitant to make a diagnosis on the basis of fragmentary information, and I am not saying that your daughter has Oppositional Defiant Disorder (ODD). However, adolescent psychologists report that the most frequent diagnosis today is ODD. The important thing is that the management of ODD can be effective in other problems of adolescent behavior.

It is important that your daughter be evaluated by a competent adolescent psychologist. Sometimes, young people with defiant behavior may have a mood disorder or ADD.

Among the symptoms of ODD are: refusal to comply with adult requests; excessive arguing with adults; frequent anger and resentment; and blaming others for his/her mistakes. These symptoms may also occur in adolescent depression, which is different than adult depression.

Certainly, the problem should be resolved so that it does not interfere with *shidduchim* and cause difficulty in marriage.

I cannot tell you how to convince your daughter to go to a therapist. Since she is defiant in other ways, she is likely to resist this, too. On the other hand, her behavior may be a cry for help, and she may be waiting for you to offer her a way to help her control her behavior.

I suggest you call a national organization, Parent Resources, 1-435-673-4057 (see Appendix). They may be able to help you with this.

OVER-PROTECTIVE MOTHER: CAN A MOTHER CARE TOO MUCH?

I have a problem, or rather my friend has. She has a son of eighteen who is physically handicapped (can't walk), but is B"H one hundred percent okay mentally. My friend, who is a wonderful person, insists on doing everything for her son by herself.

However, this is clearly too much for her. Although she loves him, she berates him, day in and day out, for not doing enough exercise. She also controls his life and doesn't let him have an opinion about anything. The problem is, my friend won't hear of getting any help from the state. She claims it's not too much for her (it's just that her son should try harder), and creates more problems than she solves. In short, she is being a martyr at the expense of her son. No one can talk her into getting help — neither her husband nor her children. Can you suggest how we can make life a little easier for both mother and son?

In situations where a child is ill or has any kind of handicap, the parents often feel guilty, fearing that they are somehow responsible for the problem, and their behavior is an outgrowth of the guilt feeling, as though they can compensate for their "fault" by doing things for the child. These guilt feelings are generally without any basis in reality, but as I have often pointed out, emotions may not obey logic. This may be why she is resistant to any logical argument.

It is, of course, unfortunate that she is flagellating herself needlessly. But what is more important is that her "helpful" behavior may actually be detrimental to her son. Many people with major physical handicaps have been able to become self-sufficient and lead independent lives. However, this requires that they develop their skills, and if someone does things for them that they are capable of doing by themselves (albeit with great effort), it stifles their ability to develop independence.

In situations where a person's behavior is detrimental, yet he/she is unable to see it, an "intervention" may be effective. During intervention (confrontation), a number of people who are involved in the case get together and present the person with the facts. In this situation, the intervention should consist of the husband, children, physician, rabbi, and several close friends.

The intervention must be rehearsed with an "intervention specialist," a competent therapist, perhaps a social worker or physical therapist who is familiar with the case. In the rehearsal, each person states his/her observation of what is perceived as being counter-productive, acknowledging that he/she knows the mother is trying her utmost for her son, but that unfortunately, her efforts may backfire in some ways. The husband, children, physician, rabbi, and friends each expresses his/her opinion.

Of course, she will rebut everything they say, and in the rehearsal, the intervention specialist will help everyone plan how to respond to the rebuttal.

The group chooses an appropriate time when they can all come together and meet with her, saying, "We feel that for both your son's sake and your own, we need to talk with you." The sheer weight of everyone stating their observations is usually effective in overcoming the resistance. At the conclusion of the intervention, the group leader states, "We know you need help, and we will see to it that you get it." Someone must then be designated to meet with her regularly and give her the support she needs. It is also important that the son receives the help he needs to develop necessary skills.

An intervention is not easy. It can be uncomfortable and stressful for everyone, yet it may be the only way to get both the mother and son the help they need.

DERECH ERETZ DEFINED?

I have a problem that has been bothering me for some time. My elderly grandmother needs a lot of care and attention. Mealtimes are difficult since she often doesn't have an appetite and will only eat or drink if coaxed and persuaded. It requires patience, skill, and often tricks to get her to eat a reasonable amount. Since I seem to have the knack to get around her and I am one of the few people in the family who she seems to listen to, this task often falls to me.

It bothers me greatly that I often bribe her and coax her to eat in a way that borders on chutzpah. Also, in other matters of caring for herself, when she asks me to do certain things that I feel she could do alone and it would even be beneficial for her to do them herself, I must refuse and insist she does them herself.

How far may I go with this within the boundaries of derech eretz and halachah?

This is really a question that should be addressed to a *posek*. I will merely comment that the Talmud says that everything depends on one's intention and attitude. Your coaxing her to eat is to maintain her life and health, and this is commendable. Similarly, if your refusal to do things for her is so that she does not become totally dependent on others, that too is with good intentions.

However, I suggest you consult a *posek* for specific guidelines.

CHILD WITH CONTRADICTORY ATTITUDES

I hope that you can help me with the following problem.

Eliezer is a 6-year-old boy who possesses many of the typical traits of "the middle child." Sandwiched between two older siblings and two younger ones, he often feels left out and is also concerned about getting his fair share. Most of his behaviors are normal; however, Eliezer has a temper, which I am finding increasingly more difficult to deal with, both as a parent and within the parameters of the family itself.

There are two areas that elicit very angry and harsh responses from Eliezer. First, when he wants something that he cannot have, or cannot have instantly, or that does not belong to him. Second, when he has to make a transition from one task to another, albeit a normal routine change, i.e., getting dressed, getting ready for school, or going to bed.

Sometimes he becomes agitated because of an insignificant matter or for one of the reasons I mentioned previously. If it cannot be or is not resolved for him immediately, he flies into an angry rage and often will throw things and yell, kick, scream ….

On the other hand, Eliezer is a very bright child and very responsible. In some ways he is much more mature than his peers. His teachers have always adored him, as he is eager to please them, very smart, and conscientious about doing his work perfectly. Because of this, we were sure he would grow out of this behavior, but it has only gotten more intense.

What is surprising is that he has such contradictory behaviors. Sometimes he is so cooperative, helpful, sweet, and calm while other times so angry and hostile. Our home has a very content and happy, loving atmosphere. My husband and I have tried numerous interventions. We shower our children with love, especially Eliezer. We give positive reinforcement whenever possible. Somehow we are always tested by Eliezer's outbursts and find ourselves walking on eggshells, hoping that he won't explode.

We want to do what is best for him but we do feel that his behavior interfering with the other children and with the calmness of our home.

Does Eliezer's behavior seem within normal range, to be dealt with more carefully, or should we seek help to overcome this anger?

I'm not sure that there is validity to the "birth-order syndromes." There are oldest children, youngest children, and middle children, all of whom have varying characteristics, i.e., some oldest children may have what has been termed "middle-child syndrome."

Giving Eliezer much love should be very helpful, but for whatever reason, it has not altered his behavior. Walking on eggshells is unwise, because it serves as reinforcement and tells Eliezer that he can control his environment by his outbursts. In addition, the other children should not be penalized because you are trying to forestall Eliezer's explosiveness.

Behavior modification is a very potent technique, wherein you use rewards and deprivations to reinforce or distinguish certain behaviors. However, it is possible that one may unintentionally reward the wrong thing. Guidance on using behavior modification is necessary.

Eliezer has many positives going for him, as is evident from the fact that his teachers adore him. Obviously, he behaves differently at school than at home, and this is probably because he feels he can get away with throwing tantrums at home.

Eliezer may not see things the way you see them, and it is difficult to know what his perspective is. His outbursts cannot be considered normal, and it is not wise to trust that he will outgrow them. It is best for you to discuss this in greater detail with a child psychologist.

DIFFICULT MOTHER

I find kibud em extremely challenging. My mother is an emotionally weak person with an attitude; she believes that everyone lies to her and that people are out to get her. She has difficulties getting along with her neighbors and her siblings, never mind my father's family. My father is a tzaddik and shows a tremendous amount of respect towards her. I think that it's in this merit that they have raised their children as they have, including sons who are talmidei chachamim, respected, and well-liked in society. We, as siblings, share a strong bond with each other, helping

each other physically and financially,
when appropriate. Our devotion to each
other, unfortunately, hurts my mother and
she always asks us why we are so good,
we'll only get a "kick" in return. At
any given moment, my mother is not on
speaking terms with at least one of us
siblings, often with reasons that are at
least partially imagined. My husband and
I try to do whatever we think possible to
encourage peace, bending over backwards to
ensure smooth sailing; however, there are
times that we are unsuccessful. She always
complains about how miserable her lot is and
how financially deprived she is, although
this is difficult to believe. It seems as
if after we are married she doesn't feel
any responsibility toward us. I know she
doesn't owe us anything, but its almost as
if we are strangers to her. In a certain
sense, her attitude is: I'll marry you off,
let the other side deal with the rest. If
any of us siblings are in need of physical
or financial assistance, her response is,
"It's not my problem. If you are old enough
to get married, you're old enough to take
care of your own problems." I always hoped
that "good will" would change this attitude
and she would come to the realization that a
life devoid of giving isn't satisfying.

Is there any way an outsider can change
such a person's attitude so that she may
enjoy her life and interactions with the
people with whom she comes in contact?
It's as if she views everyone as enemies.
Unfortunately, it's a familial thing; her
mother had the same attitude. I would think
that since it's familial, some of us siblings
would also have this issue, but we all seem
to get along with each other and our spouses'

Your mother might possibly change some of her ideas if she underwent fairly intensive therapy, but there is little likelihood that this will happen. Her perception is that she is fine, and everyone else out there has problems. Although her perspective may be grossly distorted, it is reality for her. This is a personality condition that is extremely difficult to change.

Of course, we are required to observe *kibbud em* even under the most difficult conditions. If being in her presence should prove intolerable for you, you may consult your *rav* as to whether you are required to visit her and how often. However, in her presence, you must exercise great respect and compassion for her.

Your observation that she picked up her attitude from her mother is probably correct. She is not responsible for the way she feels. I doubt that this attitude is hereditary, and if you show your children compassion and model proper relationships with family and people in general, there is no reason for concern that your children will develop her attitude.

HOLOCAUST SURVIVOR HAS BORDERLINE PERSONALITY DISORDER

To make a very long story short, my mother,
a Holocaust survivor, has a severe case
of borderline personality disorder. It
has gotten so bad that she rants abusive
insults not only at her daughter but to her
grandchildren and great-grandchildren. My
13-year-old granddaughter was present during
the latest abuse, and she suggested that

Whatever diagnosis there may be, nothing that psychiatry and psychology knows or ever knew can be applied to Holocaust survivors. The horrors that they experienced and witnessed are among the worst, if not the worst, in the history of humanity, and their behavior is beyond anyone's judgment. The miracle of miracles is that so many survivors have been able to lead normal lives.

I don't think that not speaking to her for a few weeks is going to change her behavior. A 13-year-old young woman can be told that the unspeakable horrors of the Holocaust may have affected her grandmother this way, and I believe your granddaughter is capable of understanding this. As difficult as it is to be the target of such abuse, this is a case where I think one must tolerate the suffering in silence and not react with hostility.

One does not have to expose oneself to abuse, and if staying away is possible, one may do so. In a different case, not speaking to an abusive person may be an effective punishment for his/her actions, but Holocaust survivors have had more than a maximum of punishment, and nothing should be added to this.

HOW COULD IT HAPPEN?

I was recently shocked to discover that my friend's son has gone off-the-derech. I know this boy, and he had never given his parents any cause for worry. My friend's Yiddishkeit is of the highest degree. His home operates according to the strictest requirements of halachah, and I cannot understand how this happened. My children are still very young, and I am wondering if there is anything I can do more than I am doing to make sure that this does not happen to one of my children.

We do not know all the reasons why youngsters go off the-*derech*. Sometimes there are problems within the family that are not known to an outside observer. Certainly, a true *shalom bayis* in which the parents respect one another, and where there is good communication between parents and children, lessens the likelihood of a child going off-the-*derech*. It is also important that the child's yeshivah provide a warm, caring environment in which the child can feel that he is valued. But there is nothing foolproof, and even in ideal circumstances, a child may deviate. The *yetzer hara* is powerful and unrelenting, and may succeed in misleading a youngster.

We must realize that we live in an environment with a degree of pleasure-seeking and moral decadence that is unprecedented. We try to bring up our children in ways that were traditional, but the traditional ways that were adequate in the shtetl and even in the America of several decades ago may not be adequate to withstand the onslaught of modern society. *Tehillim* (106:35) says, "They mingled among the nations and they learned their ways." As much as we try to avoid the mingling, we cannot prevent penetration of the environmental influences.

It is, therefore, necessary that we increase and strengthen our defenses against the attack of the secular world. When the enemy's weapons were spears and arrows, a shield was an adequate defense. When his weapons are guided missiles, our defenses must accordingly be much greater. In the shtetl, strict observance of halachah was adequate. That may not be enough to counteract the weapons that the *yetzer hara* has today.

The secular world is motivated by pleasure-seeking. "If it feels good, do it, as long as it is not harmful or illegal." Unfortunately, even many Torah-observant people ascribe to a similar principle: "If it feels good, do it, as long as it is not harmful or in violation of halachah."

In order to counteract environmental influences, it may be necessary to live according to the *Mesillas Yesharim* chapter on *Prishus* (avoidance of indulgence), the fourth step of Rabbi Moshe Chaim Luzzato's ladder of *ruchniyus*. Ramchal says that implementing the first three steps of *zehirus* (watchfulness), *zerizus* (diligence) and *nekius* (pureness) makes one a tzaddik. Going beyond that leads one to becoming a chassid.

One may say "I am satisfied if I can be a tzaddik. There is no requirement that I become a chassid." I can only repeat that if we wish to prevent our children from going astray, we must reject the pleasure-seeking motif of modern society, and we cannot say, "If it feels good, do it, as long as it is not harmful or in violation of halachah."

Let us be frank. Many of the pleasures of the non-Jewish culture have now been made available to *shomrei Torah*. When I was a child, the Pesach menu was essentially potatoes, meat, and borscht. Some milk products were available. The only candy we had was marmalade. Today there is *kosher l'Pesach* pizza, *cholov Yisrael* ice-cream in a variety of flavors, non-*gebrokt* ice-cream cones, all soft drinks, more than one-hundred varieties of wine, and a huge variety of confections. The availability of all kinds of permissible pleasures is present all year round.

Our *sefarim* tell us that the degree of *kedushah* we have must be as intense and powerful as the prevailing *tumah*. The degree of *tumah* that is displayed in the graphic media and that flies through the air to the screens of television, computers, and Palm Pilots necessitates a corresponding intensification of *kedushah*. Ramban (*Vayikra* ,19:2) defines *kedushah* as going beyond that which is forbidden and abstaining from non-essential permissible things.

This is asking much of a person. In fact, in our times this may be considered a degree of *mesiras nefesh*. However, if we realize the dangers to which our children are exposed, we will — indeed we must — be willing to follow the Ramban's teaching.

IS MY CHILD IMMATURE?

I have 5 children (Bli Ayin Hara), and, Baruch Hashem, we try our best to bring

them up to be G-d-fearing Jews with tznius
and good middos. My question is concerning
our first-born; he is ten years old and
his learning skills are pretty good. His
behavior is usually adequate but the big
difficulty is that he is very immature.
As much as we try, in a positive way, to
teach him responsibility, to help others
and to stop being enormously jealous of
his younger siblings, it seems he doesn't
understand what we want from him. He is
only able to focus on himself, goes crazy
for a small piece of candy, and behaves in
certain situations as a 5-year-old would!
His younger sisters (6 and 8) are so much
more responsible and mature even without our
asking them to act in such a way.

Is there any way of teaching maturity or
do we just have to have patience and let
time resolve the problem.

Although children eventually may mature, it is not uncommon to see people at age 40 who behave immaturely. It is, therefore, risky to dismiss the problem and hope for the best.

Although I am not a child psychologist, I know that immaturity may be due to any number of causes. Sometimes a child feels insecure, and believes that he must take everything for himself or else he will not get a fair share. He may feel he is entitled to things, and that if he doesn't get them he is being unjustly deprived. We all know adults who behave as though the world owes them a living.

Sometimes the self-centeredness is due to the child feeling that he has a deficiency of some sort, such as one of the learning disabilities or ADD. It is, therefore, important that the child be evaluated by a competent child psychologist. If he/she should suggest that it is O.K. to leave the child alone and assures you that he will outgrow his immaturity, then you may relax.

The psychologist may instruct you to relate to your child in a more effective way. Properly done, behavior modification — rewarding the desirable and essentially ignoring the improper behavior — may be effective, but one must be carefully guided in the use of this method, because sometimes we may inadvertently reward the wrong thing.

PREVENTING A CHILD FROM GOING OFF-THE-*DERECH*

I greatly enjoy your books, especially the one about parenting, so I was a little surprised by your comments about how to prevent a child from going off-the-derech. Your main theme was the need for extra kedushah, prishus (separating ourselves from the influences of the outside world) in the home. While I agree that this may be important, I have some questions on your advice.

Is it really realistic to expect parents to be able to get anywhere near the levels of prishus you called for and even more so to expect the kids to attain such a level?

Even if it is, I have seen much about kids going off-the-derech and seen a number of real-life cases — the main reasons generally given are not what you said, rather lack of love in the home, bad teachers, and, perhaps most of all, a severe failing in the whole educational system to give kids an appreciation of what TRUE Torah Judaism is about — of what a relationship with Hashem is; of why we do mitzvos; of the little-known fact that Hashem actually wants to make our lives better, not worse, etc. Isn't this a far more fundamental problem?

> I have heard about surveys in which frum
> kids were asked why they are frum and the
> vast majority answered that it was because
> they were brought up that way — isn't this
> kid of attitude most responsible for kids
> falling to the temptations of the modern
> world — the ta'avah that leads them there is
> more of a symptom than a cause of why they
> go off — if they were happy with Torah then
> maybe the ta'avos of the world would not
> lead them astray.

There is no question that there is much in our educational system that could use improvement. However, our educational institutions as well as our families are operating under a great deal of stress.

As important as the impact of the educational system is, the influence of the home is nevertheless primary. We must realize that a Torah-true Judaism goes beyond glatt kosher, *chalav Yisrael,* and *yashan.* We must take very seriously the words of the Talmud, which states that rage is equivalent to *avodah zarah,* and that *lashon hara* is equal to the three cardinal sins combined.

I do not doubt that parents give their children much love, but an angry outburst or speaking derogatorily about someone is a gross violation of Torah, as is carrying a grudge against someone who offended you, and this may leave the children with the impression that the essence of Torah is the ritual performance of mitzvos.

Yiddishkeit is built on *avodas Hashem. Avodah* means work. There is not much work today in observing kashrus. Everything is available with a reliable *hechsher.* There is not much work in keeping Shabbos. It's quite comfortable. *Tefillah* is supposed to be *avodah,* but I don't see anyone sweating bullets after *davening.* Where is the *avodah* in *avodas Hashem?* About the only place there is real work is in *middos.* Indeed, R' Chaim Vital says in *Shaarei Kedushah* (1:2) that it is more difficult to develop proper *middos* than observe all the mitzvos.

I repeat, "*Fun kein guts antloift men nisht*" — "No one runs away from what is good." It is the responsibility of parents and *mechanchim* to demonstrate that Torah is beautiful, and this is done primarily by refinement of *middos*. A home filled with love, true *shalom bayis* and exemplary *middos* can counteract the shortcomings of the educational system. Needless to say, *mechanchim*, who should be models for their students, must also exhibit exemplary *middos*.

I have difficulty with the question of whether it is realistic to expect parents to live a life of refined *middos* as described in *Orchos Tzaddikim* and *Mesillas Yesharim*.

R' Chaim Vital goes on to say that *middos* are the basis for mitzvos, and makes the awesome statement, "One should be more cautious about improper *middos* than about fulfilling the positive and prohibited mitzvos." Only someone with the stature of R' Chaim Vital could assert that one must be more cautious not to lose one's temper or have any other of the bad *middos* than to eat *tereifah*.

It is precisely because we do not practice what R' Chaim Vital says, as parents and as teachers, that some children may become disappointed with Yiddishkeit.

I remember the anxiety that parents had before the polio vaccine was developed. They panicked during the summer months when polio most often struck. If parents and teachers would realize that the children's Yiddishkeit is endangered by the *tumah* of the outside world just as their bodies were vulnerable to the dreaded polio, and not hide their heads in the sand and trust that their children are immune, they will take the *mussar* and *middos* of Yiddishkeit more seriously. The only way to overcome the unavoidable *ta'avah* to which our children are exposed is to make the home and cheder/yeshivah thoroughly *Torahdik* in *middos* as well as in mitzvos.

ADDICTION

PREVENTING DRUG USE IN CHILDREN

I never thought it would come to this. We often hear about drug problems in youngsters, but I felt secure that a sincere yeshivah bachur from a good, frum home would never have this problem. Recently I discovered that it could happen. What I want to know is, what should we be doing to prevent this from happening to our children?

I was told that there is a man who approaches yeshivah boys and offers them marijuana. What can be done about this?

Your question is extremely important and timely. We immunize our children to whooping cough, tetanus, and diphtheria when they are infants, giving them three injections that make them febrile and sickly for 48 hours. The possibility of a youngster getting into drugs, regardless of his environment, is far greater than the chance of his getting whooping cough, diphtheria, or tetanus. We cannot afford to have a false sense of security. Regardless of how low the incidence may be, if it does occur, it is ruinous to both the child and the family.

Because of the prevalence of drugs in our environment, it is important that parents educate themselves about illegal drugs, and know the names of the more commonly used drugs. It is also important that parents should be aware of warning signs that might indicate drug use. Many books are available that can provide this information.

We should let our children know that we are aware of the fact that drugs can be found everywhere, and that if they have any questions about drugs, they may ask us. Some people think that talking about drugs may give the children ideas and arouse their curiosity. The fact is that many, if not most, yeshivah boys (and girls!) have already heard about illegal drugs. Avoiding the topic means that they can never discuss it with their parents, and if they look for information elsewhere, they may get it from the wrong sources.

Youngsters who turn to drugs are invariably unhappy or dissatisfied about something. Paying attention to our children is the best way to be aware of how they feel. We should interest ourselves in what they are learning and who their friends are. Children should know that their parents have a listening ear to hear their troubles. It is unfortunate that economic necessity often make such demands on parents that they do not have enough time to spend with their children.

A prime factor for a child to feel happy is a secure and pleasant home. A home in which the children are controlled by fear is not a pleasant one. Children should obey their parents out of respect for them, and this respect must be earned. Parents who have exemplary *middos* are respected by their children. If parents do not have proper *middos*, and are chronically dissatisfied, indulge in angry outbursts, act disrespectfully to each other, and are self-centered, they may lose the respect of their children, and these children do not feel secure in their home.

It has been wisely said that the greatest gift you can give to your children is the consideration and affection you show to your spouse.

It is important that children should never be humiliated in yeshivah. There are ways of controlling a class with proper discipline while protecting the dignity of students. The emotional scars of being humiliated in front of others can be deep and long-lasting. The Talmud says, "Let the honor of your student be as dear to you as your own" (*Pirkei Avos,* 4:15). A teacher who humiliates a child does not belong in the classroom.

Cigarette smoking should be absolutely forbidden. It is extremely rare to find anyone who uses drugs who was not a cigarette smoker first. Fortunately, smoking has been drastically reduced in American yeshivos, but unfortunately, is still very prevalent in Israeli yeshivos, and young men who never smoked in America come back from Israel as smokers. When a *bachur* goes to Israel, he should be told in the strongest terms, *b'gzeras kibbud av,* that he dare not pick up a cigarette.

Youngsters should also know that improper use of alcohol is forbidden. They should be discouraged from the heavy drinking that sometimes goes on at weddings and on Simchas Torah. Even on Purim, the halachah in *Mishnah Berurah* (695:5) states that it is not proper to become drunk.

Insofar as someone offering drugs to children is concerned, most *poskim* consider him a *meisis umadiach* (one who seduces to wrongdoing) and possibly a *rodef* (one who threatens to kill). If this dealer is identified as Jewish, check with a *posek* about turning him over to the authorities. If you suspect that a drug dealer is "hanging out" in places where children congregate, speak to a youth office at your local police station. The police may be able to help, either by posting an officer at the location, which will cause the dealer to leave, or by arresting the offender.

INTERNET ADDICTION

Having just read the heart-rending letter that the 21-year old yeshiva bachur wrote to you last week, [regarding internet addiction] concerning the tragic double existence (for one cannot call it a life) that he is leading and about the absolutely, unimaginable daily unhappiness he must be experiencing, I felt compelled to sit down and answer.

I am writing only as a mother, of bli ayin hora, a large family, including four sons aged 13-21. I am in no way a professional and I have absolutely no experience in these matters whatsoever. However his words, his pleas, just broke my heart and I found myself crying at the end — for him, and for all the others he mentioned ....

Rabbi Twerski, his bravery and honesty were over-whelming, but the phrase that stayed in my mind was, "Your answer could save my life or not." And with all due respect, I am not alone in feeling that in no way was an answer given. If anything the lack of concrete response could indeed lead to even further desperation, c"v. Surely someone out there can help him, and like he says, the thousands like him who are so badly in need of help — now, before it's too late .... Surely there must be parents or families who have unfortunately "been there" and somehow found a way out, or other bachurim themselves who have experienced what he's going through and can help him get through it safely.

Thank you for your comments. Let me first tell you that I answered the young man's letter directly. In a subject as sensitive as this, not everything can be printed.

Though you say, "Surely someone out there can help him," that is not quite true. I polled Nefesh, an organization of several hundred *frum* psychotherapists, and no one claimed competence in treating this problem. Nefesh promptly began researching ways in which *frum* therapists can be trained to work with this problem. (See the Appendix for a partial listing of agencies that can refer one to the proper therapist.)

Your comment, "Surely there must be parents or families who have … 'been there' and somehow found a way out, or other *bachurim* themselves who have experienced what he's going through and can help him get through it safely" is wishful thinking. Do you believe that any parents or *bachurim* who had this problem would come forth? Why, things like this are kept tightly secret so that no one should ever know of them. I constantly get calls from people who are afraid to do a *shidduch* with a young man or woman because they "heard" from someone that a member of that family was once seen entering a psychologist's office (even if it was only to deliver *mishloach manos*!) I can assure you that even if we guaranteed confidentiality and made an appeal for parents or *bachurim* to help, absolutely no one would volunteer.

Internet addiction, like most other addictions, is a difficult problem. Just think of how many cigarette smokers who know that smoking kills and maims, and who do not want to die, have nevertheless been unable to break the habit. Like this young man, even after stopping, they go back to it.

Even if we will have trained therapists, the likelihood that therapy alone will help is slim. The only success I know of in addictions is with a support group, such as Alcoholics Anonymous, Gamblers Anonymous, Overeaters Anonymous, etc. It is vital to establish a support group for this problem, but again, because of the fear of exposure, this may be difficult to accomplish. Support groups may help, but the fear of exposure prevents people from participating. I am trying to arrange a "call-in" service, to which, at a given time, one can call and talk with several people who are successfully combating this problem. This will avoid the callers being identified and ostracized.

Some people believe that the answer lies in *teshuvah*, more Torah study, and *tefillah*. These are, of course, important, but unfortunately not enough. There are many truly Torah-observant people who know that Hagaon Rav Eliashiv and a number of other *poskim* have ruled that smoking is an absolute *issur*, yet have been unable to stop. I sat with one Torah giant when he cut a cigarette into small pieces, and while wheezing from smoking-induced lung disease, lit up. He said to me, "I am an *onus* [helplessly compelled]."

Regardless of what some people may think, the young man who brought the problem to public awareness is an *onus*. He has tried to stop, but, like some *dybbuk*, the problem is tormenting him. I can assure you that I am trying to find ways to help. If members of the community could change their attitude so that the fear of exposure would not paralyze efforts at recovery, significant progress can be made.

SUGAR ADDICTION

I believe that my two children are addicted
to sugar. As a sugar addict in recovery,
I am quite concerned. Ever since I started
watching my sugar intake and using a twelve-
step program, I am a different person,
B"H. I am actually starting to become more
like the mother I've always dreamed I'd be,
instead of the critical, screaming mother
who was the result of sugar addiction.
Is there a way to help them, before they
hit rock bottom (which may take years
of suffering, c"v)? Even if they could
understand how harmful sugar is for them,
they wouldn't want to be different from
every one else. As an adult it took me
years to really change my eating habits,
even after I realize that sugar affected
me negatively. I feel helpless as our kids
are bombarded with sugar outside the home.
I hope there is a way to help them so
they won't suffer through the mood swings,
fatigue, impulsiveness, and all the other

*results of this problem. Are there any books
appropriate for frum children or teens on
the Twelve Steps?*

I'm not aware of any 12-step material for *frum* youngsters.

As you have no doubt heard, there is a movement to remove candy machines and soft-drink dispensers from schools. While this might be helpful, the experience with alcohol prohibition indicates that trying to restrict availability has had limited success, although a recent experiment has shown that student obesity was reduced in schools that do not offer refined sugar in lunches and snack machines. If you make it clear that no refined sugars come into the house, you will be sending a message that children may absorb and utilize as they mature.

It might be possible to reduce the craving for sweets by providing meals high in carbohydrates. I'm sure that you have done research on nutrition.

For decades we have been discouraging kids from eating candy because it is bad for their teeth. This did not accomplish much, perhaps because people still bribe kids with lollipops. Nevertheless, it is still wise to gently tell children that sweets are not healthy for them. Having cut-up fresh fruits and vegetables ready for the children when they come home from school may help satisfy their "sweet tooth" in a healthful manner.

FRIEND IS A COMPULSIVE GAMBLER

I have a friend who is in a difficult
spot. I wanted your opinion as she often
turns to me for advice. When her husband
lost his computer job after the industry
downsized, he began gambling in Atlantic

City as a source of income. He initially did quite well, but then started losing money. My friend begged and pleaded with him to stop gambling but it didn't help. After some time we found Gamblers Anonymous (initially, I went with my friend to Gam-Anon). Her husband went to a few meetings and decided that since it is a program of self-improvement, he'll get a chavrusah and learn mussar instead. His rav endorsed the idea and was kind enough to learn with him.

After a few weeks of abstinence, he went back to gambling. It has been two years of off-and-on gambling. They are now living on tzedakah as he still has not found a good, steady job. My friend is trying to control the household money so that he will not have access to it. Yet there is always another gemach or tzedakah fund in our community of chessed so that he always manages to get money with which to gamble.

They have a large family and my friend is too afraid of being on her own and of upsetting the children to divorce him. I/we have a few questions:

1. Can people make money gambling? Are there people who are smarter (as we all like to think of our family members) than the average individual, and who are able to beat the odds?

2. Is learning mussar following the basics of a twelve-step program ever enough to cure an addiction? (Or if not cure, to curb an addiction?)

3. Is the tzedakah that my friend receives enabling? On one hand, why should she and her children suffer? On the other hand, it is relieving him of the obligation to provide basic living expenses.

4. As we live in a wonderful community, bli ayin hara, of balei tzedakah who don't understand gambling, what can be done about the access to tzedakah money a gambler has?

5. On the rare occasion that he does come home with winnings from Atlantic City, what should be done with the money? (Gam-Anon told her to throw it in his face so that he won't even have the dream of winning big and being a hero. Her rav feels that inasmuch they are living off tzedakah, by throwing it away she would necessitate taking even more tzedakah. He feels she should take the money.)

I know this is a long letter and we appreciate your response.

In about a month, my book on compulsive (addictive) gambling in the Jewish community will be out. In the meantime, your friend (and you) should read *Behind the 8-Ball*. It is vital for families of gamblers.

Our community does not know, and does not want to know, the truth about gambling. Many families have been totally crushed and ruined because of this. Most rabbonim have never learned about gambling, and consequently do not know what to advise.

Compulsive gamblers may occasionally win, but ultimately they are ruined. There is nothing they will not do to get money to gamble.

Mussar is wonderful and should be studied by everyone. However, it is not a substitute for insulin for the diabetic, nor for effective treatment for the gambler. Effective treatment must include serious involvement in Gamblers Anonymous, and, for the spouse, Gam-Anon.

Giving the gambler money is enabling. This is not tzedakah any more than giving cocaine to a drug addict is beneficial. (It is actually a form of *lifnei iver*.) People do not understand this. The wife and children may be supported by tzedakah, but the rent should be given directly to the landlord, and food money to the grocer, etc. The gambler should not be given a single penny.

If he does win and gives the money to his wife, she should do with it what she would do if he gave her money that he had stolen. She must consider this money as *tereifah*. The wife should follow the instructions of Gam-Anon. By bitter experience, they are the only ones who know what to do.

Addictive gambling is a very powerful force that the gambler cannot resist without the proper help (GA). Addicts will go for help only *b'ein bereirah*. Unless they feel the consequences of their behavior, they will not change.

OFFICE ADDICTION

This is a problem of long standing. My husband cannot detach himself from his office. When we go on vacation, he can call the office six times a day. His secretary has told me that she can easily reach him by cell phone if they really need him and there is no need for him to call in so often. This is very annoying to me. I've talked to him about it, with no luck.

We're due to go on a vacation, and frankly, his office addiction is so irritating that I am not looking forward to what should be a very enjoyable vacation. What can I do to stop him from "calling in" so many times?

This is not at all unusual. It may help to understand why some people are like this.

I've written several books about people who have low self-esteem due to unwarranted feelings of inferiority. There are several techniques that are used to escape this distressing feeling. One way is to convince oneself that one is needed and that others depend on him/her. Your husband may have a need to believe that the office cannot function without his immediate attention and control. This can boost his ego.

Some people may feel very competent in their business or profession, but may feel inadequate as human beings. I knew a physician who spent from 6 a.m. until midnight at the hospital or at his office. His wife complained, "I am a dependent person. I needed a husband to lean on, but my husband was never there for me."

This doctor knew he was an excellent physician and was comfortable in this role. He did not think he had anything to offer his wife and children simply as a human being. Because he felt inadequate as a husband and father, he avoided being home.

Sometimes it is necessary to be at the office until late, but sometimes a person feels more comfortable at the office, not just because the demands at home are too great, but because he feels inadequate there.

Your husband may fit into this category. If so, he cannot give up contact with the office, even though it is unnecessary. He can't afford to think that he isn't needed there.

You might try to tell your husband that he is a far better person than he gives himself credit for, and suggest that he read up on self-esteem. This will be especially important after he retires, when he won't have the office to give him an ego-boost, and he may then become depressed, which should certainly be avoided.

COMPUTER ADDICTION

My husband sits at the computer during breakfast, lunch, and suppertime. It seems he's hooked! He does not visit inappropriate sites but has a compulsion to gain more and more knowledge. Maybe this is worthwhile but it has taken over his (our) life. If I say anything about bitul zman, he explodes.

(His main use for the computer is for his business. I'm referring to after-business use.) Can I "un-hook" him or is he a lost case, and if yes, how can I accomplish this in a loving and peaceful manner?

It is no joke! Computer addiction is real, right along with other addictions. It is extremely prevalent and can be destructive to job and family life. Your husband's explosive reaction is very similar to that of an alcoholic who is told that he is drinking too much. However, just as the wife of an alcoholic cannot control or stop him, you cannot "un-hook" him. He is the only one who can stop — but only if he works at it. And the first step is for him to admit he has a problem.

There are various reasons for this addiction. One computer addict said, "It's the only place my opinion makes me feel important." One addicted smoker said, "My craving to go on the Internet first thing in the morning is stronger than the urge to light a cigarette."

You may profit by reading *Caught in the Net*, by Kimberly Young. Also, you may read *Co-Dependent No More*, by Melody Beatty. Although the latter deals with alcoholism, many of the dynamics apply to computer addiction as well. The Family Support groups for alcoholism may be of help, too. See the Appendix at the back of the book.

ADDICTED TO GADGETS

My husband is really a wonderful person. He is a talmid chacham and has fine middos. He treats me wonderfully. So what's my problem? He has a love for gadgets, and buys gadgets we don't need. We do not run an office, but we have an electric pencil sharpener and an electric stapler. We never use either. He

*buys gadgets for the kitchen that I don't
need or use. It seems he can't resist buying
gadgets.*

*That might seem amusing, but it's not.
Although some gadgets are relatively
inexpensive, others are costly. He bought
a robot vacuum cleaner that we don't need.
That's a very expensive gadget, and we don't
have that kind of money. I even saw him
reading an ad for an electronic translator!
There are thousands of gadgets out there,
and if he has no self-control, we can get
into serious financial trouble. What do you
suggest?*

There is actually an addiction to shopping, referred to as compulsive shopping. As with any other addiction, buying a gadget can give the person a thrill, similar to gambling.

Compulsive shopping can range anywhere from mild to very serious. When it gets to the point of going into debt, one can do irrational things, borrowing heavily and even mortgaging one's house.

In contrast to alcohol addiction, in which the person can be helped to abstain totally from drinking, compulsive shopping is more like food addiction. One cannot avoid eating and one cannot avoid shopping.

It may surprise you, but your husband might not be aware of how many unnecessary gadgets he has bought. You might collect them all and set them before him, with a calculation of how much money was spent on them, money the family needs and could have been used for important purchases.

Although your husband may not appear depressed, it is not unlikely that buying a gadget temporarily relieves feelings of depression. It is important that he seek professional help. Compulsive behaviors and addictions don't stop simply because person promises to discontinue them.

For other addictions, there are self-help support groups. I am not aware of a group for compulsive shoppers. The most appropriate group may be is Debtors Anonymous, where you may find people who went deeply into debt because of compulsive shopping. Debtors Anonymous can be found in the telephone directory. Also, books on compulsive shopping are available in the library and bookstores.

CAFFEINE TO BOOST ENERGY

My son bought a new drink at the local convenience store. It was labeled "a natural health product." The label read: "Recommended use or purpose: Developed for periods of increased mental or physical exertion, helps temporarily restore mental alertness or wakefulness when experiencing fatigue or drowsiness."

My son is 16, and attends yeshivah out of town. It seems that boys use this drink or similar products (including coffee) to pep themselves up when they need to stay awake for various tests, etc. Is this a safe practice? I fear that unwittingly my son may be stepping onto the path of substance abuse.

I am also concerned that in yeshivah or summer camp, my son may purchase over-the-counter medications for various ailments (cough syrup / cold preparations / stomach preparations, etc.) on the recommendations of his peers.

I would like to share your response with my son as soon as possible.

Thank you for your work for Klal Yisrael, and for your many wonderful books.

To the best of my knowledge the only active ingredient that may increase wakefulness is caffeine, which is equally present in coffee and some soft drinks.

Using caffeine to stay awake may cause problems if a person becomes dependent on it. Some people are sensitive to caffeine and may become agitated or tremulous even with small amounts. As one increases the dose of caffeine, such symptoms may occur. It may also cause irregular heart rhythm and insomnia.

An example of what might happen is a medical student who pushed himself to study and relied on caffeine to keep him awake. He had to increase the dose, eventually consuming fifty cups of coffee daily, resulting in severe mental symptoms. Once a person becomes dependent on caffeine, trying to reduce the intake may result in severe headaches, which causes the person to go back to it.

In my yeshivah days, when I was very tired, I would rest my head on the desk for 15 minutes. Stimulants should be avoided.

People think that because something is sold over-the-counter it is safe. That is not true. A drug is a drug, and should be used with caution. Medications of any kind should not be used without consulting a physician. Summer camps usually insist that even over-the-counter medications be held at the nurse's station and dispensed by the nurse rather than by the camper.

RX: LOOKING AT *KEDUSHAH*

I consulted a rav about my internet addiction, and he advised me to train my eyes to see kedushah, such as to look at the writing in the Torah when it is raised during hagbah, and to look at the light of the Shabbos candles and Chanukah candles.

I tried this and it has backfired. Whenever I look at hagbah or at the Shabbos candles,

*I think about the internet. Why is this
happening and is there anything else I can do?*

I t is certainly advisable to begin therapy from a *frum* therapist, who may help you with this. However, the *rav's* advice is sound, and "backfiring" is not unexpected.

Tanya explains that we have an ongoing struggle with the *yetzer hara*. When two opponents wrestle and one begins to get the upper hand, the opponent increases his force to overcome the other's advantage. Similarly, when the *yetzer hara* feels threatened, it will increase its force to mislead you. What you see as "backfiring" is actually an indication that you are getting the upper hand, and that the *yetzer hara* is reacting to this, because your tactic is successful. Continue to train your eyes to *kedushah*, and don't let this reaction undermine your efforts. In the end they will prove successful.

COMPULSIVE OVEREATING

*I have a very big problem — I overeat. I've
been overweight all my life. I've been on
every diet, read every health book, and in
my mind I know exactly what my problem is.
I like to eat! I feel like I am a slave to
food and I can't stick to any normal eating
program for any length of time. How can one
change such a horrible middah permanently?*

Y ou have made one important discovery. Diets don't work! That is to say, they do work, for a brief period of time, then one regains the weight, plus some.

I cannot understand why people are so gullible. For many years, the magazine covers have been announcing every month, "Miracle diet! Guaranteed to work." Every month there are a number of guaranteed-to-work diets, and there have probably been several hundred of them. If even one were of any value, why would there be a need for ten new diets every month?

It all comes down to this. Animals in the wild eat to meet their nutrition needs. Then they stop, and they do not touch a morsel more. Many humans, on the other hand, find that eating makes them feel better. In other words, after their nutritive needs have been met, they use food as a drug. Compulsive overeating is nothing other than a drug addiction — in this case food is the drug — but it is basically the same as alcohol or narcotic addiction. It has been wisely said that overweight is not due to what you eat, but to what is eating you. In my book, *The Thin You Within You*, I elaborate on this.

My experience with addiction has been that the greatest success is with a support group. Overcoming any addiction is not easy, but it can be done if a person is willing to put forth the effort. Without a support group, one's efforts don't seem to work as well.

DISCOURAGING INTERNET

I am well aware of the efforts to discourage and prevent access to the internet by youngsters, but I also know that these will not be foolproof. And I know that young people often don't listen to what they are told. Isn't there any way to discourage young people from allowing themselves to be drawn to something that can be so destructive to them?

How I wish that young people would understand that some things that they see as enjoyable and harmless can be deadly serious. Many youngsters who thought that they would not become addicted to drugs have lost their futures and even their lives. The internet is of no less danger.

In *Avos D'Reb Nosson* (20:1), the Talmud makes an amazing statement: "Whoever takes Torah to heart will be spared from indecent thoughts, and whoever does not take Torah to heart will be given indecent thoughts." It is as simple as that. Whatever other steps a person may take, if he does not take Torah to heart, he will have indecent thoughts. There are no two ways about it.

Note that the Talmud does not say "anyone who learns Torah," but rather "anyone who takes Torah to heart." We say *ki heim chayenu*, because Torah is our life. If one believes this, then Torah to him is like oxygen. He knows his life depends on it. There are people who have conditions that necessitate their constantly being attached to an oxygen tank. They know that if anything happens to their oxygen supply, their life is in great danger. That is how one must feel about Torah. One must feel that any deviance from Torah is life-threatening. Anything less than that, the Talmud says, will result in one having indecent thoughts.

I am certain that if, on going to an indecent website, one would get a sharp electric shock, one would stop doing it. A person who takes Torah to heart would get a sharp "shock" from exposure to anything indecent.

The restrictions that have been established by rabbonim are indeed important, but may not be enough or always enforceable. This may sound naïve, but the only solution I can see is to establish a home environment of increased *kedushah* that would discourage things that are averse to *kedushah*. This means that in addition to observance of Shabbos and the highest standards of kashrus, children will see that their parents avoid *lashon hara* like the poison that it is. They will see that observance of Shabbos includes one's speech being different than that of the work week, and that Shabbos is indeed a Shabbos *kodesh*, where one does not read a newspaper or anything other than Torah *sefarim*. They will see that their parents are absolutely dedicated to truth and honesty. They will see that their parents never lose their tempers. They will see that their parents never hold a grudge. They will see that although the parents must work for a living, there is *mesiras nefesh* for *tefillah b'tzibur*. They will see that their parents being *maavir al middos*, never returning an insult, and working toward refinement of their *middos*.

I have often said that given the drastic deterioration of morality in today's world, we must combat it with greater effort at *kedushah* than ever before. It is no longer enough simply to observe the *Shulchan Aruch*. If we want our children to be able to withstand the unprecedented *yetzer hara* of today's world, we must also live our lives according to *Mesillas Yesharim* and other *sifrei mussar*, and strenuously strive for *kedushah*. This will, of course, require great effort, but if parents are not able to make this effort, it may be unrealistic for them to expect their children to exert the effort necessary to resist the powerful *yetzer hara*.

The Talmud's words must be taken seriously. There is only one way to prevent this problem. We must live our lives in such a way that our children see that we are not only observant of Torah, but that we feel that the slightest deviation from Torah is as lethal as poison. If they develop that attitude, taking Torah to heart, the Talmud says that they will be spared from indecent thoughts.

Unfortunately, some young people might not listen to what their parents say, but they are more likely to emulate what their parents do.

GAMBLING VS. INVESTMENTS

I am writing to you in the hope that you will have a solution to help my father. Initially my father started investing in stocks and he had some success. Then, I'm not sure how it started, but he sold those to invest in other stocks that were not successful. He started borrowing money against the house from relatives and friends to continue to invest in these "great deals"

— I assume in the hope of recouping his losses. To make a long story short — my parents are now in dire financial straits, owing huge amounts of money on their house and to several individuals. My father denies the reality of the situation and continues to try to invest. I'm afraid that the only short-term solution for them is to sell their house and buy a less expensive house elsewhere. If they do get out of debt, I'm afraid that my father will just continue to do the same thing, borrowing money against the new house, and they will find themselves in the same situation again.

Is there any way he can be helped? If so, how can I get him to agree, since he denies the severity of the situation?

There are various forms of gambling: casino, horseracing, betting on sports, poker, day-trading, or the kind of gambling your father is doing with stocks. It is characteristic that the compulsive gambler (in this case the compulsive investor) goes deep into debt, and when borrowing is no longer feasible may result to desperate, even illegal measures, to get money to gamble / invest. He will continue to do so until things get so bad that he is forced to face reality.

Sometimes, to avoid a scandal and *chilul Hashem*, friends and family may bail out the person, and extract a promise that he will never again indulge in this practice. This is a serious mistake. The promise will not be kept. If the gambler does not feel the consequences of his actions, he will not change.

The family needs to learn what compulsive gambling is like. Do not deceive yourself that, because he does not go to the racetrack or casino, his gambling is any less severe. *Behind the 8-Ball*, a book by Linda Berman, is must-reading for the family.

For expert guidance on a problem like this, see the listing of referral agencies in the Appendix at the end of the book.

LACK OF *FRUM* DRUG-TREATMENT FACILITIES

My husband underwent two operations on his back, and because of the severe pain, he took massive doses of pain medication. Actually, the doctor gave him as many painkillers as he asked for. He continued to use more and more pills, and they began to affect his behavior. The doctor says that he is addicted to these pills and needs treatment for the addiction. He must go into a treatment facility, because whenever he tries to cut back, he suffers such severe pain that he goes back to the drugs.

We inquired about a treatment facility for him. He would have to be there for a month, because that's how long it takes to be weaned from the heavy doses of medication he takes. Several facilities will bring in kosher food, but there is no place with any Yiddishkeit, and in his condition, he needs much chizuk. All these places are mixed-gender, and almost all the patients are non-Jewish.

I'm sure that there must be many cases like his. I also know that there are frum people who are addicted to street drugs. Why doesn't the Jewish community provide a treatment center suitable for a frum person?

Probably the most potent force in the *frum* community is *shidduchim*. If any member of a family has a condition that would reflect badly on the health of that family, it is concealed for fear that exposure would endanger the children's chances for *shidduchim*. This is especially true in case of a psychiatric problem

If there were a *frum* treatment center, it is highly likely that *frum* Jews would avoid going there, for fear of being recognized by other Jews there. They would prefer to go to a facility where there were not other *frum* people.

One treatment center that I am aware of does have a rabbi who comes in regularly to meet with Jewish patients — the Caron Foundation in Wernersville, PA.

ADDICTED TO READING

My teenage son is addicted to reading. He admits that he has a compulsion to read and has a hard time controlling it. He stays up late and as a result sleeps late and misses hours of school. I have tried removing tempting reading material, but he then rereads old books. I would like to get to the root of the problem and would appreciate your advice.

My first take on this is that the compulsion to read is not the major problem. I readily admit that I have a compulsion to write. As long as he does not read worthless or objectionable material, this compulsion in itself might even be constructive, if it did not interfere with normal function.

The problem, as you describe it, is that it *is* interfering with normal function, because he is up late, sleeps late, and misses school. I don't think he stays up late because he reads, but rather that he reads because he stays up late.

I recently addressed a somewhat similar problem, and I explained that we all have a biological clock, known as "circadian rhythm." For most people, the clock operates so that one is awake during the day and sleeps at night. Some people seem to have a biological clock which is set differently. They simply cannot fall asleep at night because their clock is on the "awake" phase, and will power doesn't help. You can't force yourself to sleep. Of course, if one is completely alert, it stands to reason that one would read.

If this is your son's problem, you might consult an expert in a Sleep Disorder Clinic, for what can be done to "re-set" your son's biological clock. Most major hospitals have such a clinic.

NON-JEWISH SUPPORT GROUPS

I am B"H a middle-aged frum Yiddishe mama and baba. I B"H have a number of children and grandchildren K"H. I am grateful to Hashem for all my blessings; however, I have an outgoing problem since childhood. I suffer from obesity, "addictive eating disorder." I have lost weight a number of times and have kept the weight off a number of years each time, always using a different program, but I've always gained the weight back with interest. After reading your suggestions and books on this topic, I decided to give the "twelve-step" program a try. I decided to join OA [Overeaters Anonymous], as my problem seems to be that I am addicted to sugar. First I joined a group that included both Jews and non-Jews. The sharing and "pitching," as they call it, often contained inappropriate language. Also the "big book" that they gave out was full of material that I wouldn't want any of my children to read. I stopped going for a while and then heard of a frum group with primarily Orthodox women ["Orthodox Overeaters Anonymous"]. I decided to try again and joined, as you seem to think that this might be a permanent solution. This new group, which calls itself CEAHOW — Compulsive Eaters Anonymous Honest Open-minded and Willing — was even worse, as assignments were given on the basis of a book that was highly inappropriate reading for frum women. I was appalled that there were frum young girls present doing this obnoxious homework called "inventory questions." I would appreciate knowing on what basis of Halachah you recommend these programs to frum women. In my opinion these groups should be forbidden — even though they do seem to help the weight problem. The question is — weight loss at what expense?

The essence of the 12-step program, per se, is acceptable. Many 12-step meetings close with a non-Jewish prayer (not an essential part of the program), which, although it is comprised of verses from the *siddur*, is used in non-Jewish religious services, and has been ruled *assur*. The phrase "to turn our will over to G-d as we understand Him" was formulated so that it would be acceptable to all religions. For Jews, this is an inappropriate phrase, and one may say, "I turn my life over to Hashem in keeping with the Talmudic statement 'Treat His will as if it were your own will and nullify your will before His will,'" as taught in *Pirkei Avos* (2:4). In *Self Improvement? I'm Jewish!* I elaborate on the 12-step program.

It may be that some people who practice the 12 steps have added on things that are incompatible with Yiddishkeit. If so, they should be avoided. The book, *Came to Believe*, lists incidents that people believe were Divine intervention in their lives, and it is an attempt to convince non-believers to believe in G-d. For a *frum* Jew, there is no need for this. We have *emunah* in *hashgachah pratis*. If we need to strengthen our *emunah*, we have *sefarim* written by our great tzaddikim.

Literature that mentions the names of deities of other religions does not belong in a Jewish home, nor is there any need for it. We do not use passages from the Christian sources, even if they appear similar to some Torah concepts. There are many books on spirituality written by Torah-observant authors, and they can provide our spiritual needs even though they are not based on the 12-step program.

Improper language is not part of the 12-step program, but some attendees may speak grossly. A number of *frum* women have reported that they attend a *frum* OA group where there is no offensive language, but I don't know where this meeting is. You may inquire from a *frum* person in OA where this group meets. There are a number of such groups in Israel. If you cannot locate one, you could start one yourself. Two people are sufficient to start a group, and it always increases in size.

An inventory is an important part of the program, and any inventory forms should be reviewed by a *rav* to see that they comply with *tznius*. Of course, the inventory is very private. Sometimes very personal material comes up in an inventory, just as it does when a person is serious about saying the *al chet*. Here, too, one should be guided by a knowledgeable *rav*.

The 12-step program can be very helpful, and there is no reason why it should be contaminated with objectionable material

MIDDOS

IS A BABY MONITOR AN ACCEPTABLE BABYSITTER?

Something has been bothering me for a couple of months now and it is preying on my mind constantly, so I decided to seek some guidance.

It is called the "baby monitor dilemma." *Baruch Hashem,* we have many married sisters and brothers. Each and every one of them uses the baby monitor as a babysitter, leaving the intercom with their neighbors when they go out during the evenings and all their little ones ka"h are sleeping. Recently one of my family members said that I should also use it and I replied, "Chas veshalam! What would happen if a fire breaks out, c"v? How can you expect your neighbor to save both her own family and yours in time? What if a thief were to break into your home and a child would wake up! I feel that Hashem gave me these precious

*kinderlach, ka"h. It's my duty to safeguard
them as best as possible.*

*My relative shouted that I have absolutely
no bitachon, while I was thinking that
they have the same lax attitude. They
leave 5/6-year-olds at home with the babies
for 10 minutes during the day to do a
bit of shopping, and allow a 5/6-year-old
to cross the roads alone during the dark
winter nights. Each time I witness these
things, I am taken aback by their lack of
responsibility. I wonder whether I deserved
to be shouted at like that — do I really
lack bitachon? To what extent does my
bitachon have to reach?*

I don't see this as an issue of *bitachon*.

I doubt that your relative means that you should have *bitachon* in her that she would save your children in case of a fire, *chas veshalom*, or confront a thief. That would be pure foolishness. (Incidentally, I don't know how a baby monitor could convey that a fire has broken out or a thief has broken in!)

If your relative means that one should have *bitachon* that there will not, *chas veshalom*, be a fire, then why does everyone I know, including great *talmidei chachomim*, have fire insurance? You might ask your relative if she carries fire insurance for the remote possibility that there may, *chas veshalom*, be a fire. If she does, why should there be any less concern about the safety of her children?

Almost every *mussar sefer* has a discussion of *bitachon* vs. *hishtadlus*. Although we have *bitachon* in Hashem as the great Healer, and we testify to this three times a day, nevertheless, if an insulin-dependent diabetic refused to take insulin or a person with pneumonia refused antibiotics, they would be committing the *aveirah* of neglecting their health. Halachah requires that we seek treatment for an illness and pray to Hashem for recovery. Similarly, it is not a lack of *bitachon* to carry fire insurance, or for that matter, life insurance.

There are some things for which worry would be foolish. An extreme example: we don't stay in the house for fear that a lion may have escaped from the zoo (Shlomo *Hamelech* cites this as the rationalization of a lazy person [*Mishlei,* 26:13]. What are things one should consider? The kinds of things one pays money to insure: theft, fire, flood. I'm sure that one could buy insurance from Lloyds of London against a lion attack, but this is so remote a possibility that one does not consider it. However, since most people do insure against fire, it is obviously a consideration. You therefore have every right to apply the same consideration when it comes to the safety of your children.

A baby monitor is meant to give parents peace of mind when they are not in the same room as the child; it is not meant to be a substitute for proper supervision. As you say, our children are a precious gift from Hashem. They should be guarded as diligently as possible. Not only is it irresponsible to leave young children alone or in charge of other, equally young children, it is illegal and these people are running the risk of being arrested and having their children taken away from them by Social Services. Your attitude is correct — you should safeguard your children as much as possible.

YICHUS — ASSET OR LIABILITY?

There is a question in my mind that has begged for an answer for a long time and I find your forum is a great place to express it.

I always wonder why people born into rebbeshe or chashuvah families get credit for being so upright and good. After all, they have zechus Avos, they inherited admirable middos, and they have received (usually) a real yiddishe chinuch at home. So from the time they are young (and I have witnessed it), they had an easy time battling their yetzer hara. My problem is not one of jealousy — adarabah, on the contrary — I wish them many more upright good people. My question lies in the area that why is it that people who come from non-yichusdige homes tend to feel as if they are on a lesser level when they are in the proximity of chashuvah/yichusdige people. (I'm speaking about women who frequently feel this way.) I've heard from many people that they feel looked down upon — for example, my friend told me that she doesn't want to go to a particular bungalow colony for that very reason.

I'd like you to clarify this for me. Do rebbishe people have a right to feel so good about themselves — do they get credit for being so helig (holy)? Isn't it a much greater madreigah (level) when people who don't have major zechus Avos battle the yetzer hara?

L et me address your most important point first. No one has any right to look down on any one else. Period!

In the letter to his son, Ramban emphasizes that a person should always look up to others and consider them as superior to himself. "If he is wise or wealthy, you should respect him. If he is poor and you are wealthier or wiser than he, you should consider that you are more culpable than he and that he is more meritorious than you, because if he sins, it is considered an inadvertent act, whereas if you sin, it is considered an intentional act."

True gedolim never looked down on anyone. We were blessed to observe Reb Moshe and Reb Yaakov. Never did anyone feel "less than" when in the company of these Torah giants. They did not allow anyone to feel inferior to them. Anyone who feels superior because of his Torah knowledge or yichus is abusing these positive attributes.

Insofar as people born into chashuvah families being at an advantage, it is actually a "double-edged sword." The Shelah cites the verse in the *tochachah*, which lists the harsh punishments for deviating from the Torah: "I will remember My covenant with Jacob and also My covenant with Isaac, and also My covenant with Abraham will I remember" (*Vayikra*, 26:42), and asks, why are these comforting words included in the *tochachah*? The *Shelah* answers, when a person is judged for his misdeeds, his background is taken into consideration. If he came from a home that was lacking in spirituality and he did not have the opportunity to learn proper *middos*, he will be treated more leniently. However, if his background was one of Torah and fine *middos*, and yet he acted improperly, he will be treated more harshly. Therefore, the *tochachah* says, Hashem will judge us as the descendants of Abraham, Isaac, and Jacob. With such illustrious ancestors, if we deviate from Torah, we will be judged very harshly.

From your question it is unclear if those individuals who come from *yichus* feel they are superior, or if you are discussing unwarranted feelings of inferiority in others.

Yichus has its problems. If a person does not live up to his *yichus*, he is far more derelict than a person who does not have *yichus*. Therefore, people who have *yichus* have no right to consider themselves superior, and they are totally mistaken if they look down upon anyone. If on the other hand, one looks at all they have — in your own words — *zechus Avos*, inherited admirable *middos* (it's questionable if good *middos* can be inherited, but one who lives in proximity to those of exemplary character and behavior definitely have an advantage — those behaviors seep into their very bones) and real *yiddishe chinuch*, and subconsciously one is jealous or feels at a disadvantage, then a person need to work on his/her own self-esteem.

Every descendant of our Holy Forefathers is entitled to be given (and obligated to give others) an optimum level of respect. Each and every human being was created in the image of G-d (*tzelem Elokim*) and is worthy of basic *derech eretz*.

It might be wise to consult with a professional regarding your feelings. Several of my books that deal specifically with issues of self-esteem, such as *Ten Steps to Being Your Best*, can certainly prove helpful.

CAUTION: CHILDREN AT PLAY

The following problem sounds so trivial, yet it really affects our lives. I would greatly appreciate it if you could take the time to address the following situation.

We are B"H blessed with five beautiful children. They however, sometimes play in a very boisterous and noisy manner. They love running, jumping, and laughing. They spend many hours in quiet play as well. They enjoy cutting out pictures and coloring. They love pasting stickers and reading books. They also like hearing stories. However, when they are at active play, things can get very noisy. In general, this does not bother me at all — unless it gets out of hand. However, we have had major issues with our landlord about this. Do you think that this is an unusual manner of play? Do you think my children are wilder and noisier than the norm? What could be causing this? Must I punish them when they still play this way even after being admonished? Do I have to feel guilty about this disturbing the neighbors or the landlord?

It is obviously impossible to render an opinion on whether your children are noisier than others.

If the landlord's complaints are not unreasonable, and the noise disturbs others, then it is an issue of teaching children to be considerate of other people's feelings, instructing them that we must sometimes make sacrifices for other people's comfort. If the complaints are unfounded, then the other people should be considerate of children who play normally.

Teaching children consideration for others is as important as teaching them proper behavior in other ways. Of course, you may not be able to convey this to a four-year-old, but the older children can be spoken to individually and told about needing to consider other people. Remind them that boisterous behavior can disturb another person's rest or be irritating and must be curtailed. As with any other behavioral lessons, this should be able to be presented, not as a "punishment," but rather as a guide to proper *middos*. Perhaps you might say, "Just as you want us to be considerate of your needs, you must be considerate of others." If the older children get the message, they can set a pattern that the younger ones will follow. Putting down thick carpeting in the play area may help to muffle the noise. The children must take care not to play over the bedrooms in the evening or on Shabbos day when your landlord may want to rest. Try to put yourself in your landlord's place. Running and jumping can sound like a herd of elephants are loose over your head.

You may have to help the children with alternate means of play that will not be boisterous. You might try to find them a place where their noisy play won't affect anyone (e.g., a basement), or talk with the landlord about whether there are hours when their play will not disturb anyone. But your primary focus must be on developing good *middos* and sensitivity to others. Whether or not your landlord's complaints are valid is not the issue. Their behavior is obviously disturbing to him and you must make a concerted effort to explain to your children that when you live over another family, certain behavior should be confined to the outdoors. This may involve diligence on your part but eventually they will learn what is acceptable and what is not. Tell your landlord that you are working on diminishing his discomfort and that you hope he will be tolerant in the meantime.

Consideration for others is a lesson that will serve your children will throughout their lives. It is worthwhile to instill this *middah* while they are still young.

TALKING IN *SHUL*

The man who sits next to me in shul likes
to talk to me during the Torah reading.
This is very annoying. I have repeatedly
told him that I want to hear the Torah
reading and to please not talk to me, but
it doesn't help for long. My only solution
is to sit elsewhere in shul, but I think
that if I did this, it would be malbin
pnei chavero b'rabbim (public humiliation),
which, I think, is worse than not hearing
the Torah reading. What do you think I
should do?

This is really a halachah question which you should address
to a *posek*.

You might tell your neighbor, "I don't want to embarrass
you by moving to another seat, but if you persist in talking to me during the Torah reading, you will leave me no alternative." If you warn
him of this several times, then it is clear that he accepts your moving
elsewhere.

However, because *malbin pnei chavero b'rabbim* is so great an *issur*,
you should consult a *posek* before doing this.

WHAT PRICE DILIGENCE?

At weddings, I often see a person sitting at
a table looking into a Gemara while everyone
else at the table is socializing. This is
O.K., but when I greet the person, instead
of getting a response, I get only a nod of

the head, as though he were in middle of davening. Is this right?

This is a halachic question which should be addressed to a *posek*, but I will share my opinion with you.

Much time is wasted at weddings. Certainly a person should participate in some of the dancing (unless one is restricted by health reasons), because this is the mitzvah of being *mesameach chasan v'kallah*. However, when there is no dancing, using the time at the table for Torah study by a person who is *makpid* on *bittul Torah* is certainly appropriate. As far as socializing is concerned, a person can determine just how much he wishes to socialize.

Responding to a greeting is another thing. There is a halachah regarding how someone should respond to a greeting in the middle of *davening*. The Talmud says that Rabbi Yochanan ben Zakkai never went even four cubits without Torah study, yet he was always the first to greet someone, even a non-Jew. (*Sotah*, 28a; *Bereishis Rabbah*, 17).

One *Erev Yom Kippur*, Rabbi Yisrael of Salant met a person who did not greet him, and whose face reflected the solemnity of Yom Kippur. Rabbi Yisrael said, "Just because you are preoccupied with *teshuvah* does not mean that you should show me a sour demeanor." *Chovas Halevavos* says that a chassid should have "solemnity in his heart, but cheerfulness in his face." It is important to greet a person pleasantly (*Pirkei Avos*, 1:15).

On the other hand, perhaps the person who is learning does not wish to be distracted and lose his train of thought. He knows that if he greets you warmly, he will find himself drawn into a pleasant conversation and will lose the time he has set aside to learn during the wedding. Perhaps he fears that he will inadvertently hear or speak *lashon hora* and therefore has decided not to get into conversation with anyone. You can be *dan l'kaf zechus* (give him the benefit of the doubt) and eliminate your feelings of annoyance.

UPROOTING ANGER

I am a bit confused. In a pre-selichos derashah, the rav said that it is extremely important that we rid ourselves of bad middos, and he especially stressed anger. He said that one should totally uproot feelings of anger.

I read in one of your books that a person can control how he reacts, but that the feeling of anger when one is provoked is beyond one's control. If so, then one cannot uproot it.

I know that I was born with anger. I used to throw tantrums as a child. I now know how to avoid having angry outbursts, but I can't eliminate the feelings of anger. Who is right, the rav or you?

This is a case where we are both right.

I have mentioned elsewhere that the Chofetz Chaim would come into the *beis midrash* late at night, open the *aron kodesh*, and plead tearfully that Hashem should take away his anger. No one ever saw the Chofetz Chaim express anger, and there is no question that he was in complete control of his actions. However, the feeling of anger when provoked was something that only Hashem could remove.

The *sifrei chassidus* and *sifrei mussar* state that one is obligated to do whatever is within one's ability to rid oneself of bad *middos*. *Nesivos Shalom* says that one should search within himself to find which *middos* are his weak points, and he should work to eliminate these. He also states that once a person has done all within his/her power to eliminate a *middah*, Hashem will do the rest for him/her.

One might ask, certainly the Chofetz Chaim had done everything within his power to eliminate anger. Why, then, did Hashem not eliminate it for him? Why did he have to keep pleading to Hashem for this?

The answer is that as long as we struggle to improve our *middos*, we grow in *ruchniyus*. There is no end to how much one can advance in *ruchniyus*. If a negative *middah* is eliminated and one no longer needs to work at overcoming it, one's growth in *ruchniyus* in that particular area is brought to a halt.

The *Midrash* says that the reason the matriarchs were barren for so long is because Hashem desires the *tefillos* of tzaddikim. But is that a reason to make them suffer? The answer is that intense tefillah elevates a person's *ruchniyus*, and Hashem wanted the matriarchs, who were the mothers of *klal Yisrael*, to be at the highest possible level of *ruchniyus*. Therefore, it was necessary that they continue their *tefillos*.

Similarly, the extraordinary high level of *ruchniyus* achieved by the *Chofetz Chaim* was due to his intense *tefillos*. As with the matriarchs, continuing his tefillos brought him to increasingly higher levels of *ruchniyus*.

As far as you are concerned, you are to be commended for your ability to control your anger and refrain from outbursts of rage. You should avail yourself of what the *sifrei mussar* and *chassidus* teach us about anger and implement what they say. You should pray intensely for *Siyatta Dishmaya* to be free of it altogether.

SUFFERING FROM BOREDOM

I am B"H married and have ba"h seven
healthy (and lebeidige) kids, but have
a problem which has been with me since
teenage years. I am constantly looking for
change. I get dragged down by monotony. I
am always thinking about and planning my
next trip away, and, understandably, this
causes difficulty in family life. If I wake
up in the morning and realize that this

is just going to be a day like any other, I fall into a depression, and I will wish for anything to happen (sometimes even bad things) just in order that there should be change. When I travel, if I am traveling to the same destination, I will fly with a different airline or different class each time, stay at a different hotel, etc. When I change my car, within a few months I get fed up with it and want to change it yet again, and when I cannot fulfill these desires, I get depressed. What can I do to help this?

This is not an unanticipated problem. In *Devarim* (11:13), on the words that we say twice a day in *Krias Shema*, "... that I command you today," Rashi says, "The commandments should always be as fresh and beloved to you as if you received them today." This may be difficult to do, but we are required to work toward achieving such a feeling.

In *davening* we say that Hashem renews the works of creation every day. The Talmud says that for every breath we take we should be grateful to Hashem.

However, it is human nature that we become accustomed to things and take them for granted. Hagaon Harav Chaim Smulevitz has an excellent essay (*Sichos Mussar*, 5731:16) on the danger of taking things for granted because of their regular occurrence. He cites the words of the prophet (*Isaiah*, 29) that Hashem chastises us for serving Him in a routine way. It is an essay worth reading, because it addresses the problem.

I must commend you, because you are aware that you are displeased with the routinization of life, and this awareness is the first step to doing something about it. Unfortunately, many people are not in tune with their feelings and do not realize why they are edgy.

Like many others, I fall into the pattern of routine. When I see the many conditions in the world from which Hashem, in His infinite kindness, has spared me, it enables me to be grateful for what I have.

When I say *Modeh Ani* each morning, I think about those people who do not wake up to another day.

Taking care of your household and raising children to be *yirei Hashem* is a mitzvah of the highest order. Every day you are performing this great mitzvah. With *ba"h* seven healthy children, you can find a wealth of excitement in them. Take some quality time, even if only fifteen minutes, to find out what they're thinking and what they're feeling. It's a great contribution to the children's self-esteem when they see that their parents not only tell them what to do, but are sincerely interested in their thoughts and feelings. Each child is a world of his/her own, and you will find plenty of novelty in them.

What can one do about the boredom of routinization? Some people look for thrills, which is hardly a solution. No other way equals what Harav Shmuelevitz says, that the only way to overcome it is with the study of *mussar*. These teachings can stimulate us to see every day as a new opportunity and a new challenge.

As I said, I think that because you are aware of the boredom, you are ahead of the game. Follow the advice of Harav Shmulevitz.

WHO'S THE BOSS?

In your book, Successful Relationships, you are very critical of a husband who tries to exert control over his wife. How, then, do you interpret the words of the Torah, "vehu yimshol bach," that the husband should be master over his wife (Bereishis, 3:16)?

Neither I nor you can interpret the words of the Torah. Only *Chazal* can do that.

Rambam (*Hilchos Ishus*, 15:19) cites *Chazal*: "The sages commanded that a person should respect his wife even more than himself and should love her as he does himself. If he is wealthy, he should favor her according to his means. He should not cause her to have great fear of him, and should speak calmly to her. He should not be tense nor short-tempered."

In *Bava Metzia* (59), the Talmud says that a husband should be most cautious not to annoy his wife, because a woman is sensitive and easily moved to tears. Being controlled is certainly a severe annoyance. *Raavad*, in the introduction to his work, *Baalei Hanefesh*, states that inasmuch as Chavah was fashioned out of Adam's rib, a husband must consider his wife an integral part of himself, and care for her and protect her as he would any other part of his body.

The Jerusalem Talmud states that if a person were to feel pain because his left hand was injured, he would hardly strike it with his right hand to avenge the pain it caused him (*Nedarim*, 9:3). Similarly, even if a husband were to be angered by his wife, to act out against her is as though he were acting out against himself.

In the *tenaim* (articles of engagement), which have the force of a *neder*, it says that husband and wife shall have equal rights to manage their assets. If the husband can sign checks and have a credit card, the wife likewise has the right to sign checks and have a credit card. Denying these rights to a wife is a serious violation of the *tenaim*.

Given the above halachos, what is left for the husband to be the master, as the Torah states? It is for him to sit at the head of the table, for him to recite the *kiddush* and the *hamotzi*, and be *motzeh* his wife, rather than the reverse, but not to control her!

TEACHER WAS ABUSIVE TO STUDENT

I have been teaching for six years and I'm doing wonderfully. I know I'm very well liked by all. I'm writing to you because unfortunately during my first year of teaching I was very hard on a 3-year-old boy in my class. I subjected him to unwarranted physical and emotional abuse. I don't know what had gotten into me then but to this day I can't forgive myself! I have never treated any child since then in this manner. Just the opposite. I'm extra warm to them, I never punish, hit, or say anything derogatory. I really love kids!

I'm turning to you, Doctor — please help me get over this. I can't sleep, I cry every night about this. I feel so down when I think of it. When I see this kid now and talk to him, he talks to me so normally, but who knows what he thinks inside. I worry about how much damage I did to him.

The Chozeh of Lublin once took several talmidim for a trip. The coachman was unable to control the horse, and it took off in another direction, getting lost in a forest. On Friday afternoon, they entered a village and went to *shul*. When everyone had left, the elderly *shammes* invited them to his home. "I don't have much to serve you," he said, "but for guests who are dressed in weekday clothes, it will be enough."

"Where are you from?" he asked. When they said Lublin, the *shammes* said, "I hear there is a tzaddik in Lublin, whom they call *Chozeh*. Have you met him?" When they said yes, he said, "You have a *zechus* to know Yaakov Yitzchok."

"Have you ever met Yaakov Yitzchok?" the Chozeh asked.

The *shammes* sighed. "Yes, Itzikl was a bit wild. I was his *melamed*. He often ran away from *cheder*. I would punish him and beat him. One day I went to look for him, and found him in the outskirts of town. He was lying on the grass and his hands stretched to the sky and repeating 'Shema Yisrael.' I realized then that he was not a usual child. I never beat him again, but I am heartbroken that I beat him so many times. How can he ever forgive me?"

The Chozeh said, "I am Yaakov Yitzchok, and I forgave you many years ago."

So, my friend, you are in good company.

There was an incident involving Reb Zalman of Volozhin, who never forgave himself for having offended someone. The Gaon of Vilna told him that a person has an obligation to do *teshuvah* and ask forgiveness from someone he offended. If one cannot locate the person to ask forgiveness, and sincerely regrets his action, he can be sure that Hashem will put it in the other person's heart to forgive him.

By presenting children with extra sensitivity and kindness, you have found your way of *teshuvah*, of rectifying a mistake. Continuing to castigate yourself and feeling miserable will not help the child. It is appropriate that you ask *mechillah* and tell the child that you are sorry for having treated him that way. Inasmuch as he is still a minor, you should ask *mechillah* again when he turns 13.

IRRESPONSIBLE SON

My son is 21, and he is really a very sweet young man. However, he seems to be irresponsible. For example, we ask him to do something; when we find out he hasn't done it and we ask him why, he just says, "I guess I forgot." We've stopped asking him to do things because he is unreliable. He does not think ahead; for example, he lost his driver's license, and instead of getting a duplicate, he drove without a license and was caught making an illegal right turn on a red light. He can drive with an empty tank and get stuck on the highway. He will take books from the library and forget to return them. I can't speak angrily to him, because he's not bad. It's just that you can't rely on him to do anything.

My wife says this is because he never really had real responsibility, and that if he marries and must care for a family, that will straighten him out. I'm uneasy about that. What do you think?

Y ou have good reason to be uneasy. I have repeatedly said that marriage is not a hospital, and it is a serious mistake to think that marriage will solve any problem. Often, problems are accentuated after marriage, and may lead to a break-up of the marriage.

Your wife's statement that he has never had responsibilities is incorrect. He had a responsibility every time you asked him to do something. He had a responsibility to get a replacement for his driver's license. He had a responsibility to return books to the library. If he cannot fulfill smaller responsibilities, there is no reason to assume that he will fulfill greater ones.

Your son should be evaluated by a psychologist. Sometimes a person who is absorbed in thinking simply does not pay attention to what may seem to him as trivial. The "absent-minded professor" is an example of this.

Although marriage is unlikely to change him, there are women who are happily married to absent-minded professors. However, when the *shidduch* is suggested, the young woman must be alerted. She must know that she cannot expect him to turn off the stove or deposit a paycheck. His good qualities may outweigh this and he may be desirable as a husband, but she should be forewarned.

WITHDRAWN TODDLER

I see that a majority of your queries are about adults. I was wondering if you can help me with my issue.

My approximately 2½-year-old child is dynamic and leibedig at home, but when he goes among people he becomes very shy and a little withdrawn (similar to his father's personality). In addition to this, he also doesn't defend himself, i.e., when someone older or younger than he is takes away something he has, he will start crying rather than grab it back or he does not hit back when he is hit by someone — he just cries.

This happens at home also where he is comfortable in his surroundings and even with younger siblings.

I do not want him to be a bully, but I want him to stand up for himself. Is it right to tell him to go take back his toy when it is snatched from him?

The reason most of the queries I receive are regarding adults is because my clinical work was with adults. Children require a special expertise. If there is a significant problem, I suggest you consult a child psychologist. However, I will address your query to the best of my ability.

You raise two issues: 1. the child does not defend himself when someone takes something from him, and 2. he is shy and withdrawn among people.

The first point needs careful understanding. The Talmud has the highest praise for a person who is *maavir al midosov*, who does not react when offended. A careful understanding of this means that the person feels offended, but does not react. He feels angry, but does not react. Only the greatest tzaddikim reached a level where they did not even feel angry when provoked. It is related that the Chofetz Chaim used to enter the *beis midrash* at midnight, open the *aron kodesh*, and plead tearfully that Hashem should take away his feelings of anger. No one ever saw the Chofetz Chaim angry, because he never reacted with anger. However, not to feel anger, which is a natural emotion when one is offended or provoked, is something that one cannot eliminate by one's own efforts, and for which one needs *Siyatta Dishmaya*.

When the Rambam says that *kaas* is like *avodah zarah*, he is referring to the Talmud that says, "One who breaks thing in rage is like an *avodah zarah*" (*Shabbos*, 105b). He is not referring to the initial feeling of anger. If a person believes that even to feel anger is evil, he is likely to repress the feeling, in which case it is buried in the subconscious and he cannot deal with it. If this happens, the anger is not eliminated, and can affect one's behavior without one realizing it. In order to be *maavir al midosov*, one must know what *middah* one has.

Your child undoubtedly feels angry when someone takes something from him. At this point, he needs to have his feeling validated. You may say to him, "It makes you feel angry when someone takes something from you, doesn't it?" Rather than sulk, it is better for him to say, "It makes me angry when you take my things from me." He needs to know that it is appropriate to feel angry when provoked, so that he does not repress the anger. He also needs to know that feeling angry does not mean that you act out your anger. He can learn this if he sees his parents controlling their anger. He is then in a position to decide what to do when someone takes his things. You might play a game with him, whereby you take something from him and say, "O.K., now what do you want to do?" and teach him to say, "That's mine, please give it back to me." He does not have to attack the other person. Even a 2½-year-old child can be taught this. Both extremes, sulking and attacking, are not good.

As he matures, he can be taught to be *maavir al midosov*. Also, as he matures, he needs to be taught that even if one feels angry when provoked, one should be able to subsequently divest oneself of the anger, because the Torah says that we should not carry resentment in our heart (*Vayikra*, 19:17).

As I said, this should be understood carefully, because it might be misinterpreted to mean that I am saying that it is good to be angry. That is not true. What I am saying is that we must learn how to manage anger, and we cannot do so unless we identify the emotion we are experiencing.

As far as the shyness is concerned, it seems that children come into the world with some inborn traits, and parents should help them to cope with them. See the Appendix for sources that will help you deal with parenting a shy child.

RABBIS' *DERASHAHS*

I have attended a number of very frum shuls, where the rabbis, instead of giving mussar, gave interesting derashas about the parashah or about events in Eretz Yisrael. This reminded me of what the Talmud says, that if you see a rabbi who is well-liked by his community, it is because he does not reprimand them about their laxity in Torah observance (Kesubos, 105b).

Nowhere does it say that a lack of derashas about the parashah is responsible for all our tzaros in galus. We are repeatedly told that the obstacle to the geulah is the lack of proper middos, the bein adam lechavero. Why aren't the rabbis condemning the divisiveness among frum Jews, the holding grudges, the envy, and the lashon hara? Why are they not speaking out against the indulgence in gashmiyus, even "kosher" gashmiyus?

The furor about the tereifah meat scandal was justified, but why isn't there the same furor about Torah middos that are so often transgressed?

I am in complete agreement with you. I have several times quoted Rabbi Chaim Vital's statement that one must take greater caution with *middos* than even with mitzvos and *aveiros* (*Shaar HaKedushah*). *Nesivos Shalom* explains that this is because, although committing an *aveirah* is a grievous sin, it does not become part of one's personality, and it is more amenable to *teshuvah*, whereas bad *middos*, such as uncontrolled anger or *ga'avah*, do become part of one's personality and are more difficult to uproot.

I was recently at a *shul* where the rabbi's *derashah* about the *parashah* was about Joseph's brothers' hatred of him, and he quoted a *Midrash* stating that throughout our history, in every generation, we suffer the consequences of this sin against a brother. He pointed out that we cannot be relieved of our suffering until we correct that sin, which means that we must be very diligent in *bein adam lechavero*.

Many rabbis do speak out against *lashon hara* and bad *middos*. It would certainly help if members of a shul would tell the rabbi, "Please give us *mussar* so that we can be inspired to improve our *middos*."

I have repeatedly stressed that observing the *Shulchan Aruch* is not enough, and that we must study *Mesillas Yesharim* and other *sifrei mussar* regularly, and integrate their teachings into our daily lives. Ultimately, the onus for expanding our study of these topics lies with the individual and not with the *rav* of his *shul*. We cannot change anyone but ourselves, so each person must set aside time for this.

FELLOW SHOPPERS SOMETIMES INCONSIDERATE

I don't know if this is the proper place for this issue, but I don't know of any other.

I shop at a store where everything is glatt kosher, chalav Yisroel, and pas Yisroel, and I assume that others who shop there rather in the supermarkets are also machmir on these. Sometimes, I want to pull into a parking space, but there is a shopping cart in the way, because the customer who unloaded groceries did not have the consideration and courtesy to put the cart back where it belongs. I am sure that if that person found a parking place blocked, he/she would be very displeased.

This is a frank violation of "veahavta lrey'acha kamocha," which Rabbi Akiva says is the all-encompassing rule of the Torah.

> Inconsiderate behavior is a violation of a mitzvah d'Oraisa. It seems to me anyone who is machmir on matters that may be even less than a d'rabbanan and violates a d'Oraisa is a hypocrite.

The *baalei mussar* bewail the fact that some people who are very *machmir* on *ben adam laMakom* are far less cautious about *ben adam lechavero*. The Chofetz Chaim said, "What goes out of your mouth is at least as important as what goes into your mouth."

Your complaint is reminiscent of the proverbial joke about the man who was enraged at the proprietor of a *sefarim* store for refusing to open his store on Shabbos. "I need a *Shir Hamaalos* for my new baby," he said.

There is little I can offer in the way of comfort. Bear in mind, all you can do is to continue to do that which is right and proper and not allow your annoyance to drag you down to the level of those unthinking (if not downright inconsiderate) individuals.

One other thing — we most often go shopping accompanied by our children, from toddlers to teenagers. When we do encounter a situation that frustrates us it is of the utmost importance not to say anthing negative about another *yid*. Don't ever verbalize "Look how inconsiderate some *yidden* are." Instead, use the opportunity to teach your children a valuable lesson in consideration. Tell them, "Let's put this shopping cart back in its rightful place so that another person won't be inconvenienced. I'm sure that if the person who left it here would have realized, he or she would have made every effort to do the right thing, so let's be *dan l'kaf zechus*, they must have been in a terrible hurry."

Let's not lose sight of the fact that the overwhelming number of shoppers do make the extra effort to put the shopping carts back. Let's hope that the few who do not will be alerted to be more thoughtful.

INTERPERSONAL
RELATIONSHIPS

TOO LATE FOR FRIENDSHIP?

*I have a friend whose company I enjoy,
but she has one habit that drives me to
distraction. She is never on time. If I pick
her up, she's never ready. If she picks me
up, she is always late. (Somehow, she shows up
for her job on time.) I've told her the event
we're going to is starting an hour earlier
than the actual time, but it doesn't help.*

   *Recently, there was the straw that broke
the camel's back. I was going to take a
flight, and she offered to drive me to the
airport. I should have known better, but a
taxi to the airport is very costly, so I
said, "OK, but this time you must come when
you promise to." I nearly went out of my
mind waiting for her, but I thought that
with little traffic, we could just make it.
Well, traffic wasn't all that bad, but I
missed my plane. She was quite apologetic,
saying, "I'm sorry, what can I do to make*

*up for it?" It was about all I could do to
keep myself from saying, "Get lost!"*

*I'd like to keep this friendship. Is it a
lost cause?*

Y our friend has a severe form of procrastination. People with this problem seem to be as helpless as an alcoholic is with his drinking. Just as an alcoholic is unable to keep a promise that he won't drink, neither can a procrastinator keep a promise not to be late.

It is not unusual that she can be on time for her job. An alcoholic can delay drinking until after work.

Let's suppose your friend was an alcoholic. You could say, "Dear friend, you are harming yourself. There is help available," to which she might reply, "No, thank you, I don't have a problem," or "Yes, I realize that, and I'm going to cut back on my drinking" In either case, nothing happens. If her drinking somehow affects you, you may say, "I value our friendship, but I just can't continue it as long as you're drinking."

Now just substitute "procrastination" for "drinking." She can't help herself. You might say, "Stop apologizing. That's not going to change anything. If you feel badly about what happened, you should realize that this is a pattern that has been going on for a long time. You might decide that you're going to be on time next time, but it won't work. You need to do something to overcome this problem."

She may say, "No, thanks," in which case you must decide whether the friendship is worthwhile and if you will tolerate her procrastination. Without help, she is not going to change. Should she indicate that she does want to change, the Appendix at the back of the book contains a partial listing of referral agencies.

HESITANT TO COMMUNICATE

---

*Thank you very much for providing us with
this question-and-answer forum.*

I love people and I love being social, but here comes my problem. I can not make easy, naturally flowing conversation. When I go to simchos, visit people, etc. I dread what to say, so many times I just don't go, which makes me feel awful. I'd love to sound more friendly and know what is appropriate to say and how to make close friendships.

By the way, I come from a home where my father is highly respected in the community, but doesn't talk much, even to us children. It's not because he hasn't got time — he just doesn't have anything to say. My mother is very bitter and unsociable for various reasons, which has surely affected us. Can I be helped? If yes, how and where?

Children often adopt parental traits, and from your description of your parents, it is not difficult to understand why you might have a problem with conversation, but it is certainly possible for you to change.

A common reason for hesitancy in making conversation is a lack of self-confidence, thinking that you don't have anything worthwhile to say. You should remember that most of the people you meet are very much like yourself. There are not many Nobel prize-winners around. You have at least as much knowledge as anyone else.

Closely related to this is an intense fear of making a mistake, saying something wrong. This is much like immigrants who are so fearful that they will mispronounce an English word or use the wrong word that they never try to speak English and never learn the language. It is a self-esteem issue. People who feel better about themselves know that a mistake is not a catastrophe, so they speak and make mistakes and eventually become fluent in English. Most of the books I've written deal with self-esteem, and if you can elevate your self-esteem, it will be much easier for you to make conversation. You might find *Ten Steps to Being Your Best* helpful.

There may also be a feeling that silence is awkward. Some people cannot tolerate being next to others and not speaking to them. There is nothing wrong with silence. If the other person has something to say, he/she will initiate conversation. If not, silence is fine, too, as long as you feel comfortable with it.

Finally, there are a number of books on this problem (which shows that you are not alone in this). One of them is *How to Start a Conversation and Make Friends*, by Don Gabor. Any of the books on this subject can be helpful, but you must practice what you read.

Don't allow your fears to keep you from socializing. Use the techniques suggested. It's too important a part of life to miss out on.

CHATTERING THROUGH SPEECHES AT A DINNER

I was recently at a bar-mitzvah dinner and I became extremely upset. There were a few speakers, each of whom spoke very briefly, but you could not hear a word because of the chattering that went on. Some of the speakers were prominent Rabbonim, but people talked anyway. Even when the bar mitzvah boy himself gave his talk, on which he had certainly put in time and effort, the chattering did not stop. It was simply disgusting.

The entire crowd was frum. I'm certain that everyone there is makpid on pas Yisroel, but they didn't have the decency to keep quiet for even a few minutes out of courtesy to the speaker.

There was only one consolation. As I looked around the room, I noticed that there was not a single non-frum Jew there, and I thanked G-d, because a non-

frum Jew, seeing the rudeness of the
people, would have walked away with the
impression that all frum people lack
elemental courtesy, and that would have
been a chilul Hashem.

Thank you for calling our attention to this.

I too, have witnessed such occasions. Everyone knows
that *derech eretz* is a prerequisite to Torah. *Derech eretz* is
the foundation upon which Torah stands, and without *derech eretz*,
Torah cannot survive.

I hope that our readers will take note of this. If, during an event,
someone speaks to you while a speaker is talking, signal him that you
wish to remain silent.

TRYING TO AVOID *LASHON HARA* DURING A VISIT

Thank you for your weekly column which I
find very interesting.

I am writing regarding an issue which
has been bothering me for a while. I have
an elderly widowed neighbour whom I often
visit. As she has not got many visitors, she
feels lonely and therefore appreciates my
visits very much.

My problem is: although I have told her
explicitly that I do not want to listen
to lashon hara, she insists on telling me
things about other people. Can you please
suggest a solution as to how to tackle this
problem.

I am looking forward to your reply.

This is a halachah question that should be addressed to a *posek*. I can only give you my opinion.

While it certainly is a *chessed* to keep a lonely widow company, this mitzvah does not override the most serious *aveirah* of listening to *lashon hara*. If the lonely widow would say, "I can't eat alone. Please eat with me," and would serve food that is not kosher, you obviously could not possibly accommodate her.

You might say, "I really enjoy spending time with you, but I am not permitted to hear things about other people, and if you talk to me about other people, I will have to leave." Because she may have nothing else to talk about, you might suggest that you can bring her reading material that you could discuss or that you would read to her. It would also be helpful if you are prepared with a list of several interesting topics to discuss with her while you are there. You might find something that interests her so that your visits can continue.

WORRISOME FRIENDSHIP

I have a friend with whom I have been very close for many years. We went to elementary school together. Then we attended different high schools and were taught different hashkafos. Now she's much more modern than I am. This doesn't bother us. But she's very opinionated and I don't want to be influenced by her. She is a very good speaker and is capable of convincing others to agree with her. In general, I would not be feeling apprehensive, but her brother recently went off-the-derech and moved out of her house and she's bitter about frum people. She often attacks frum ways and I don't always have an answer to her confusing messages. We are very close and we talk almost daily. I don't want to break a friendship, but should I if it could be damaging my ruchniyus?

W e must be extremely careful about our *ruchniyus*. We have a lifelong battle with the *yetzer hara* that tempts us to do many things that would be pleasurable but which the Torah forbids, and we must be constantly on guard. Any ideas that might arouse a doubt in our minds about our commitment to Torah may weaken our resistance to the *yetzer hara*.

One can have a friendship with the agreement that there are certain areas that are not open for discussion. I know people who have made an agreement with friends not to talk about politics because they are on opposite poles, and discussion may lead to personal attacks. We may not exercise good judgment if someone attacks something in which we believe.

What purpose can there be in your friend maligning Yiddishkeit? She may be doing it defensively, perhaps to defend her brother or to justify some things that she does. She is hardly doing so out of genuine concern for you.

You may continue the friendship with the understanding that you have differences in your *hashkafos*, and that issues of Yiddishkeit are out of bounds for discussion. If she persists in bringing these issues up, you may tell her, "I value your friendship, but we have agreed that this subject is off-limits." If she nevertheless persists and is not honoring the agreement, it indicates that she has some agenda, and at that point I believe you should discontinue contact. If your friendship is important to her, she will then agree to honor the agreement. If it is not important to her, you lose nothing by dropping a worrisome friendship.

ANXIETY

ANTI-ANXIETY MEDICATIONS

You've often written about anti-anxiety medications, saying that they are addictive. My husband is currently being treated for anxiety and panic attacks, and I was wondering how long he can take the medication (Lexapro) without it becoming addictive, as I am concerned about that.

The doctor feels he should stay on the medication for a year or two. Isn't that long? He has been taking the medication for about six months, and is doing well.

Isn't it time to stop?

My cautionary remarks were about the classification of medications known as "tranquilizers," which may be abused or addictive. Antidepressant medications, such as the one you mentioned, are generally not addictive. Antidepressant medications are helpful even if the person is not depressed. They were given this name because they are widely used for depression as well for as other conditions.

It is recommended that one take the medication for at least a year, and perhaps two years. After that, even if some anxiety recurs, the person is much better able to cope with it.

Panic attacks are actually a physiological condition, just as any other physical disease. However, manifestations, or symptoms, of panic are emotional or psychological. Panic is usually not the result of early life experiences or other psychological causes, but of a chemical imbalance. However, because panic attacks are so frightening, there is anxiety about having a panic attack, or "anticipatory anxiety."

As the person realizes that a panic attack is not a heart attack and that he is not going to die, the anticipatory anxiety may disappear. Therapy can also be helpful for the anticipatory anxiety. Some people who have stopped taking antidepressant medication after a year or more say that they sometimes get anxiety episodes, but they can ignore them, whereas before treatment the attacks were disabling.

SOCIAL PHOBIA

I am very socially capable and have many friends and significant relationships, or at least this was true until the past few years. I developed a problem: when I speak I become very self-conscious. I start to focus on how I am speaking and how I am being perceived, as opposed to focusing on what I am saying and how I am conveying my ideas to the listener. The feelings of self-consciousness cause me to analyze how I am making eye contact, when I am making eye contact, my facial expressions, the listener's facial expressions, etc. This causes me to feel tremendous anxiety and my

*natural personality is hampered. In turn, it
has caused me to fear certain social settings
and events, even everyday social encounters.*

*On the other hand, I do not experience
these feelings of self-consciousness at
all when speaking on the phone. I am much
more relaxed and feel much more at liberty
to express myself. I do not know why this
problem started. It does not occur all the
time. However, it has been occurring with
increased frequency even though I have been
attempting to deal with it. I have read
many of your books, but I feel that I need
something specific to fix this problem; it
has started to take over my life for no
good reason.*

As you say, "this causes me to feel tremendous anxiety."
Anxiety problems may develop at any time in a person's
life. Sometimes the reasons are apparent, at other times the
reasons might be ferreted out, and in some situations, the reasons
may never be known. Therefore, the focus should not be so much on
looking for the underlying cause, as on finding what to do for relief.

The feelings you describe are characteristic of a "social phobia."
Some people might think that taking a tranquilizer to subdue the
anxiety is the answer. Unfortunately, this may result in a more difficult problem, because many tranquilizers may be addictive if they
are used with any regularity.

Some people may have anxiety only under very specific circumstances, such as when they must give a public address or lead the
tefillos in *shul*. It is possible to block the effects of occasional anxiety
by taking a medication such as propanalol prior to the event. This
must be checked out with one's physician. Use of this medication is
not practical for anxiety that occurs more frequently.

Some people experience an almost constant anxiety, which is not
triggered by any particular situation. Some of the antidepressant
medications can be helpful, and these are not addictive.

In your situation, I would recommend a treatment known as "Systematic Desensitization," which can be done with or without a therapist. In an earlier issue of *Hamodia*, I described the treatment. Essentially, it consists of learning a relaxation technique and then applying the relaxation to anxiety-provoking conditions. You may get a copy of this treatment by contacting *Hamodia* and asking for the "Systematic Desensitization."

GO VEGETARIAN AFTER MEAT SCANDAL?

Following the horror story of not-kosher meat sold in an Orthodox community at a supposedly glatt kosher butcher store, I told my wife that if something like this can happen, I want to go vegetarian. How can I ever be sure that some person without a conscience might manage to circumvent even a reliable hechsher? My wife says that I'm neurotic, and that my fear is unfounded. Does this make me neurotic?

We are all still reeling from the shock of the unthinkable catastrophe. Although your reaction is a bit extreme, there is no reason to consider it neurotic. After all, many people are vegetarians for any number of reasons.

There are halachos about what one should suspect and what not. We should be guided by halachah rather than by emotion. Consult your *posek* about what the halachah requires.

I must mention, however, that being vegetarian does not assure one is safe. As terrible as the *issur* of *tereifah* meat is, the fact is that the *issur* of eating vegetables that are infested with insects is even worse. For some reason, people accept a *hechsher* on vegetables without the same concern they have for meat, whereas the reverse should actually be true. The only reasonable thing to do is to seek the advice of a *posek*.

FEARS EXPRESSING DEEP FEELINGS

As a teen with very strong emotions and difficult situations, I often have the need to express my deep feelings in very bold and absolute terms. I can hear myself say "I won't ever …" or "I can't …." It makes me feel good just to say what I so strongly experience. Still, I know the concept of al tiftach peh lasaton. What is the source for this pasuk? Will bad things really happen to me because I said something in desperation? Is this rule different for people in special circumstances like mine?

The origin of this concept is in *Berachos*, 19a.

In many areas of Yiddishkeit, we find that words should not be treated lightly. We value a *berachah*, although it is only words. Making a *neder* (promise) is a serious obligation. Swearing falsely is a grave sin. *Lashon hara* (defamatory speech) is equivalent to the three cardinal sins. Words can be more far-reaching than some actions. A lie is only words, yet it is the only sin about which the Torah tells us, "Keep your distance from it" (*Shemos*, 23:7).

Psychologically, words have an impact on how we think and feel. Negative words can result in negative thoughts and feelings.

There are some "I won't evers" that are positive. For example, if a person has done something wrong, he may say, "I won't ever do that again." The Talmud says that tzaddikim would take an oath to fulfill a mitzvah, because this motivates them and strengthen their resolve to do it (*Chagigah*, 10a).

Try to find a positive way to deal with an emotion. For example, suppose you're irritated by the way a salesperson treated you, and you feel like saying, "I won't ever set foot in this store again." Instead you might say, "Next time I come here, I expect to be treated more respectfully."

Blurting out a negative comment happens without thinking. If you pause to think of how you might express the feeling in a more positive way, you have already gained something. You have learned to think a bit before you speak. Much misery could be avoided if people took the time to think before speaking.

SEVERE *SHIDDUCH* ANXIETY

Last year my daughter went through a terrible breakup. It was traumatizing. In our circles this is a big thing. We agonized for several weeks. Should we do it? Should we not? She just wasn't happy. Yes? No? Yes? No? Indescribable agony for weeks.

Finally the decision was made. Her decision was to call it off. We all agreed with her. She was back single and happy as ever. I truly felt, "Wow, she's strong!" She was on top of the world, always smiling. She was really taking it well. Too well.

A shidduch was mentioned to her and she went out. She came back from her date and boom! She was shaking. She said her date went well but she just had this nervousness. I figured since she was traumatized the first time it was normal. The next day when she woke up she was shaking like a leaf. Anxiety to no end and something must have snapped in her brain. She was shivering, jumping out of her skin, and needed to be calmed down quick. She started taking Valium for about three months. Not a big dose, but *it was still Valium. That's the only thing that seemed to help. She spoke to someone and he just said, "It takes time, it will go away. Time heals all wounds." After these few months of terrible anxiety, dizziness, headaches, weakness, and sadness, she stopped the Valium. It's been months and she's finally calmed down. Her appetite is back and her mood is back. No depression at all.*

However, certain symptoms are just not going away. She has this worriedness every morning. She wakes up nervous, but she's not worried about anything specific. Her legs are always very weak and she feels extremely light-headed and unsteady. I don't know what it means but even if she is standing, for example, while speaking to a friend, she just has to constantly move back and forth. If not, she just doesn't feel right. She cannot stand in one place. When she moves she feels better. I have spoken to several psychologists and they say it takes time; it will go away. However, it's been seven months and it's not going away. It's like she's just stuck in this hole and can't get rid of these few symptoms.

Is anti-anxiety medication a solution or should we stick it out and wait till it goes away by itself? I personally don't want her to take medication. If you feel she should, what would be the best anti-anxiety medication? Is her reaction normal? We are sick, watching our daughter suffer for almost a year. It just has to end already.

Proper shidduchim are being redt, but how can she continue when she has these terrible symptoms that don't seem to leave? Please give me a lead as to what I can do.

ymptoms of anxiety can occur for a variety of reasons, many of which are not logical, but the emotional part of the mind does not necessarily follow the rules of logic. It is not possible to guess what triggered her anxiety and why it is still persisting. You mentioned that you have spoken to a number of psychologists, but you did not indicate whether she consulted a psychotherapist.

The first place to begin is always with a thorough medical examination. Many years ago, I wrote a book describing a number of cases that appeared to be neuroses, but were actually due to an undiagnosed medical condition.

If she is found to be in good physical health, she should consult a psychiatrist. It is good that she is not relying on Valium, which, while it may be helpful for a short-term problem, should not be relied on for the long term because it can be addictive. There are a number of non-addictive medications that are effective for anxiety.

I don't believe in "sticking it out" and waiting for time to heal. Anxiety can bring on anxiety, and one can be caught in a vicious cycle. The sooner her symptoms are brought under control, the better.

Some psychiatrists do psychotherapy, while others primarily manage medication and refer patients to a psychotherapist for therapy. She should certainly be seen for therapy. Referrals can be obtained from ECHO, 845-425-9750 or RELIEF 718-431-9501 (see Appendix).

FAILING MEMORY

I am 52, and I assume I'm not in the age range for Alzheimer's disease, but in the past year or so I find that I'm having memory problems. I sometimes can't remember names of people I know, and sometimes I grope for a word I know but can't remember it, although it does come to me at a later time. Why is this happening and what can I do about it?

People might not like to hear this, but we actually begin losing brain cells in our 20's! Yet we have enough mental acuity to function well even through advanced age, unless, of course, one *chas veshalom* develops Alzheimer's disease.

Failure to remember people's names or words is not dementia. It's a "glitch," which may be due to the fact that our minds are cluttered up with so many things. Now, if a person has driven from his home to the post office countless times, and then one day cannot remember how to get there, that is a more serious problem.

The inability to remember names or words usually remains fairly constant over many years. Dementia is progressive, and worsens in a matter of months.

I do much writing and often grope for words I know. I leave the space blank and fill it in when the word comes to me. This can be frustrating, but it's not serious.

To remember names, there are some "tricks" that can help. For example, when meeting Mr. Silverberg, you look at him, try to fix his appearance in your mind, and repeat a few times, "Silverberg, Silverberg, etc." Or, while looking at him, think "He reminds me of a mountain of silver" (silver + berg). For Fox, Green, or Schwartz, associate the face with the image of a fox, a shade of green, or the color black. Sometimes you can make associations to the name that are ridiculous, but it's precisely these that can be most helpful, because they stick in the mind.

Anxiety is the leading culprit in many problems of thought. Learning how to relax and how to put things in better perspective so that one does not become overly anxious can ease memory problems.

Finally, books on memory improvement can suggest some techniques that are useful.

MOMENTARY PARALYSIS

I had a terribly frightening experience a few days ago. I woke up from a nap, and I felt I was paralyzed. I couldn't move. I wanted to scream for help, but I couldn't open my mouth. After a few seconds, it went away. Does this mean there is something wrong with my brain?

S top worrying. This is a common occurrence. It is called a "hypnogogic" or "hypnopompic" phenomenon, and occurs in the "twilight" stage when one is either falling asleep or waking up. Sometimes it occurs after a frightening dream, which a person may or may not remember.

These phenomena are normal, although they may be frightening. One may have jerking or twitching sensations. Sometimes one may hear sounds, such as the ringing of a bell, a name, or a song. There can be visual sensations of various kinds. While these are actually hallucinations, they do not indicate any abnormality.

Sometimes people have a sense of predicting things in this state. While it may be an eerie feeling, it is normal and there is no reason for concern.

TRAUMA TRIGGERS DEPRESSING THOUGHTS

I never had a problem until about six months ago. My father, who is 82 (to 120), became very ill, and was not expected to survive. B"H, he recovered miraculously. He and I are very close, and when I was afraid I would lose him, I panicked, and throughout his illness I had panic attacks. But now that he has recovered, even though I rarely get panic attacks, I keep on thinking, "What happens if next time he doesn't recover," and I begin to cry. I can't fall asleep. My family doctor has given me two medications, which help a little, but I still get very upset when I think of this. Is there anything I can do?

I t is not unusual for an emotionally traumatic event to trigger one or more of the anxiety-depression disorders, including panic attacks, obsessive-compulsive disorder, depression, and sometimes all three. Medications are often very effective. If you have not had much relief, you should consult a psychiatrist, who may change or regulate the medication to help you feel better. It is also helpful to consult a psychotherapist.

I can understand that your close relationship with your father makes it difficult for you to think of being without him. May Hashem bless him to live to 120, but we must realize that the natural order is for children to survive parents. It is the joy of parents that their children survive them. G-d forbid if a parent loses a child, that is an inconsolable loss.

You have been blessed with the relationship of a loving father, and may Hashem grant you many more years with him. Of course, it is painful when one loses a loving parent. Rather than panic at the thought of the inevitable, concentrate on spending as much time with him as is feasible and enjoy the blessing of your relationship. It is possible that the recurring thought that you cannot shake off may be a symptom of OCD (Obsessive Compulsive Disorder), which can be relieved with treatment.

FEAR OF ANIMALS AND BIRDS

My 8-year-old son is afraid of animals. Originally he just did not like dogs, but now his fear has spread to cats, and more recently to birds as well! I thought he would soon grow out of it, as my older

*children did. None of them like animals, but
they tolerate them and get on with doing
what they have to do! Not so with this son.
What worries me is that his fear of all
creatures is greatly affecting his life! He
avoids going to parks, for walks on Shabbos,
anywhere he thinks there may be a dog, cat,
or bird! When we go to a park as a family,
he often stays in the car, unless he is sure
that there is a fence around the playground,
and that both my husband and I will be there
so that one of us can watch the younger
children and one of us can watch him! He
rarely goes to Mesibos Shabbos on Shabbos
afternoon, as he is worried about what
animals he may see on the way. What prompted
me to write to you now is that last night
we went to Kaporas. He could barely read the
"Bnei Adam" — he was too worried to take his
eyes off the surrounding areas checking for
chickens! There was not one loose chicken!
They were all being held or in cages! When
my husband held the chicken over my son, he
took the baby's blanket and covered his head
while I was holding him against me!*

Zoophobia, or fear of animals, is one of the most common phobias, affecting both children and adults. As you point out, it can be very restricting and can affect a person's life style very negatively.

There are several psychotherapeutic approaches to this phobia. Medication is not the answer. You should find a psychologist who has expertise in treating this condition. You may call ECHO or RELIEF for a referral (see Appendix).

If the fear was limited to tigers or even snakes, animals which he is unlikely to encounter in the course of his day, it might be possible to ignore the problem or wait until he outgrew it. However, his phobia involves animals that will cross his path frequently and the problem should be resolved.

I understand that some parents may be reluctant to have their child treated by a psychologist because he may then think that he is mentally ill. Some parents may worry that consulting a psychologist, even for a child of 8, may be an impediment to a *shidduch* 12 years later. This is a very unwise consideration. The effects of an untreated phobia, which may paralyze the child's activity, is far worse than this unlikely possibility.

TEENAGE FRUSTRATION AND ANGER

I am a 15-year-old teenager. Recently I have been suffering from strong emotions such as nervousness, anger, frustration, and helplessness. These emotions overtake me completely and at times I even have an urge to do outrageous things. I have tried to let out my feelings by doing intense exercise or listening to music — but nothing helps. I am anticipating your response.

Many teen-agers have strong emotions. The transition from childhood to adulthood involves many issues.

Young children are relatively free of responsibility. They are dependent on their parents for many things, and they have little difficulty with this. As one becomes an adolescent, one takes on more responsibility for one's actions. In addition, this is a time when one wishes to assert one's independence, yet the reality is that one is still dependent on parents. While one may wish to be independent, that idea can be quite scary, and the adolescent is caught in a bind, both wanting independence and fearing it.

As a child, one is generally known as "so-and-so's son/daughter." In adolescence, one begins to establish an identity of one's own. When life was simpler, this was not too great a problem. But life today is so much more complex that a young person may be confused, not knowing exactly what it is he/she wants to be. Adolescents realize that they will be making important decisions that will affect their future.

All this is normal. You can be assured that your nervousness, anger, frustration, and helplessness are shared by many other young people. It will help to remember that all adults have survived adolescence.

The best thing to do is to discuss your feelings with a mature person. If you are not comfortable sharing your feelings with your parents, you should be able to find someone who can listen to you and help you clarify your thoughts and feelings. If your *rebbe* does not have the time to do this, he can suggest someone to whom you can talk.

UNDERSTANDING ANXIETY

I've been suffering from anxiety for several years now. As our community looks down upon those who need assistance in mental health, it took me many years to make the connection between the way I was feeling physically and the possible (probable) connection to the way I was feeling internally. After several years in therapy, combined with taking medication, I've experienced many ups and downs, as is normal to one who suffers from anxiety. Some days are better than others, while I struggle to work through my feelings of anxiety and its underlying causes, the result of numerous experiences and crises that I've experienced in my early life.
During the past few excruciating years, I've been subject to much animosity and ridicule from my family. How do I make them understand that these feelings and its

symptoms are real; they are caused by past experiences and cannot simply by dismissed with remarks like, "You're just full of self-pity; stop creating your own problems; there really is nothing wrong with you; it's all in your head, etc."? I know they read your column and will respect your advice.

Also, in general, how can I educate the community at large, teaching them that mental health is equally as important as physical health, that conditions like anxiety, depression, etc., are no different than physical illnesses, in that the feelings are real and those who suffer from them need not be embarrassed; Hashem is testing them the same way He tests someone with a physical sickness, which a person does not cause him/herself.

Anxiously awaiting your answer as each day brings with it more and more ridicule, and less and less and less understanding of and concern about my situation, never mind the support I so desperately need.

A nxiety is a very broad topic. A simple definition is that anxiety is the same sensation as fear, but whereas in fear the object of the fear is known, such as being in a building that is on fire, in anxiety there is no known object. This is why anxiety may be difficult for people to understand. Why would someone be fearful if there is nothing to fear?

Some psychologists say that there is indeed an object of fear, but that the person is not aware of it because it is in the subconscious mind. The object of fear may be a repressed memory of trauma, or a very threatening thought that may occur to the person.

Sometimes the anxiety is restricted to a particular situation, in which case it is referred to as a phobia. There are countless phobias, some of the more common being agoraphobia, anxiety when in a public place; claustrophobia, anxiety caused by being in an enclosed space; acrophobia, anxiety in high places, and many more.

Severe anxiety can occur suddenly, without any trigger. A person suddenly feels overwhelmed by an intense fear. This is known as panic disorder, and appears to be due to a chemical imbalance rather than to psychological causes.

Our bodies are provided with a mechanism to help ward off an attack or escape from it. This is known as the "fight-or-flight" reaction, in which there is a surge of adrenalin, rapid heartbeat, rapid breathing, elevated blood pressure, a shift of blood supply to the muscles, and several chemical changes. This reaction can occur in anxiety, where there is no assailant, just as it can in fear. Because there is no one to fight or flee from, these changes may linger, causing a variety of physical symptoms and diseases.

Psychotherapy can be helpful in treating anxiety. Caution must be used when taking medication. Antidepressant medications are often effective and are relatively safe. Tranquilizers, on the other hand, present a risk of addiction if used regularly.

It is possible to overcome anxiety with self-help methods. One of these was formulated many years ago by Dr. Abraham Low in his book, *Mental Health Through Will Training.*

People who have not experienced anxiety may not be able to understand why a person should feel anxious when there is nothing disturbing him. It is to be hoped that they will become more understanding if they learn about it.

AIR HUNGER

We flew to Israel for Pesach, and on the flight I suddenly felt that I could not get enough air and I felt a tightness in my chest. I began to feel faint and I had the sensation of pins and needles in my face. I was sure I was dying. My husband alerted the

flight attendant. Fortunately, there were two
doctors on the plane. They checked me and
said I was not having a heart attack. They
had me breathe into a bag, which made me feel
better, but I still felt I could not get
enough air. I could not take a deep breath.
They were able to get a tranquilizer from one
of the other passengers, and I felt better.

The doctors said I had "air hunger and
hyperventilation" and that it was due
to anxiety, but I wasn't anxious about
anything. In fact, I was looking forward to
a great time in Israel. On return, I had a
checkup with my doctor, who said I was in
perfect condition, and that the doctors on
the plane were right.

What can I do to prevent such an episode?
It was very frightening.

In the absence of disease, "air hunger" — feeling one is not getting enough air — can be a symptom of anxiety. In order to get more air, one breathes faster (hyperventilates). When you do this, you exhale carbon dioxide, which changes the alkalinity of the blood slightly, but enough to cause a drop in blood calcium. This can cause dizziness, feelings of pins and needles around the lips, numbness of the fingers, and tightening of the muscles. Understandably, these are frightening feelings. When you breathe into a bag, you inhale the carbon dioxide that you had exhaled, thereby replenishing the blood calcium level.

Anxiety attacks may occur for no apparent reason. The best way to avoid anxiety is to learn how to better relax, and there are a number of books available on relaxation methods. Of course, the more one has *bitachon* and feels secure under the protection of Hashem, the less likely one is to feel severe anxiety.

Taking a tranquilizer for an occasional anxiety episode is acceptable. Frequent use of tranquilizers is unwise, however, because one may become dependent on them and become addicted. Tranquilizer addiction is difficult to treat, and one should avoid it. If anxiety episodes occur with some frequency, one should consult a psychiatrist. Non-addictive medications may be prescribed, or a course of therapy may be recommended. See the Appendix for a partial list of referral agencies.

FEAR OF BEING AN ABUSIVE MOTHER

I have been married for about a year-and-a-half to a wonderful man. We are now, G-d willing, expecting our first child in a few weeks. We are, of course, very excited — and nervous as well. My question is as follows: I have always been an aggressive person. When I am frustrated or angry, my first reaction is to tense up, and I feel like I have to hit someone, throw something, etc. This, of course, is not widely accepted as an appropriate means of behavior, so I do not go around hitting people often, but the feeling is there. I guess this makes my question obvious. I know that babies are a lot of hard work, and can test a person's patience to the limits. I know my baby will cry for no reason, wake me up when I have only had a few minutes of sleep, and demand every bit of my attention. I am very nervous that I will get frustrated and chas veshalom do something to harm my baby. I would like to nip this problem before it starts, or at least get some tips on how to channel my aggressiveness in another way so that I do not end up taking it out on my helpless baby. The last thing I want is to be an abusive mother, G-d forbid!

The fact that you are aware of the problem is a great part of the solution. Don't doubt the efficacy of your controls. We all have feelings which we do not allow to progress into action.

It is related that the Chofetz Chaim used to pray tearfully for Hashem to divest him of his feelings of anger. No one ever saw the Chofetz Chaim angry, because he was in control of his feelings. You may say, "But I'm not the Chofetz Chaim." Just think of how many times you had any number of feelings that you did not act on because you felt they were inappropriate.

Nevertheless, there are some steps you can take to ease your tension. Relaxation exercises are very helpful, because tension and relaxation cannot coexist. Relaxation can diffuse tension. You may learn how to adopt a state of relaxation by following the exercises in books on relaxation techniques. They work if you follow instructions. You can learn to give yourself signals that will make you relax when you're tense. Additional techniques can be learned through biofeedback or with a therapist who can help you with hypnotic relaxation.

We must prepare ourselves in advance for dealing with an anger episode. An airplane pilot must know in advance what to do if the landing gear is stuck. Whatever technique you are going to use should be practiced every morning, so that when you feel anger you can promptly activate the control mechanism.

Feelings of anger are very common, and there are a number of books on anger management. The book by Rabbi Zelig Pliskin is excellent.

You should be aware that having a new baby can be exhausting. Try to get extra help so you are not overwhelmed and overtired, which could lead to episodes of anger. Discuss this issue with your husband before the baby is born so that he can help you deal with it.

OVERREACTING TEENAGER

I am 17 years old. When something upsetting happens, although it can seem like a minor issue, I get very upset and I feel like I can't control myself. I end up yelling, or crying in my room until I calm down. I feel like every part of my body is crying and shaking. I'm often down and depressed and find it hard to smile and be cheerful. My mother says I shouldn't be such a grouch, but I'm just feeling sad and upset about real things. Now, I was wondering, is it just bad character, pessimism, or can it indicate something more serious?

Y ou say that you over-react to "something minor." Obviously, if when the upsetting thing happens you knew that it was something minor, you would not react to it by yelling or by crying. It is only in retrospect that you understand that it was something minor, but at the time it happened, it felt like something very major.

On a windy day, a speck of dust may fly into your eye, and it is terribly irritating. It feels like it is the size of a boulder. When you take it out with a cotton swab, you see it was a very tiny speck of dust. The reason you felt it to be so big was because it affected a very sensitive area, the conjunctiva of your eye.

This is also true emotionally. If one is very sensitive emotionally, even something that is objectively minor can feel very large.

It is not unusual for young people in adolescence to have heightened emotional sensitivity. I suspect that the most upsetting things are those that make you feel in some way inadequate or inferior. This is most often due to having unwarranted low self-esteem. I discuss this concept in my books, *Life's Too Short* and *Angels Don't Leave Footprints*. In *Ten Steps to Being Your Best*, I suggest some steps to elevate one's self-esteem. You might want to check these out.

IRRITATED BY OTHER'S HABITS

I would like to ask you about an interesting

problem that I have had for about 15 years, and has probably gotten worse over that period of time. Very succinctly, I become nervous due to other people's habits. But not just simply nervous — I become anxious, tense, concerned, and nauseated. What makes it even worse is that it's also normal, regular things that people do that make me feel that way — the way people clear their throats, chew, sniff, etc .... It has gotten to the point where my relationships with people who get me nervous (basically my family) have deteriorated. I avoid my husband at meal times and shout at my son for the stupidest reasons .... Sometimes I try to control or ignore it but even if I'm successful for a short while, it soon comes back in full force. I am not always like that. In my public life, no one would dream I have such an issue. I am vivacious, outgoing, a charismatic teacher, someone looked up to and respected. At home as well, I do have peaceful moments when I don't feel that anxiety and tension. I guess it's my skeleton, which does not stay in the closet, and I wish it would! I am so normal otherwise but when that tension comes upon me, I feel like the weirdest, most immature being ever. Please help me find a solution.

This is not an unusual problem and has nothing to do with being immature. It is a result of one of the "tricks" our subconscious mind can play on us.

Our conscious minds think logically and can reject illogical thought. The subconscious mind cannot do that. Sometimes a "short circuit" occurs in the subconscious. It can go something like this:

At some time, a person experiences an event that causes him anxiety or other unpleasant sensation. At the same time, or very close to it, he happened to see purple flowers. It is possible that after that, every time he sees purple flowers, he may experience the same anxiety or unpleasant sensation that he had the first time. The subconscious mind has connected the two.

Associations like this can cause problems such as the one you describe. Probably some time in the past, you experienced some kind of unpleasant sensation or thought at the same time you observed a particular act. The subconscious has fused the two, and that act now evokes an unpleasant feeling.

It is possible to "stonewall" the symptom and it may eventually leave. Another possibility is to think of a very happy feeling, and when you see the act that provokes an unpleasant sensation, immediately think of and concentrate on the happy feeling. You may be able to dissociate the act from the unpleasant feeling.

If this doesn't work, psychological treatment may help you get rid of the problem.

ANXIETY

I wonder if you might be able to help me with my anxiety problem. It started about 3½ years ago, a year after my first child was born. I lost a lot of weight and started to have trouble sleeping. I was sure it was a hormonal imbalance or other physical problem, but after doing various blood tests, my doctor referred me to a psychiatrist. He diagnosed me with General Anxiety Disorder and prescribed an SSRI (Celexa) for one year. He said that after this amount of time, 90% of the people are able to discontinue the medication and function well.

Three-and-a-half years later, I am still taking it although I have tried a least three times to stop. Every time I eventually get the "sleep anxiety" again and go back on. When you are a mother of young children, its difficult to function with inadequate sleep.

My question is, how can I successfully discontinue the medication? It is supposedly not physically addictive and I have recently been taking a very low dose — one that is, theoretically, not even therapeutic (10 mg). Am I psychologically addicted?

Since I began motherhood (Baruch Hashem) in my mid-30's, I guess that this new role triggered something in me (although I was never the most tranquil, self-confident person). Sometimes I worry that I'm going to have to continue the medication at least until my children grow up. I think I could benefit from some therapy, but an English-speaking therapist is not so easy to come by in the city in which I live. The psychiatrist didn't seem to think that this was a crucial part of the treatment. But how does a person break out of the anxiety?

Maybe there are some books you could recommend to strengthen bitachon. Maybe they would help me build the inner strength to cope without the medication.

To the best of my knowledge, SSRI's are not physically addictive. However, there can be uncomfortable symptoms when reduced or discontinued. One should do so very gradually. Some people have had relief from withdrawal by using a Catapres patch. This can be prescribed by your physician.

One can become psychologically habituated to anything. The best method to overcome this is to be in a support group. In some areas there is a group called, "Pills Anonymous." If there is none in your neighborhood, you may follow the lead of people with pill habituation who have actually gone to Alcoholics Anonymous and have been helped even though they never drank.

There are a number of books on self-help for anxiety. They probably all have something to offer. Many years ago, Dr. Abraham Low wrote a book, *Mental Health Through Will-Training*. Based on this book, there are meetings of Recovery Inc. in many cities. These groups can be helpful in dealing with anxiety. See the Appendix for a partial list of referral agencies.

SHIDDUCHIM

PRE-NUPTIAL JITTERS

A friend of mine confided in me that her daughter's wedding is in a week, but that the daughter is constantly crying that she does not want to marry this man. She says she was pressured into the shidduch. My friend says that she cannot tolerate the shame of calling off the wedding. They are telling this young woman, "He's a fine boy. I'm sure you'll get to like him." Do you think this is right?

This is unfortunately not an uncommon problem. There have been several instances where the couple separated within weeks of the wedding.

We need to distinguish between pre-marriage anxiety (jitters) and genuine resistance. Frequently, a young man or woman may get "cold feet" as the wedding day approaches. This may be due to their realization of the seriousness of committing oneself to marriage. In some cases they may say, "I'm not sure he/she is the right one," but this may just be their way of expressing anxiety. With discussion and some assurance and encouragement from parents and a *rav*, they can go on to have a happy marriage.

It is much different when the young man or woman states, "I don't have any feelings for him/her," and maintains this attitude after discussion. The person may feel that he/she is being pressured into an unwanted relationship, and the resentment, added to the antipathy for the other party, makes it rather unlikely that the marriage will be successful. The nature of the hesitancy should be evaluated by a skilled *rav* or therapist.

Calling off the wedding after hundreds of people have been invited is indeed painful, while if the couple separates, it will usually initially be known to only a few friends. However, the experience is traumatic, and young lives can be ruined.

Greater caution in making a *shidduch* may avoid such tragedies. I again plead that there be complete disclosure and that no information that could adversely affect the other partner should be withheld. If people are asked for their opinion about the prospective *shidduch* and the families involved, and they know some important negative information, they should not give false or doctored information because they wish to avoid *lashon hara*. They should inquire from a *rav* what their obligation is according to halachah. The Chofetz Chaim, the leading authority on *lashon hara*, says that there are times when a person **must** disclose negative information.

Young men and women should not be pressured into *shidduchim*. If they have doubts, they should discuss these with a *rav* who is competent in marriage problems or with a Torah-true therapist, so that their misgivings can be resolved, or, if they are not, the *shidduch* can be terminated.

While the embarrassment involved in calling off a scheduled wedding is indeed very painful, it should not be the determining factor. A *rav* should be consulted and the issue thoroughly discussed.

The issue of *shanda* (disgrace; shame) can have serious effects. Some people refuse to get necessary psychological help for a son or daughter because consulting a therapist is considered to be a *shanda*. This can result in tragedy for a couple when problems arise after the marriage, and children of such a marriage are innocent victims.

The idea that marriage will cure a problem is a grave mistake. Marriage is not a hospital! Problems that exist before marriage may actually become worse after marriage.

I feel profound empathy for parents who confront these problems. It is of utmost importance to pay close attention to what your daughter is saying so that you can distinguish between pre-nuptial jitters and a potential serious problem. In the event that there really is an issue that cannot be readily resolved, we must be able to set aside our own feelings for the sake of the children's welfare. Thoughtful consultation with a *rav* can help arrive at the proper decision.

DATED WITHOUT PARENTAL KNOWLEDGE

I am 21, and so far the shidduchim I have been redt have not worked out. A woman who works in the same office with me suggested that I meet her cousin, and I did. He is 23, a fine yeshivah bachur with good middos, and comes from a fine, frum family. I have met him twice, and I think it is a far better match than any of the others that I've encountered.

My dilemma is that I did not tell my parents that I met him, and I think that if I tell them now, they will be very upset that I had not asked them first. I'm sure they would have approved, and I don't know why I didn't tell them. I guess I thought that nothing would come of it. Maybe to avoid upsetting them, I should just drop the whole thing and forget about it. On the other hand, this may be an opportunity I should not overlook. What do you think I should do?

You don't address the issue of how this *shidduch* came to be *redt* without your parents' approval. Why didn't your co-worker speak to your parents about this boy? Did "the fine yeshivah *bachur*" know that they were not consulted? If so, his willingness to deceive your parents speaks volumes about his character. If not, he is also a victim of your co-worker's thoughtlessness. You may be attracted to him because of the secrecy of the way this has been managed. How did you meet him without your parents' knowledge? Did you deceive them about where you were, or did you meet him at the office without telling them? You can see that one deception leads to another, and you have been living a lie. You should immediately turn to your parents and be honest with them.

Don't compound one mistake with another. It was a mistake to meet someone without consulting your parents. The best thing one can do when making a mistake is to own up to it. Tell your parents exactly what happened and apologize for deceiving them. If you know that they would have approved, they may be angry that you did not tell them, but I am sure they will understand and forgive you.

I don't think you should drop a possible *shidduch* that may be appropriate. If you have been impressed with this young man, you may try to compare others you may meet with him, and set yourself up for disappointment. So tell your parents, and then proceed with their approval.

READINESS FOR MARRIAGE

I am 19 years old. My parents are pushing me to consider a shidduch, but I have been resisting. I don't think I'm ready for marriage. Several of my friends are engaged or married, but that doesn't bother me. I think I'm afraid of the responsibilities of marriage and that I'm not ready for them. Do you think I should go ahead with shidduchim anyway, or should I wait until I feel more ready? How can I get my parents to understand me?

Readiness for marriage is a vague term, and just waiting until you feel ready does not suggest a time period. Is that likely to take one year, five years, or more?

It is not unusual to have concerns about the responsibilities of marriage. You may even have an advantage over some young women who have no such concerns, and later discover that they do not feel able to cope with the responsibilities of marriage.

Marriage requires maturity, and the fact that you are worried shows a level of maturity, but I believe you should consult someone with whom you can discuss your concerns and get proper guidance. You might talk with one of the *kallah* teachers, who may be able to help you herself or may refer you to the proper person. When your concerns are clarified and you receive the proper guidance, your fears will dissipate and you will feel ready.

SHOULD MY PARENTS RETHINK THEIR DECISION?

I am a 22-year-old bachur in beis midrash, and I am in the parashah of shidduchim. Recently, I was present when a shadchan suggested a young woman to my father. The shadchan praised her highly. She comes from a Torah'dig family. She is a Bais Yaakov graduate and attended seminary in Israel. She is well-liked by all and has very fine middos. She works mornings as a secretary in a lawyer's office, and in the afternoon, teaches English subjects in Bais Yaakov.

*It sounded promising to me, but before
my father had a chance to react, my older
brother said, "This is not a shidduch
for a kollel young man. She is obviously
interested in a secular career, otherwise
she would not be working in a lawyer's
office, and would be teaching limudei kodesh
rather than English subjects." My father
agreed with him and rejected the shidduch.*

*I have my doubts that they were right.
Is it appropriate for me to contact the
shadchan and arrange to meet her? Perhaps I
would find out that she is not interested
in a secular career, and my father would
reconsider.*

S uggest that your brother look at the Rashi in *Bereishis*, 24:50, about a son who preempts his father in rendering an opinion.

Your brother's concern may or may not be valid. It is a mistake to jump to conclusions. Your father may be able to find out more information. Too often, *shidduchim* have been rejected because of a knee-jerk reaction. There is always need for *yishuv hadaas*.

It is inappropriate to proceed with a *shidduch* against your father's wishes, although the halachah is that if the father's objections are groundless, the son is not obligated to obey. At this point we don't know whether his objections are groundless.

I suggest that you discuss this with your *Rosh Yeshivah*. There may be a way of finding out more about the girl's long-term goals. She may feel that this type of employment will more realistically enable her husband to learn in *kollel*. If that is her intention, it gives it another slant to the issue.

Of course, tell your father that you wish to discuss this with the *Rosh Yeshivah* and why. I'm sure he will not object to that.

LACK OF ATTRACTION

Several months ago, I became engaged. The young woman is from a fine family, and has wonderful middos. Everyone likes her, and I was told that I was very lucky to have made such a shidduch. Her parents are crazy about me. I was very happy, because she has all the maalos that I was looking for, even though in the three times we met, I did not feel an attraction toward her

We have met several times since, and I still do not feel any attraction. The wedding is two months away. I am having doubts. How can I marry someone to whom I don't feel attracted? I haven't shared this with my parents, because they are just enamored of her. What is your advice?

A while back, there was a very similar situation, where the young man consulted *daas Torah*, who said that as long as he did not see anything negative, the absence of attraction should not be a concern. The attraction will come later. They were married, and indeed have a happy marriage.

There may be more reason for concern when the relationship is based on strong attraction. These feelings may cause a person to overlook significant incompatibilities, which come to the fore when the passion wanes.

It is commonly believed that a marriage should be based on emotion, and perhaps that is why there is a nearly 50% divorce rate in the U.S. When a marriage is based on *sechel* (intellect), and the character traits of both parties are compatible, there is greater likelihood of an enduring relationship. The *daas Torah* was right. The proper emotions develop later.

This is borne out by Rambam (*Hilchos Yesodei HaTorah*, 2:2) who says that the way to develop *ahavas Hashem* is to contemplate the wonders of Hashem's creation, and by having some concept of the greatness of Hashem, *ahavah* develops. In other words, when there is great respect and appreciation of another person, along with a sharing of *hashkafos* and long-term goals, *ahavah* develops.

You do not state that you have any negative feelings of dislike that would have to be overcome, and inasmuch as your *kallah* has all the *maalos* you were looking for, your respect and admiration will bring about the emotion.

I realize that some people will disagree and say that when there is no feeling, one should not marry. I happen to agree with the opinion of the *daas Torah* in the above-mentioned case, but that was his advice to that individual. In a decision as important as this, you should consult *daas Torah* on your own.

WANTS A BEN TORAH PROFESSIONAL

I'm not sure what I want. I know for certain that I want a ben Torah, and I certainly want my husband to learn for two years after we're married, but after that, I'm not sure. I don't know whether I want someone who plans to learn in kollel long-term, or someone who will be kove'a ittim, but will be doing something for parnassah, either as a professional or in business. I don't know whether I would be happy being a kollel wife. If I asked a rav, I think that it's a foregone conclusion that he will tell me to go for a long-term kollel life. I'd like to consult someone who is willing to consider both options.

Y ou may be ambivalent because of societal pressures to conform, and therefore you feel that you must marry a young man who will be learning in *kollel*, yet at the same time you recognize that the lifestyle of the *kollel* is not for you.

I don't think your conclusion that a *rav* will automatically tell you to go for long-term *kollel* is valid. Our tradition has been that there is a Yissachar and a Zevulun. A person who is *kove'a ittim* and is supportive of Torah is very dear to Hashem.

The question is what is more compatible with your needs, and you can explain this to *daas Torah*, who will be sensitive to your needs. The *daas Torah* may give you his opinion, or if necessary, suggest someone with whom you can discuss at greater length and depth your needs and feelings, and help you decide what is likely to give you the greatest happiness.

Your parents can refer you to *daas Torah* who can relate to your question.

DOESN'T ADMIRE HER FATHER

I am a 22-year-old single girl. Baruch Hashem, I have not grown despondent about finding my marriage partner. I do not let things break my spirit. I firmly believe that my partner will come from Hashem alone, and the right shidduch is not in the power of any human being.

I have my mother as my coach, my teacher, and my best friend. She is a very smart woman with whom I discuss absolutely everything.

I have a very different relationship with my father. I guess I must admit that I don't admire him tremendously. You see, my father is a good person. With regard to worldly affairs, he's an intellectual, yet he is lacking the intuition, the on-target feelings about the whole shidduch process. My father has complaints about every single shadchan, and he voices them in public. When he voices his opinion he does it with venom. I shudder. I've tried to stop him and explain that I am grateful to any shadchan who calls. Nothing at all has changed. I am hesitant to approach my mother and tell her how my father's attitude in general hurts me.

My mother is a smart woman. She sees this. Do I have a right to interfere? Rabbi Twerski, I need some advice. What may be said? What should be said? Are there any books you can recommend?

I would love for you to give me advice on how to work on building an inner respect for a person whom I don't respect greatly. Again, I love my father but I really want to respect him as well.

When you feel you must differ with your father, you should consult a *posek* on how to do it. There are halachos on how to go about this, preserving *kibbud av*.

There is nothing wrong with confiding in your mother, telling her that your father's behavior bothers you. Whether she can do anything about it is questionable.

Kibbud av is required even when a father has some character defects. You must follow the halachos regarding proper behavior toward your father. However, while halachah regulates behavior, it does not govern feelings.

Nevertheless, it is possible for you to improve your feelings toward your father. *Mesillas Yesharim* and other *mussar* authorities state that our actions can affect our feelings. By following the halachos of how you should relate to your father with respect, you may develop feelings of respect.

Your father may have a change in attitude, but this is not something that you can bring about. You are fortunate in having a good relationship with your mother, who can be the one most involved in *shidduchim* and who has a positive attitude.

INFORMING FUTURE PROSPECT OF MENTAL CONDITION

I am writing in response to your answer to the girl who wrote to you regarding her suffering from OCD (Obsessive Compulsive Disorder). Of course, I'm not an expert, but I find your response somewhat puzzling. This young woman is seemingly doing well and her symptoms obviously don't interfere with her day-to-day functioning. Why would she need to inform her future prospect, who might very likely be scared off, as many people are totally unaware of what OCD is and they might be afraid that she's mentally unstable? Granted it is a mental condition, but so are phobias, anxiety, etc. and I don't believe these are very uncommon conditions.

I personally suffer from a form of agoraphobia but it does not interfere with my ability to travel — even short distances — and I often take medication when necessary. However, I don't believe my husband resents not being told beforehand and he has his "mishugasin" too (like everyone). An acquaintance of mine suffers from her husband's excessive moodiness. Did he need to inform her beforehand? I personally feel that if one's spouse has a bad temper, his/her spouse suffers more than with OCD and no one expects that to

The basis of a healthy marriage is mutual trust, and anything that can jeopardize this trust must be assiduously avoided.

There have been problems wherein one spouse has manifestations of OCD that may not cause dysfunction, but the rituals and other symptoms may be very annoying. If this condition develops after marriage, it can be managed just as if a spouse were to develop any medical condition. The healthy marriage relationship obviously can withstand many stresses. However, if it is discovered that this condition existed before marriage and was not disclosed, a spouse may feel that he/she was deceived by the withholding of information, and this may cause a breach in trust.

Assuming that the symptoms of OCD are not disruptive, there is no need to say "I have OCD," or "I have a phobia," because, as you say, people might misinterpret these terms. However, one may say, "I just want you to know that I have the habit of rechecking things a number of times," or whatever else the behavior might be. Or the person may say, "I just want you to know that I have a fear of enclosed spaces, like an elevator." If the two are sufficiently fond of each other to consider marriage, they may not end the relationship.

If, however, after marriage the husband wants to visit a favorite uncle and aunt who live on the 15th floor of an apartment building, and the wife says, "I'm sorry. I can't take the elevator, and 15 floors are too much to walk," the husband may say, "How long has this been going on?" The wife may say, "Since I was 10," and the husband says, "You mean for the rest of our lives we can never go higher than the 4th floor?" This may not result in a break-up of the marriage, but he may be very angry that she did not tell him about something that could restrict their freedom of movement.

If any behavior that one has is really not significant, there should be no problem in disclosing it. If, on the other hand, it may in any way restrict their freedom or cause any kind of stress, it should be disclosed. Discovery of such things after marriage may be handled differently by different people. Some may take it in stride, and others may feel deceived. There is no way to predict how one will react, and the risk of undermining mutual trust is too great a risk to take.

Yes, if a person knows that he has a bad temper, he should say, "I want you to know that I have a short fuse, (or that I may lose my cool, or that I may fly off the handle when provoked)." It's one thing if a partner knew about this and accepted it. It's another thing if he/she is shocked by an unexpected outburst of anger.

We are living in a time where the number of marriages that fail is unprecedented, with serious consequence to both spouses and to the children. Every effort should be made to avoid any misunderstandings.

CONCEALING INFORMATION IN A *SHIDDUCH*

My daughter was married four months ago, and is now on the verge of divorce. Her husband has a serious nervous condition that she cannot cope with. This was kept secret from her before their engagement or marriage.

He claims his parents asked a rav or a rebbe and were told that they did not have to disclose this. I think that is criminal. They have traumatized my child, and they did not do their son any good by leading him into a marriage that was likely to fail

I feel sorry for this young man. Except for this nervous condition, he has a pleasant personality. He is now going to be a divorcé, and how much good will that do him?

I appeal to parents. I truly feel for you if your child has a problem, but if you are not up-front with this, you will be causing your own child harm and inflicting harm on

*another person. Do not do to others what has
been done to me and my child.*

———————————————————————————————

This issue has come up several times. As far as what the rav
or *rebbe* said, we have no idea what he was told. He gave his
advice on the information that was given to him.

I have pointed out that the Chofetz Chaim says that conditions
that the other party would consider as serious impediments to a relationship must be revealed, not only by the parents but also by anyone
who has valid knowledge of the problem.

My heart goes out to parents who feel that if they would disclose
a condition that their child has, he/she would never be able to find
a *shidduch*. I can understand that this deep concern for their child
influences them not to disclose it. However, as in your case, it is ultimately not to their own child's advantage, and they also cause hardship to the other partner.

What is a young man or young woman to do about a *shidduch*
if he/she has or has had a medical or emotional condition? Many
conditions have no long-term effects and will not impact on the
individual's ability to live a long, healthy, and fruitful life. In addition, many, if not most, medical conditions are not passed on to
future generations.

It is imperative that all relevant information be shared. The interested party may opt not to pursue the *shidduch* based on this information. If this is the case, you must understand that the outcome of
whatever we do is in Hashem's hand. Our job is to do that which is
right and *ehrlich*.

Should the condition indeed prove to have a lasting impact, there
are *shadchanim* who specialize in these types of *shidduchim*, and have
made many successful marriages. Keeping such conditions secret does
not result in a successful marriage. The basis of a good marriage is
trust, and if there is no trust because important information has been
withheld, the marriage is off to a very shaky start.

SON ON MEDICATION

When our son was 17, he had an episode which resulted in his being diagnosed as bipolar. He was put on medication, and B"H is functioning normally. The doctor said that he must stay on this medication indefinitely in order to prevent recurrences.

Several months ago, my son stopped the medication, not out of refusal, but he "just forgot," and because he saw no difference in the way he felt, so he discontinued taking it. He would take it if we told him he must.

He is soon going to be in the shidduchim parasha, and I'm concerned that if he is on medication and discloses it, it will spoil his chance of a shidduch. What do you recommend?

I am fully aware of the overwhelming importance of *shidduchim*. However, to make a decision about a psychiatric medication based on what effect it may have on a *shidduch* is really no different than making medication for diabetes contingent on the effect it may have on a *shidduch*.

Secondly, if there is a likelihood of recurrence of a psychiatric problem, this would have to be disclosed prior to finalizing a *shidduch*. If there was an isolated incident which would not recur, one may or may not reveal it, because it would probably not affect the *shidduch* at all. But if there is reason to expect a recurrence, such information cannot be withheld.

What you should do is get a second opinion from another psychiatrist. If he, too, says that there is a possibility of recurrence, then your son should continue the medication to prevent it. A recurrence of the problem any time after the marriage can be very serious.

DIVORCED BECAUSE HUSBAND CONCEALED PSYCHIATRIC CONDITION

I hope you will print this to save other young men and women from my fate.

After I was married for two weeks, I discovered that my husband was taking medication. He told me that he had been diagnosed as bi-polar and that he may have to take medication for the rest of his life.

I was shocked. I insisted on meeting with his psychiatrist, who told me that although the medications are effective, it is possible that he can have recurrences even while on medication.

I was furious. My husband said that his parents told him not to reveal it, because he might never get married if he does. If a husband or wife develops a bi-polar disorder after their marriage, of course the spouse should stay with him/her. The problem here is that the fact that he kept such important information from me indicates that my feelings mean nothing to him. I'm just an object that he acquired. I cannot live with someone who feels that way about me.

We went to a rav who agreed that I should get a get. My husband did not object, and we are divorced. But my life has been ruined, I am a divorceé, and like it or not, this is a stigma. No one had the right to do that to me.

I want you to put this in bold capital letters. **NEVER WITHHOLD IMPORTANT INFORMATION IN A SHIDDUCH. THIS IS A CRUEL BETRAYAL. RABBONIM SHOULD COME OUT FORCEFULLY THAT IT IS FORBIDDEN TO MISLEAD ANYONE.**

This is an issue we have discussed previously in this column. Parents who tell their child not to reveal information about himself/herself should ask themselves how they would feel if it was the other way around, and that their child's spouse had withheld important information.

I agree that it would be proper for *rabbonim* to come out with a sharp condemnation of withholding information. However, even if they did so, many people would not obey. Parents are deeply invested in their child making a good *shidduch*. Regardless of what *rabbonim* may tell them, they are influenced by their emotions, their strong desire to have their children make a good *shidduch*, and, if emotions conflict with intellect, emotions usually triumph.

The Torah forbids a judge to take a bribe because "a bribe will blind the eyes of the wise and distort the words of the righteous." Regardless of how wise or righteous a person may be, a personal interest is a "bribe" and can totally distort one's judgment.

The Torah forbids selling a piece of merchandise that has a defect without alerting the customer. How much more so if a person has a problem that can affect another person's entire life and withholds that information!

Some parents have said that they consulted a *rav* who said that they do not have to disclose this. I don't know what it is that they told the *rav*. If it is a condition that is over and done with and there is no reason to expect recurrence, there is no need to reveal it (although revealing this kind of thing is not likely to affect a *shidduch*). But if there is a possibility of recurrence, it should be revealed and the other side should decide what they wish to do.

I suggested to a respected *gadol* that he come out with a declaration to all *rabbanim* that they should not advise concealing any physical or emotional condition unless they know all the facts and are certain that the condition will not cause a problem in the marriage. He said there was no need for such a declaration, because no *rav* would ever give such advice without knowing all the facts.

The parents of the young man in the case above certainly thought they were acting in his interest. However, he is now divorced and that may make it more difficult for him to make another *shidduch*.

I feel the anguish of parents who must reveal that their child has a problem. I wish there was someway of avoiding this pain. However, there is no choice. For everyone's sake, there must be truthful disclosure of problems.

SELF-ESTEEM

SHOULD I GET IN TOUCH WITH MY "INNER CHILD"?

First, I would like to thank you for your wonderful books and for this helpful column. You should continue to have the Siyattah Dishmaya to help change lives for the good.

I am a single girl. After going out with several boys, I realized that something was amiss … in me. I stopped dating and started seeing a frum psychiatrist. It wasn't easy, but because I took myself out of the "shidduch scene," it was easier for me to concentrate on healing myself from my emotional setbacks. The psychiatrist explained to me that since my parents weren't able to express their love for me (my mother suffered from depression), at a very young age, I picked that up and began to feel unloved. He introduced me to the concept of "The Inner Child," in which I have to work to make the hurting two-year-old in me feel loved.

I never felt a true feeling of "belonging," even in my own home. I would often stop myself from saying things, for no good reason. I'm fine standing up in front of a crowd and giving a speech, but when it comes to talking with people one-on-one (including friends), I feel extremely uncomfortable and my mind works overtime thinking of the right things to say. I'm overly conscious of what others think of me. I can't express myself well and I'm constantly telling myself that I'm not welcome. I can't stick to tasks that I set for myself to do. I don't work well with others and find it hard to concentrate on things.

Of course, for the outside world (besides at home), I put on a confident mask. I hide any feelings of inferiority or low self-esteem. As you can imagine, it is not a good feeling to hide my emotions and not be me. Girls have told me that I appear to be aloof and unapproachable. Great — exactly what I don't want to be!

I feel most uncomfortable talking to my parents. It sounds pretty crazy, but I wish I could just talk to them normally, and have a normal (and even close) relationship with them, but … I can't! And now that I know that they are the "cause" of what I'm going through, I feel like getting back at them. I know I sound like an angry teenager, but that's exactly what I feel like these days. Angry, empty, sad.

I must mention that my parents are the best parents anyone can ever ask for. They love me — I know they love me. They do more for me than any of my friends' parents do for them.

Some of my good friends are already engaged. It not that I'm in a rush to get married. In fact, now I realize how serious marriage is and what a long way I have before I can be "ready" to have such a deep relationship. But I keep thinking, "What if a year passes, and I'm still going to therapy, and I'm still in the 'freezer' and ... nothing's changed! I'm still dealing with the same problems that I had when I started out!"

Rabbi Twerski, I'm turning to you. Do you know about the "Inner Child" therapy? Am I just wasting my time having my dreams interpreted and talking about my inner child? I'm so frustrated with my life — I wish I could go live in a hotel, or fly off to Israel for a long time. I'm jealous of people who know how to make their lives worthwhile and not eat cake till 1 a.m.

I want to commend you on your insight and on taking steps to maximize yourself before marriage.

Although I was trained psychoanalytically, I do not feel that dream interpretation and excessive groping into childhood experiences are the solution. It seems that you are aware of having a self-esteem problem, which puts you way ahead, because most people do not realize this.

Low self-esteem means that a person is actually far better than he/she feels about him/herself. The feelings of inferiority are unjustified, yet they haunt a person.

I have written about self-esteem. My books, *Life's Too Short* and *Angels Don't Leave Footprints,* describe the condition. In *Ten Steps to Being Your Best,* I suggest exercises to elevate one's self-esteem.

Although books can be helpful, they may not be enough. A therapist skilled in self-esteem problems can be very effective, particularly if one uses group therapy. Therapists from the cognitive school are usually good at this. See the Appendix for a list of organizations that can steer you to a therapist in your area.

CARING FOR CHILDREN ENHANCES THEIR SELF-ESTEEM

You write a lot about the importance of self-esteem. This week I spent some time with two friends. One said she'd really love to go to work, but cannot because she has no one to look after her children. The other said that she had to turn down an invitation for a cruise because she has no one to look after her children. Now I ask you, how can children develop self-esteem if they feel they are standing in the way of their parents' wishes?

With all due respect, I don't see how you could possibly be more wrong.

If a person spends $30,000 for a fine car, are we to say that he resents the car because it cost $30,000, or rather, the fact that he spent $30,000 indicates how much he wants and values that car?

Parents love their children, and from infancy on, perhaps beginning with being awakened several times a night, continue to sacrifice their own comfort in many ways, in the interest of the children's welfare. Children are aware of this, and it *enhances* their self-esteem to know that their parents love them and value them and are willing to make sacrifices for them.

Sometimes a parent may say, "Look at what I've done for you and yet ..." That is unwise, because it is trying to control a child by making him feel guilty. There are much better ways to discipline children.

Parents know that by having children they will be curtailing their own freedom and assuming obligations. That they do so gladly and willingly shows how much they value their children.

Clearly, parents who are abusive or neglectful and put their own selfish interests ahead of their children may affect a child's self-esteem, because their actions indicates how relatively little the child means to them. But good parenting, which involves setting aside one's own comfort for the child, is a plus for the child's self-esteem.

HOUSEWIFE WITH LOW SELF-ESTEEM

I read your column with great interest every week and it has given me a greater understanding about people. I hope you can help me on this.

I have a friend I think very highly of and with whom I have a very open and honest relationship. However, she sometimes complains that she is not up to standard in certain areas, e.g., her house is messy, her children look neglected (though they are not — I think people can learn from her what it means to give children quality attention), etc. When I point out that it is not as bad as she is making it, she agrees with me but only for that moment. She admits she has a complex. How can I help her raise her self-esteem, because she really is a wonderful person and she has helped many people?

I have written quite extensively about self-esteem problems. In my books I point out that people who are gifted may, paradoxically, have very low self-esteem.

A person's self-concept is a perspective; i.e., that is the way one sees oneself. This perspective can be distorted, just like physical vision can be distorted. If a person's vision was affected so that he sees everything as green, you could not convince him that snow is white, because he sees it as green. That is why your assuring her about how good she really is has no long-term effect. She "sees" it otherwise.

Low self-esteem can be overcome. I address this problem in *Angels Don't Leave Footprints,* and I suggest self-help exercises to overcome low self-esteem in *Ten Steps to Being Your Best.* Some people who have diligently followed the instructions in the latter book have reported that it has elevated their self-esteem.

Inasmuch as your friend "admits that she has a complex," she has an advantage because she knows that her self-perception is distorted. However, this knowledge alone does not relieve the situation, anymore than knowing that one has a headache relieves the pain. One must do something about it. If the self-help approach is insufficient, she should see a therapist who is competent in dealing with self-esteem problems.

I'M NOT POPULAR

Can I be helped or should I just try to accept myself the way Hashem made me?

I'm a young married women and feel very unpopular and unliked. The reason, I think, is that I lack communication skills, haven't got interesting topics to speak about, and can't express myself well. Also, I'm not friendly by nature, although I'd love to be. When I actually speak with somebody I feel they are talking to me as a favor.

I have read your books, especially Ten Steps to Being Your Best, which I found very useful — but I still suffer very much because I can't socialize like other people. Besides davening to Hashem, is there anything else I can do? If so, what and where?

The feelings you describe are classic symptoms of unwarranted low self-esteem. The person is convinced that all the negative feelings about oneself are absolutely true. I described this in a number of books, especially *Life's Too Short*. I have also pointed out the paradox that people who are highly gifted may have the most profound feelings of inferiority and inadequacy. I have come across many bright people who think that they have nothing to offer in a conversation, whereas what they have to say may be much more valuable than what others say.

While books may help, they may not be the entire solution.. Suppose that unbeknown to you, someone put green contact lenses on your eyes. You would see everything as green, including snow and eggs, and no one could tell you that these are not green, because you know what you see, and they are green. It is necessary to have the green lenses removed so that you can see reality correctly.

That's how it is with the self-image. If a person *sees* him/herself as being unattractive, dull, and inferior, no amount of argument will change his mind. A person looks at him/herself through "psychological lenses" that distort his self-perception. It is necessary to correct the misperception. This can be done with the help of a psychotherapist, either in individual therapy, or better yet, in group therapy.

You may call ECHO (845) 425-9750 or RELIEF (718) 431-9501 for referral to a therapist (see Appendix).

LOW SELF-ESTEEM LEADS TO DEPRESSION

I have a friend who seems to be depressed. She is unhappy, lonely, and disinterested in life in general. She is of marriageable age, but has no desire to get married (she still dates and seeks her bashert, but does not display the normal interest shown by other girls her age). She also has issues with her self-esteem. My question is this: What can I do for her as a friend? I know she will never consent to see a therapist or anything of the sort. Also, I cannot really fix her loneliness because the fact is that she does not have many friends. She does have a loving family, but sometimes that's not enough. Please help.

M uch of what I have written focuses on problems of low self-esteem, which, as I have defined, refers to feelings of unworthiness, inadequacy, and inferiority *that are unwarranted by fact.* Indeed, sometimes people who are most gifted have the most intense feelings of inferiority. Why do so many people have such feelings and why are they worse in gifted people?

In *Angels Don't Leave Footprints,* I cite the Talmudic statement, "The *yetzer hara* grows stronger every day and tries to destroy the person" (*Kedushin,* 30b). I postulate that the way the *yetzer hara* tries to destroy a person is by giving him such unwarranted feelings of inferiority. A person who has these feeling may be, as you describe, "unhappy, lonely, and disinterested in life." It is typical that one has difficulty in making relationships when one feels, "Why would any-one want me?" Because the *yetzer hara* in a gifted person is particu-larly powerful (*Sukkah* 52a), that person may have more profound feelings of inferiority.

As a friend, you may say to her, "I see that you're suffering need-lessly. You are a far, far better person than you give yourself credit for." She is not likely to accept this, because she is convinced that her self-perception is accurate.

I don't mean to come across as commercializing, but I address these problems in a number of my books. *Life's Too Short* and *Angels*

Don't Leave Footprints describe these problems. Even though your friend may not consider seeing a therapist, she may agree to read these books. If she does recognize that this is her problem, she may get some help by reading *Ten Steps to Being Your Best*. She may then be willing, if necessary, to consult someone for counseling (see Appendix for a partial listing of referral agencies).

LOW SELF-ESTEEM

I am 16 years old. I am learning in yeshivah. I learn very well. I have a problem and I would like your advice. I don't have any self-esteem and I always watch what I do so nobody will say anything bad about me. A lot of times I do things that are not comfortable for me so that no one will say anything bad about me. I always fear that some one may be speaking about me. Some times they do speak about me but I fear that they must be talking negatively. I get upset even though sometimes it's only my imagination. My self-esteem and confidence are so low that some times I am afraid that I can't solve things, because I am afraid I'll make a mistake. I am also very embarrassed to solve things. So please give me advice right away and please give me the names of books about this problem that would be good for me to read.

Your problem strikes a familiar chord. The theme of low self-esteem is constant in my books, and as I indicated there, I suffered from low self-esteem until age 38, although I had no idea that this was my problem. Inasmuch as you are 16, you are fortunate in recognizing the problem 22 years earlier than I did.

To respond in detail here would be to rewrite a book. Suffice it to say that many people have severely distorted perceptions of themselves. They are pleasant, bright, and gifted people who are unaware of their personality strengths. Seeing themselves negatively causes them to be extremely sensitive to the opinion of others. Not having a positive self-image, they are dependent on what others think of them. Low self-esteem may cause a variety of behaviors. It is interesting that Rabennu Yonah says that *ga'avah* is actually a desperate attempt by a person to escape his feelings of low-self esteem (*Rabennu Yonah al haTorah*, p.156).

No one likes failure, but for a person with low self-esteem, failure may be devastating. Some people avoid trying anything, because if one doesn't try, one can't fail. But not trying is the worst failure of all.

It is paradoxical that people who are most gifted may have very severe feelings of inadequacy and inferiority. I address these issues in detail in *Angels Don't Leave Footprints*, and in *Ten Steps to Being Your Best* I suggest a self-help approach to elevating one's self esteem. If this does not do enough for you, you should consult a therapist to help you develop true self-awareness.

EMDR FOR ANXIETY

I am dealing with issues of childhood abandonment and low self-esteem. I am currently working with a therapist who is helping me come in touch with my memories and feelings so that I can understand what went on. Unfortunately, my lack of trust is getting in the way, and doesn't allow me to stay with the intense emotions for more than fifteen seconds. Soon after, I find myself not even remotely close to the emotions any longer. I am not sure that this trust issue will be different with anyone else. Someone suggested EMDR; what do you think of it? I

*feel that I am wasting my life at age 28,
not being able to create a marriage or hold
a productive good job.*

———————————————

Issues of abandonment are particularly stubborn, and these feelings may recur even long after they seem to have disappeared. Sometimes these feelings may get in the way of marriage, because of the fear, "What happens if he/she will abandon me?" Some people will avoid making a relationship because of the risk that the relationship may end.

Working with a therapist is the best way to overcome these feelings and fears. The fear of trusting someone may be similar to the fear of abandonment, i.e., "What happens if I trust someone and he/she lets me down?" However, if you feel that your therapist is trustworthy, there is no way other than to force yourself to maintain trust in him/her.

It is only natural to want to avoid distressing emotions. But if one avoids consulting a dentist because of the fear of painful treatment, the loss of teeth is far worse You have to stay with the emotions even though they may be painful.

EMDR is rather specific for severe anxiety, especially for post-traumatic symptoms. The trauma may be a severe, shocking incident, or something relatively "minor," such as being disparaged by a parent, humiliated by a teacher, or teased by peers. These are "minor" compared to a life-threatening accident or attack, but can be very "major" to a person. Here is a very brief description of the process.

EMDR stands for Eye Movement Desensitization and Reprocessing. It is a psychological treatment employing external stimuli, whether eye movement, auditory stimuli, or tapping. To put it briefly, the client is asked to identify the most vivid image related to a negative belief about him/herself and also, that of a positive belief.

The client is then asked to focus on the negative thought or image, and on the sensations one feels. The therapist then has the client move the eyes back and forth for 20-30 seconds, listen to an auditory stimulus, or tap with the fingers or foot. This is repeated until the negative image or memory no longer causes emotional distress.

The client is then asked to focus on the positive belief, again with eye movements.

The theory is something like this: If one is a victim of an attack or trauma, even though the person may logically know that one is a victim, there may be strong negative associations in the mind that interfere with logical processing of the information. The person has an illogical feeling of being at fault or guilty. It has been found that eye movements while recalling a negative incident allow the mind to *reprocess* the incident, which allows one to rid oneself of the guilt or the feeling of fault.

While this may not sound too logical, the fact is that the system works. The Veterans Administration uses this method for soldiers who have experienced war trauma.

I have written extensively about self-esteem. You might look at *Life's Too Short* and *Ten Steps to Being Your Best*. People have reported improvement in their self-esteem by diligently following the recommended exercises.

YOUNG WOMAN DOES NOT FEEL ACCEPTED

You're the first person I'm revealing this to. After much indescribable suffering, I'm sure there are plenty of others who feel the same way as I do.

I'm an 18-year-old girl going to seminary, im yirtzeh Hashem, this year. I don't have any "true" friends. I'm a very normal, cute, friendly, outgoing, sweet girl. But somehow my classmates don't think that I'm someone whom they can have fun with, the one to be excited to tell news to, or the "popular" one. Why can't I be accepted this way? What's wrong with me, with who I am? I wish they could've told me before. This is what I keep on asking myself. It's ruining my self-esteem, day by day! This is causing me to be depressed, so that I have become a very moody and stubborn person.

When something really troubles someone, it's hard for him, and he tries to escape from it by doing bad things that he thinks will give him satisfaction. This is the biggest risk I am getting myself into. Since I feel I'm not accepted by my classmates the way I want to be, I have a strong will to find others who will like me and who will accept me. And you know, I really do understand myself.

Although you describe yourself in positive terms, it may be that at a deeper level you do not think so well of yourself. Please listen.

My first book, almost 30 years ago, was entitled *Like Yourself, and Others Will, Too.* This was based on the verse in *Bamidbar* (13:33), in which the spies returning from Canaan reported that it was inhabited by giants. "There we saw the *Nephilim*, the sons of the giant from among the *Nephilim*; **we were like grasshoppers in our eyes, and so we were in their eyes**!" One of the Torah commentaries says, "The way you feel about yourself is the way you think that others see you."

This comment was an awakening for me. The Torah is telling us that if we do not have good feelings about ourselves, we will think that others feel negatively about us. You see, I was very much like you as a youngster. Even though I had loving parents and was an excellent student, I had the idea that people would not like me. Looking back, I can recall how I used to walk around the playground alone during recess, afraid to ask the other kids if I could join because I was sure they would reject me. I was unaware that my self-image was incorrect.

Subsequently, I have written many books, but they are all on the same theme: building self-esteem. We may be totally unaware that we may be doing things that distance us from other people. Sometimes we become "people pleasers," trying to do things for others to gain their friendship and affection. If we try doing things only to be liked, that indicates that we don't think of ourselves as likeable.

At the risk of sounding commercial, I suggest you read *Angels Don't Leave Footprints* and *Ten Steps to Being Your Best*. When you become aware, at a deeper level, that you are really a wonderful, likeable person, you will have many friends. A true self-awareness will be a very happy discovery.

Beginning seminary will give you new surroundings and new acquaintances. I believe that as you improve your self-esteem, your problem will be solved.

EMOTIONAL DISORDERS

ABUSE BREEDS ABUSE

My nephew was an abused child. My brother-in-law, alav hashalom, was simply cruel to the child, and the boy sometimes sought refuge in my home, crying. He often said, "When I grow up and have children, I'll be so good to them that I'll spoil them rotten."

Well, my nephew is now married, and I recently spent Shabbos at his home. I was both shocked and horrified to see him mistreating his son exactly the way his father did to him. I said, "Don't you remember how you promised that you would never mistreat your children? Why are you abusive to your son?" He looked at me, totally bewildered. "I'm abusive?" he said. "How can you say that?"

I feel sorry for the child just as I did for my nephew. What can I do to make my nephew realize what he is doing?

You are dealing with a psychological mechanism that is difficult to overcome.

Let me point out something about the uncanny efficiency of the human mind. You are asleep, and in your dream there is a scene in which a bell is ringing. Perhaps it is the doorbell or the telephone. As the ringing continues, you awaken because it is the alarm clock that is ringing. The ringing in the dream was something concocted by your mind to allow you to continue sleeping. Your mind disguised the alarm-clock ring as part of the dream.

But consider this. Your mind's manufacturing of the scene in the dream had to occur within one-thousandth of a second of the first ring of the alarm clock! Within a split second, your mind was able to produce a scene in which the ringing of a bell would be natural so that you should not be aroused by the ring of the alarm clock. That's how your subconscious mind tries to protect your comfort.

There is a psychological defense mechanism that the mind employs to protect one's comfort, and that is "identification with the aggressor." When you are victimized and feel helpless and powerless, your mind may try to relieve this distressful feeling by making you feel that you are an aggressor rather than a victim. You may then take on some of the qualities of the aggressor. That is why a child who suffered abuse from a cruel parent is likely to become an abuser himself. He may swear to himself, "When I grow up and have children, I'll never be abusive to them." Yet, surprisingly, he may turn out to be an abusive parent. This is because his resolve not to be abusive is a product of his conscious mind, whereas the need to identify with the aggressor is a product of the subconscious mind. (The *sifrei mussar* refer to this as "*tatt hakarah.*")

When the conscious and subconscious conflict, the subconscious often triumphs. The abused child becomes an abuser, but the subconscious mind prevents him from recognizing this. That is why most abusers do not recognize that they are abusive, and refuse to admit this when it is pointed out to them.

You may sit down with your nephew and say to him, "I know it may be painful, but it is important that we do this." Then remind him in great detail of some of the scenes you witnessed when he was a child. He may remember them. Then you say, "Now, I know this may be difficult for you, but I want to go over with you some of the things I saw on Shabbos when I was with you, in regard to how you acted with your son." As gently as possible, and with as much empathy as you can gather, go over the scene with him. Remember, it will be very painful to him to accept that he is abusive, because he hates this thought. If he can see the similarities between his and his father's behavior, you can say, "It is very common that people who were abused as children repeat that behavior without being aware of it. You are a good and kind person, and I know you don't want to be like that. It is difficult to change your behavior by yourself, because you are unaware of it, but counseling can help you to be what you really want to be." Encourage him to see a psychologist. That's about all you can do.

At a later date, you might ask him whether he has consulted someone, but don't nag him about it because that is likely to make him more resistive.

POSTPARTUM DEPRESSION

I gave birth to my first baby B"H three months ago. I often feel depressed even though there's nothing that should be bothering me. Some days I feel like crying all day but I cover up when I'm around people.

I'm also more sensitive and less confident than I was and I feel that this is affecting my shalom bayis. I would appreciate some advice on how to raise my spirits when I'm feeling down and how to develop more meaningful and deeper relationships.

Can you please also suggest one of your books that would address my problem?

You are describing a condition — post-partum depression — that frequently occurs anywhere from several weeks to several months after having a baby. "Baby blues" that last more than a few weeks can become depression that should be treated with medication and therapy. It is very good that you are inquiring about this now so that you can get prompt relief.

The human body is a very delicate system, with very complex hormone functions, which may be easily upset. Perhaps you remember the tale about a princess who slept on a pile of mattresses, and was able to feel the discomfort caused by a pea that had been placed under the bottom mattress. That's how sensitive the human mechanism is.

When you were carrying the baby, your body produced a number of hormones, and when the baby was born, there was a sudden cessation of these hormones. This gives the body quite a jolt, and this may upset the body chemistry. This chemical change may result in emotional symptoms such as those you describe.

We can easily understand that chemical changes may cause fever, joint pains, or changes in the sugar metabolism. No one looks for psychological "reasons" why these occur. When we experience emotional changes, such as depression, lack of feelings, crying, and exhaustion, we tend to look for psychological causes, and we may implicate things that have nothing to do with the symptoms.

Don't look for reasons "why" you feel that way. It is purely a chemical imbalance that can be corrected. Contact your doctor promptly for the proper medication. A number of antidepressant medications are available that can relieve your distress.

Most of these medications take from 7-16 days to take effect. It is also important that they be taken in adequate doses. Sometimes the first antidepressant prescribed may not work and another antidepressant must be tried, but there *is* a medication that can restore the chemical balance and you will feel well. Do not discontinue the medication until your doctor instructs you to do so.

Understandably, it is also important that you get adequate rest. If you can have help in caring for the baby for a few weeks until you feel better, that would be very good. Some doctors also suggest taking vitamin B-complex and vitamin C, which may increase the effectiveness of the medication. I describe this condition in *Getting Up When You're Down*. Do not delay. There is no reason to suffer unnecessarily.

ANOREXIA / BULIMIA

I do some counseling at a frum girls' high-school. A 16-year-old girl, whose grades were dropping, confided in me that she has the eating disorder anorexia-bulimia and that it has taken over her life. She cannot think of anything other than binging and purging. This is why her grades have fallen — she cannot concentrate properly on her school work.
Her parents are unaware of it. She made me promise not to tell her parents, because she is afraid of their reaction. How can I get her help without her parents' knowledge?

Legally, a 16-year-old person has the right to confidentiality, and you cannot tell her parents without her permission.

It would, of course, be much better if she could share this with her parents. I am sure that she is living in the fear of "What happens if they find out?" and this tension aggravates her problem. With proper counseling, her parents can be supportive. Furthermore, the reality is that if she sees a therapist, she will most likely have to pay for this and her parents will have to know. For her to continue without therapy is very foolish. Not only will her schoolwork suffer, but it will also affect other areas of functioning.

She does have a right to privacy, and she may consult one of the Bikur Cholim services that can provide therapy without a fee, or she may find a *frum* support group. She will then have the added worry of keeping her parents from knowing that she is going for therapy or to meetings.

She may be thinking that she is the only person with this problem. She may not know that it is very common, and that some of her peers have this condition and are covering it up just as she is doing. Eating disorders can be life-threatening and this girl surely needs help to overcome it. Anorexia and bulimia can cause serious health problems and cannot be ignored.

As a counselor at a girls' high-school, you are certain to encounter this problem. If you attend a *frum* eating-disorder support group, you may find young women who are coping with this problem, and who are willing to share their experiences with someone who is looking for help.

Your student's fears about her parents' reaction may be unfounded. You may tell this young woman that if she permits you tell her parents, you will meet with them and help them understand this problem.

Many young people today have a variety of problems. Parents should tell their children that if they have any kind of a problem, to share it with them, and that they will be supportive and do whatever is necessary to overcome the problem.

WORRY WART

I guess you can call me a "worry wart." I've been like this ever since I can remember, but it is taking a toll on my life. When the phone rings, I fear that it is going to be terrible news. It might turn out to be very good news, like a mazal-tov in the family. When I see any kind of official letter in the mail, or if G-d forbid, I get a notice about a certified letter, I panic. One Shabbos night I found a notice from the post office informing me that there was a certified letter, and I was "meschuge" until the post office opened Monday morning. You can be sure I was at the door the moment *it opened. I feared it was a notice of an income-tax audit or some similar calamity. It turned out to be my renewed passport. How can I get rid of this torment?*

The reasons that people have morbid expectations is not clear. Some people may harbor unwarranted guilt feelings and expect that G-d will punish them. Others may have an attitude that if they expect the worst, they will be pleasantly surprised when it doesn't happen. In others, it may be a symptom of OCD (Obsessive-Compulsive Disorder).

In case of OCD, a person should consult a therapist for help. In absence of OCD, building up one's self-esteem is useful, and one should get help in ridding oneself of unwarranted feelings of guilt.

In the event a person has realistic grounds for guilt, one should do whatever is necessary to do proper *teshuvah*, after which one should be confident that Hashem has erased one's sin. Consultation and guidance by *daas Torah* is extremely important.

The Scriptures give us an example of excessive and inappropriate worry in the person of Iyov, who would bring offerings for forgiveness "just in case his children might have blasphemed Hashem." Blasphemy is a rare occurrence and totally illogical in people who were obviously enjoying life as Iyov's children were. Why would anyone expect so absurd a happening? Although Hashem's forgiveness is abundant, there can be no forgiveness for a non-existent sin. *Daas Torah* can clarify whether one's guilt feelings are justified. If they are not, one should consult a therapist for help.

It is important to strengthen one's *bitachon* (trust in Hashem). There are many essays in the works of *mussar* on the development of *bitachon*.

It is helpful to recite Chapter 112 of *Tehillim* every day, and when reading the verse, "He does not fear evil tidings. His heart is secure in trust in Hashem," to pray that Hashem gives one the strength of *bitachon* so that one will be free of morbid expectations.

CHUMRAH OR OCD

*I am one of the oldest of a large family,
k"ah, and most of the Pesach preparations
fall on me. By nature I enjoy working
and cleaning the house but because of how
nervous I get, I feel that I will add more
stress to the house by pitching in — but I
know my help is desperately needed. I have
spoken in the past to someone knowledgeable
in the area of OCD [Obsessive Compulsive
Disorder] because my nervousness occurs in
other areas, such as kashrus or washing
netilas yadayim (which could take a good
three minutes). She feels that it comes from
a lack of knowledge in halachah — knowing
what's required and what's not — but I am
not sure if that is the cause.*

*I really can use some advice on what to
do next. Thank you.*

As I have pointed out in the *Hashkafah* section, even extreme precautions on Pesach are not necessarily OCD. There are some very strict *chumros* that are practiced by different people. Of course, one woman who would not allow bread in her home all year round cannot be considered to be legitimately *machmir*.

There are clear halachos regarding *netilas yadaim* and kashrus, and an authoritative *rav* can clarify them for you. If, in spite of knowing that you have completely fulfilled the halachah, you are still bothered by unreasonable doubts, that may be a symptom of OCD. This should be evaluated by a Torah-observant therapist, and if it is OCD, you should have it treated. The doubting in OCD can be a torment and can drain one's energies.

I know of a woman who threw out three sets of dishes, unable to accept the reassurance of a *posek* that there was no *sh'eilah* whatsoever about kashrus. So, if the problem is lack of knowledge of halachah, that can be remedied by a *rav*. Inability to be at peace with the ruling of a *posek* does suggest OCD.

PROCRASTINATION POSES PROBLEMS

I've been a procrastinator all my life, but I was always able to get away with it, although I knew it was wrong. I suffered some losses here and there — nothing really big — so I never did anything about it. Actually, I knew I should get help with it, but I've put that off, too.

But now my wife is getting fed up with me. She says that she can't put up with it, and I don't like what that implies. So my question to you is, what can I do to overcome this habit? Do I have to see a psychologist, and if so, who?

Procrastination is very common, and there is a wide spectrum of degrees of procrastination. It is a habit much like drinking or overeating, where classically one says, "I'll start dieting next week." Furthermore, if one does begin dieting, there is frequently backsliding after a few days or weeks.

The Talmud warns us about postponing learning Torah. "Do not say I will study when I will be free, because you may never become free" (*Pirkei Avos*, 2:5). Even when you do become free, you will find other things to do, so that you may never really be free.

It is interesting that *Mesillas Yesharim* cites procrastination as a bad trait, and uses very sharp words: "There is no danger as great as the danger of procrastination." Someone who simply refuses outright to do something he doesn't like even though it may be important is at least not deceiving himself. The procrastinator has a worse problem because he is not refusing to do it outright. Rather, he deceives himself. "Of course I will do it, but not just now. I'll get around to it a bit later."

The procrastinator may come up with many reasons to justify postponing something. "Tomorrow I have a free day, so I can do it then," or "I'm a night person. I do my best work at night, so I'll do it then." At night, he may say, "I'm too tired to concentrate on this now. I'll do it the first thing in the morning."

There are a variety of reasons why a person procrastinates. Sometimes it is because of fear of failure, based on the idea that if you don't do something, you can't fail at it. This person may think he is being judged by what he does, and if he fails at it, he will be criticized. But not doing what he should be doing gives rise to guilt, which makes a person feel worse about himself, increasing the fear of failure. Or, it may be that what he should do is boring, and he'd rather do something more interesting and exciting.

Conversely, a person may procrastinate because of fear of success. Achieving something may add to one's responsibilities. This is illustrated by a story my father used to tell. A *melamed* pointed to an *alef* and asked the child to say what it was. When the child stubbornly refused, the *melamed* first shouted at him, then threatened him, then lost patience and went on to another student. An observer asked the child, "Don't you know what that letter is?" "Sure," the child said, "it's an *alef*." "Then why didn't you say so? Why did you subject yourself to so much punishment?' "Because," the child said, "if I told him it was an *alef*, then he would want to know the *beis* and *gimmel* and so on." Some procrastinators avoid "saying the *alef*" so they should not feel compelled to go on.

There are self-help methods to overcome procrastination (see the Appendix). But remember the words of *Mesillas Yesharim*. There is danger in self-deception, and you may backslide. If you can stick with the determination to really help yourself, and not procrastinate on this, you may be able to overcome other procrastinations.

CHRONIC UNHAPPINESS

I wonder if you have any suggestions for my husband. He is 36, and we have lovely children. We are far from wealthy, but B"H we have parnassah. Neither of us has aspirations for luxury and we do not feel deprived.

My husband is an unhappy man and doesn't know why. He saw a psychologist for one year with no change. He tried several antidepressant medications that did nothing. He saw a second psychologist for six months, who has said that he can't figure out what is wrong and doesn't have any treatment to offer. What do you do in such a case?

It seems that what you are describing is "discontent" rather than depression. The latter probably would have been helped with either medication or therapy.

If a competent psychologist and psychiatrist have said that they have nothing to offer, we must consider that the reason for the discontent is beyond the areas of their profession.

There are two other possibilities to consider. The first is "low self-esteem." I have addressed this in several books. Low self-esteem can occur in highly gifted and even very successful people. It is a nagging feeling of not being good enough, and it can drain a person's enthusiasm and enjoyment of life. There may be many reasons for this distorted self-concept. In *Angels Don't Leave Footprints*, I cite the Talmud that states that a person's *yetzer hara* grows stronger every day and tries to destroy him. One mechanism the *yetzer hara* uses may be to crush a person's self-esteem. In *Ten Steps to Being Your Best*, I suggest ways in which one may get a true self-image and better self-esteem.

I want to preface the second possibility by describing the phenomenon of the growth of lobsters. A lobster is a soft animal that lives within a rigid shell. Inasmuch as the shell does not expand, how does a lobster grow? The answer is that as a lobster grows, its shell becomes very confining and oppressive. It then casts off its shell and produces a larger, more spacious one. Eventually, this shell also becomes too confining, and the lobster repeats this process numerous times.

What is important to realize is that the signal that the lobster must cast off a confining shell so that it may grow is — discomfort. We humans may not recognize that discomfort may be a signal to us that we must grow. (If lobsters could get tranquilizers or pain-killers, they might never grow at all!)

Even though we may be students of Torah and observe mitzvos, we may be at a spiritual plateau, and may not be growing in *ruchniyus*. Just as the body needs nutrients to grow, so does the *neshamah*. Whereas the body stops growing in early adulthood, the *neshamah's* need for growth never stops, and if we do not supply the *neshamah* with growth, we may experience discontent.

Every professional and every artist, regardless of how accomplished, tries to improve him/herself. We may be Torah students and have fine *middos*, but we may not be advancing. A careful study of *mussar sefarim* shows us that for all of us there is great room for growth. Spiritually, one does not remain stagnant. If one is not advancing spiritually, one is regressing, and that can cause discontent.

SHALOM BAYIS PROBLEMS — CAUSE OR EFFECT?

I have had shalom bayis problems off and on, and my wife is insisting that I see a psychiatrist to get medication. She says that I have always been discontented, and that is why I pick on her, and that if I will eliminate my discontent with medication for my nerves, I will be easier to get along with. I don't want to take medication, and we agreed to ask your opinion.

There are several major types of psychiatric medications. 1. Tranquilizers, which may be used briefly for relief of severe tension. These should only be used for a short time, because continued use may result in addiction. 2. Antipsychotics, which are primarily used to control the behavior of a person who has broken with reality. 3. Antidepressant medications, which can be of great help when a person suffers from depression that is due to an imbalance in the body's chemistry. 4. Mood stabilizers, for people who have more extreme than normal mood swings.

Shalom bayis problems that are due to incompatibility or poor communication skills are not going to be helped by medication. For these, one or both spouses should get proper counseling to resolve their differences and learn how to get along more harmoniously. Problems of spousal abuse are similarly not treated with medication, but require changes in one's behavior.

Chronic discontent is usually an attitudinal problem. A person may feel that the world has not been treating him fairly. The discontent may be due to a person not fulfilling himself, especially if a person is not pursuing *ruchniyus* (spirituality). I have coined the term "Spirituality Deficiency Syndrome" to describe the discontent that occurs when a person is not giving the *neshamah* what it needs. Just as deficiencies in vitamins and minerals can cause a person to feel physical discomfort, deficiencies in not giving the *neshamah* its nutrients can cause spiritual discomfort, felt as chronic discontent. This, too, is not helped by medication.

It is, of course, possible for a person to be depressed, with or without good reason. If such a depression is due to a chemical imbalance, it can often be greatly relieved by antidepressant medication. Unfortunately, there is no laboratory test for this imbalance. The only thing one can do if the possibility of a chemical balance is suspected, is to have a doctor prescribe an antidepressant and see if it provides relief. One must wait three or four weeks for a result. Sometimes more than one type of antidepressant must be tried.

You should discuss with your doctor whether there is reason to suspect that you may be depressed due to a chemical imbalance and whether medication will be effective in your case.

OCD AND ITS IMPACT ON LEARNING

I am an avreich who has learned in yeshivos and kollelim for over 12 years. I have had personality problems and intrusive thoughts that have affected me since childhood, but these problems were not recognized by me, my parents, or mechanchim as anything that needed professional help.

Around a year-and-a-half ago, after I had already been in contact with a frum psychologist due to a family problem, I came to realize that it would benefit me to discuss what I believed to be a "small problem" with him. I am very pleased that I did, because he helped me, Bechasdei Hashem, more than I imagined possible, and showed me how obsessive thoughts and anxiety had affected me. Gradually this, together with medication, has relieved my OCD.

This process has also led to what seems to be a reduction in the intensity of my learning of Torah and mussar. Part of the problem is that since childhood I had subconsciously believed myself to be someone destined for greatness. I had used mussar and closeness to an eminent Mashgiach to try to rectify my personality problems, which had largely been caused by this subconscious belief.

I am now trying to be "someich bechelki," and to find a direction, with professional advice and Da'as Torah, in which to continue. However, I find it difficult because, due to the stigma that surrounds psychological problems, I am unable to explain my changed behavior and resultant comparative lack of hasmodah to anyone *but a few close confidants. I have also developed, unfortunately, an aversion to mussar — which my therapist has described as an "allergic reaction" — due to how I used to pin so much hope on it as a way to change myself.*

I feel a need to be able to be more open about my problem, but know that this could be harmful to me and my family. Would establishing a support group for sufferers of such conditions be a good idea? How could this be done in a close-knit yeshivish community without compromising the need for confidentiality?

How can I make the necessary changes while remaining a ben Torah, in learning (possibly becoming a mechanech, according to the advice I have been given), but to be relaxed, without being bitter about the past? How can I use my experiences to benefit others? 1 would be grateful for your advice.

I am pleased to hear that you have been relieved of the agony of intrusive thoughts, but it would seem to me that this should free you so that your *hasmodah* and learning should increase.

I'm sorry that you now find difficulty with *mussar*. I am an avid student of *mussar*, and I have found that many of the *baalei mussar* had profound insights into human psychology and emotions. I believe that the more contemporary works of *mussar*, notably by Harav Dessler and Harav Wolbe, are exceedingly valuable.

Your "allergic reaction" to *mussar* may be due to the fact that you were led to believe that *mussar* would relieve your intrusive thoughts. I have pointed out previously that, whereas *mussar* is helpful in dealing with *machshavos zaros*, the kind of alien thoughts that tend to pop into one's mind (especially during *davening*), the nagging, intrusive thoughts of OCD require medical treatment. The fact that *mussar* does not relieve the repetitious intrusive thoughts of OCD is in no way a reflection on the value of *mussar*. I suggest you try a fresh approach to *mussar* and try to detach it from your disappointing experiences.

It is unfortunate, but the stigma of any kind of psychological problem persists, and as long as it does, you should share this only with close confidants.

I think that a support group for yeshivah students with OCD would be very beneficial. The problem is in organizing such a group. Understandably, people are hesitant to reveal this problem to others, and we would have to find a way to assure confidentiality. Perhaps if one of the *Roshei Yeshivah* or *mashgichim* would be willing to be the person to whom people apply, such a group could be formed. As I mentioned in another response, it might be possible to establish a telephone "hotline" with trainee counselors manning the phones to offer advice and lend emotional support.

Whether or not such a group is formed, you can certainly give *chizuk* to others with OCD and share your recovery with them. You can look back upon your past as a difficult but valuable learning experience. Of course, some way would have to be devised so that others with OCD could reach you.

By all means, continue your growth in Torah.

BORDERLINE PERSONALITY DISORDER IN A PARENT

My father has borderline personality disorder but won't go for help. Is there any way the family can help him? How can we protect ourselves from his onslaughts of anger or periods of deafening silence?

Is the condition hereditary? Should we be on the lookout for it and if we do see evidence of its emergence in the next generation (in ourselves or our children) how can we curb or help it so it doesn't become worse?

I t is difficult to address this problem in the confines of a column. It requires a book!

Borderline Personality Disorder (BPD) is a condition that has baffled many mental-health professionals. There are diverse opinions on what may be the cause, and even what the symptoms are. The most common manifestations of BPD are:

• rapid cycling moods. In contrast to bi-polar disorder, where changes in moods are usually of weeks' or months' duration, the borderline person can have radical shifts of mood from hour to hour, making him/her totally unpredictable. The person may be profoundly depressed, but one hour later may be euphoric.

• intense, inappropriate, and seemingly uncontrollable anger

• self-destructive acts, such as self-mutilation (cutting or burning oneself) and suicidal threats or gestures

• poor impulse control

• desire to have complete control over others

• chronic feelings of emptiness or boredom

• unstable, chaotic, and intense relationships

• feelings of needing someone else in order to survive

• inordinately strong need for affection and reassurance

There are, of course, varying degrees of BPD, from mild to severe.

The title of a book about BPD is *I Hate You, Don't Leave Me.* These few words describe the borderline person's behavior.

While some medications may be used, there is no specific medication for BPD. BPD and other personality disorders are different than psychiatric conditions of a biological origin, such as major depression or psychoses, even though some of the behaviors may be similar, and the treatment is different.

BPD sufferers may refuse medication or therapy because they feel there is nothing wrong with them. They feel that "Everybody else is crazy." Any suggestion that one needs therapy may be seen as an attack, provoking retaliation.

Some people with BPD recognize that they have a problem and seek help. There are specialists and clinics for BPD and some patients have very good results.

The impact of BPD behavior on children can result in their feeling that they are bad, inept, stupid, and unlovable. The children need help to realize that they are not what their parent says they are. When they become adults, they may be in a position to protect themselves by distancing themselves, and even then they need guidance on how to relate without being hurt. With therapy, they may be able to correct the impact of earlier experiences.

To sum up, all effort should be made to help the children survive and be emotionally healthy. Efforts at changing the BPD patient are usually futile, unless the person recognizes the need for help.

If one parent has BPD, the other parent should consult a mental health specialist for guidance in how to help the children. If children appear to be adopting BPD behavior, they should be seen by a therapist to try and prevent these traits from becoming engrained in them.

There is no reason to believe that BPD is hereditary. However, someone growing up in the presence of a borderline person may adopt BPD traits.

INTELLECT VS. EMOTIONS

I am a person who has come far in life, considering my difficult childhood. I now have several children and am running my household, well, not perfectly — there is room for growth — but fine.

My problem is that I am critical and can be grumpy. I think it's the flip side of the middah that helped me improve my character and accomplish so much.

Often when confronted with a decision to make, I take the harder route, the commendable one, with long-term advantages (i.e., staying firm but gentle and kind with my children, and not giving in when they want something they shouldn't have).

Or I'll do something the way my husband/ mother-in-law, etc. want me to, for the sake of shalom. Another example: I'll stop myself from saying something critical that's on the tip of my tongue, or I'll forgo a luxury that we really can't afford, rather than put it on my credit card.

While I know I am doing the right thing and I am happy to do it, there is also often a feeling of "I know it's right but ..." It reminds me of the "ess is shver tzu zein a yid" [It's hard to be a Jew] of the past generations.

What can I do and think when I know I should be happier with my decision, but the feeling is not there?

I sometimes feel that my intellect is smarter, more developed than my emotions and it is in pursuit of emmes and yashrus, I feel compelled to do what my intellect demands, yet my emotions are not yet on that madraigah. Any advice? Thanks.

You are to be commended for behaving according to proper *middos*.

Our *sifrei mussar*, and especially *Tanya*, point out that we are in a lifelong battle with the *yetzer hara*, a foe whom we can never vanquish, yet our triumph consists of preventing it from dominating our behavior. Although in a war, fighting to a draw is not considered a victory, it is different in our battle with the *yetzer hara*.

When we do a mitzvah that does not conflict with an emotion, as when we say *birchas hamozon* or eat matzah on Pesach, it is relatively easy to have *simchah shel mitzvah*. In such instances the *yetzer hara* does not have much ammunition to stop our simchah. However, when we have to overcome an emotion, the *yetzer hara* uses that to prevent *simchah*. When the *yetzer hara* realizes that you have resisted its force and you behave according to proper *middos*, it feels defeated, and strikes back by making you feel unhappy.

This is why we must *daven* for *simchah*. In *Tehillim* King David repeatedly prays for *simchah* (e.g., *Tehillim*, 86:4).

You are right, and you are fortunate that your intellect is "smarter and more developed" than your emotions. Let us remember that many of our emotions stem from our animal-like body, and that our uniqueness as human beings is in our intellect.

You should recognize the source of your negative feelings. Do something to act "as if" you were really happy, e.g., sing or dance. *Mesillas Yeshorim* says that our actions generate our feelings. If you act "*simchahdig*," you will eventually feel *simchah*.

MEDICATION IN POSTPARTUM DEPRESSION

I've recently been diagnosed with a mild form of postpartum depression. (I had a stillborn child about three months ago). I am seeing a psychologist who suggested that I see a psychiatrist to prescribe medication. My OB wanted to spare me the expense of a psychiatrist and offered to prescribe Zoloft for me. I have a weight issue and the psychologist said she believes that Zoloft can cause weight gain. She said that there is an SSRI (she couldn't remember the name of it) that actually curbs appetite and can aid with weight loss. My OB says he will only prescribe Zoloft or Prozac because he doesn't know about any of the other SSRI's. What should I do? Do Zoloft

and Prozac cause weight gain? Is there
a better option for someone who is very
overweight and the weight is connected to
the depression? Is it necessary to pay the
very high fee of a psychiatrist (my husband
is learning in kollel) to be evaluated? What
do you suggest?

I am not aware of any SSRI that does not have any weight-gain side effect. However, Wellbutrin (bupropion) is an antidepressant that is not an SSRI, and does not have any significant weight-gain effect. In fact, some claims have been made that adding Wellbutrin to an SSRI can minimize the weight-gain problem. This can be prescribed by a family physician. Of course, the effects of medications may vary with individuals.

You might try Wellbutrin, beginning with 75mg daily and working up to 225mg over a period of 10 days. The antidepressant effect may not occur for three weeks.

Incidentally, it is wise to take vitamin B-complex with C twice daily. It is also beneficial to take Omega-3 (there is a kosher product available). The dose is two or three capsules daily. Its mood-elevating effect is very gradual, beginning after about 6-8 weeks.

NO "GET UP AND GO"

My husband has no "get up and go." Every
morning it takes him hours to get dressed
and daven. He davens shacharis after chatzos
without a minyan. (He goes to bed very late
at night, sometimes 4 a.m., and although he
gets up to say Shema bizmano and Birchos
Hashachar, he sometimes goes back to sleep.)
He claims he can't find a minyan where
they daven with proper kavanah at a slower
pace. (We live in a large Jewish community

where there is no dearth of minyanim, so I
don't buy that excuse.) He finds all kinds
of things to busy himself with before he
finally does daven and I keep telling him
that nothing is so important that it has
to be done before davening. Of course, he
doesn't like to be nagged and he gets very
annoyed at me for telling him this. Although
we have parnassah he is not regularly
employed, which is why he is in no hurry
to do anything in the morning. He has no
problem getting up on Shabbos and going to
minyan then. He claims he is depressed due
to a number of things; he was partially
disabled from an accident years ago. He has
good days and bad days, days when he can
function quite normally and days when he is
in a lot of pain and can barely walk.

We also went through some very bad times
concerning some very close relatives, which
he claims added to his depression. In that
case, I should also suffer from depression
because I went through it with him. However,
I manage to go to work, keep house, and
function quite normally and get on with my
life, so I don't know why he can't either.
In fact, I think I should be more depressed
than he is!

He is always criticizing me and tells me
that his problems are due to my not being a
supportive wife and that I don't take care
of him properly as a wife should. He is very
capable of taking care of himself, when I am
not available to "take care" of him (getting
his meals, making Shabbos, etc). He always
blames all his problems on others and nothing
is ever his fault. I think he suffers from
low self-esteem and depression, but I don't
know how to help him. I don't want him on
medication and neither does he, so there

has to be a different way to get him out of this slump. He looks and acts normal on the outside so I don't think anyone else knows about this problem. I just want to know how to get my husband to daven with minyan in the morning and go to bed at a normal hour. Everything else I can deal with.

I t is impossible to know what your husband's problem is unless he undergoes a personal evaluation, which must be done by a competent mental-health professional. I can only list the possibilities.

If his failure to get up for *minyan* is simply laziness, then he needs guidance from a *rav*. If it is due to a psychological problem, there are essentially two possibilities.

1. He may have a physiological depression. As I explain in *Getting Up When You're Down*, a person may have a chemical imbalance that causes depression. The symptoms of depression may vary. One may have good days and bad days. It is common that a depressed person feels worse in the morning and better toward the evening. If the depression is due to a chemical imbalance, there are medications that can give significant relief.

Unfortunately, we do not as yet have a laboratory test that can confirm the presence or absence of a chemical imbalance. The only thing one can do is to take antidepressant medication in adequate doses for several weeks. If the depression is not due to a chemical imbalance, the medication will not do anything. If there is a chemical imbalance, the person is likely to feel significant relief.

2. Psychological causes for depression vary greatly, and require evaluation and psychotherapy for improvement. Low self-esteem is very common. Things that a person with good self-esteem can shrug off may depress a person with low self-esteem. However, it is classic that depression due to a chemical imbalance may cause a person to feel inferior. A person suffering from depression is likely to look for things to blame for why he feels depressed, and these may not be in any way causative.

A person who has chronic pain may understandably be depressed, but it is also possible that depression may accentuate the pain.

As you have discovered, your urging him is of little value. I suggest that he sees a competent therapist for evaluation. There is no reason to suffer when help is available.

EMOTIONAL NUMBNESS

I'm worried about my 15-year-old son. He has always been and still is a good student, and a respectful boy with fine middos. Two years ago, he lost a friend who was in a car accident. Initially, he took it very hard, but after a week, he showed no signs of grieving, and since then he has been very reserved, by which I mean that things I would expect to make him happy don't seem to have any effect. He has done very well in yeshivah, but I don't see him having any pride in his accomplishments. I know he loves us, but seems unable to show it. Is this a normal reaction to losing a friend? I don't want to send him to a psychologist, because I don't want him to think that I feel he has a mental problem.

This strikes a familiar note to me, although I cannot say that the two cases are identical. Let me share an incident with you.

In *Tanya*, the Alter Rebbe mentions the inability to feel emotion. I first encountered a glaring example of this phenomenon when one of the therapists in my rehabilitation center asked me to evaluate one of his clients. "He just is incapable of emotion," he said. "He sits in group sessions like as rock."

An interview with this young man revealed that when he was ten, his father died of a heart attack. "I looked at myself in the mirror and said, 'You are not going to cry,' and I didn't," he told me.

Fortunately, just several days earlier, an incident occurred at my home which gave me insight into this young man's problem. I tried to repair a leaky faucet, but I was unable to turn off the water supply to the sink. A plumber had no better luck. "That valve is frozen," he said. "It has probably not been turned since this house was built 75 years ago. If I force it, the pipe may break and you'll have a flood." The only thing to do was to turn off the main valve that controlled the flow of water to the entire house.

It turned out that the inside of the faucet was corroded, and the plumber had to go back to the shop to get a replacement. The water supply was off for several hours. When the water was turned back on, the opening of any faucet in the house was followed by an explosive discharge of rust-colored water.

This served as a model for me to understand the young man. At age ten, he wished to spare himself the distress of feeling grief. However, he was unable to block the grief emotion while leaving all other emotions intact. In desperation, he turned off his entire feeling system, so that for years he had felt nothing. Therapy was going to open the "main valve," but after years of being without any feeling, he feared the emergence of any emotion, which, like the opened faucet, might emit emotions with explosive force. Even pleasant feelings like love, pride, and friendly affection were threatening to him. He just did not know how to manage feelings, so he developed a rock-like insensitivity.

This may be what is happening with your son. He may have tried to avoid the grief caused by the loss of his friend by "turning off" his feeling system, which is why he seems to be unable to feel anything.

In this case, since it has only been two years, it should be much easier to re-open the feeling system than it was with my patient. If he has a relationship with one of his teachers or a *rav*, the latter may ask a psychotherapist how to go about easing your son's readjustment to feelings, and how to help him deal with the grief that he may have blocked. Should it be necessary for your son to consult a therapist, this can be handled with via the teacher or *rav* who would be working with him.

INABILITY TO CRY

I have a problem that disturbs me greatly.

The problem is that I cannot cry. Nothing makes me cry. I watch friends and family members go through such difficult times, yet I can't cry. I have lost close relatives, but I didn't cry at all. My own personal problems and worries don't make me cry. Nothing makes me cry.

However, I am an emotional person. I am easily moved by things, but never with tears. Watching people, friends, and family suffer hurts me so much. My heart really feels and hurts, yet I don't cry.

I often wish I could cry; it would release my feelings, my heart pangs. I know I would feel better afterwards. I want to cry to show my close ones I feel for them in their pain and sorrow, but I can't. Dwelling on their pain and thinking about their pain doesn't help me either. I haven't cried in many years. Please help.

The inability to cry may be due to either physical or emotional causes. There is a condition in which the lacrimal (tear-producing) glands simply fail to produce tears. Sometimes this results in the "Dry Eye Syndrome." This requires evaluation by an ophthalmologist.

There can be a number of emotional reasons for the inability to cry. You may recall a man, described in the previous segment, who lost his father at age 10. He remembers looking in the mirror, saying "You are not going to cry." He simply turned off his ability to cry.

There are men who don't cry because the culture considers male crying a sign of weakness. Some years ago, a leading presidential candidate had to drop out of the political race because he cried in public.

Some people who are depressed say that they would feel better if they could cry, but are unable to. There may be an emotional block to crying because of an incident earlier in life that resulted in suppressing crying.

Check out the possibility of a physical cause first. If there is none, you may want to investigate the possibility of an emotional block.

DISRUPTIVE MOTHER

I have been wanting to write to you for quite some time, but the article about Borderline Personality Disorder really pushed me into gear. Baruch Hashem, I am happily married to an absolutely wonderful man and we have five beautiful children. Looking at me now, you would never know the crazy, dysfunctional childhood I endured.

My mother has been diagnosed with depression, paranoia, and, most recently, bipolar disorder. The article about BPD gave me pause to think that maybe that is the correct diagnosis. For the past twenty years, since I was 20 years old, she has been on Lithium. She says she feels quite stable on this medication. Aside from (or perhaps in relation to) her psychiatric issues, she is emotionally unstable, unpredictable, and extremely difficult to be around. As I said, my childhood was one of utter instability, never knowing if Mommy would run away today and/or try to harm herself, or if she would not be speaking to me because of some "terrible" slight on my part, or if she would be loving and generous. Much of this behavior continues today, even though she is 81 and I am 41.

Baruch Hashem, my father was an extremely stable and loving person, the rock in my

*life, who, although not a demonstrative
person, always let me know that as long
as he lived I would be loved and taken
care of. Three years ago my father passed
away, leaving me alone to face my worst
nightmare — my mother to contend with
(I am an only child; no aunts or uncles
either). My father left all the assets to my
mother, the remainder to me upon her death.
Throughout his life, my father handled all
the finances, and my mother never so much as
wrote a check. She is an extremely gullible
person, and as I've said, quite unstable
and unpredictable. Because of this, we
transferred all the money to my name. It's
in a separate account, and we regularly
transfer funds into her personal checking
account as she requests.*

*There has been no foul play whatsoever,
although my mother is quite upset at our
"lack of confidence" in her ability to
manage her finances and our "wrongful taking
of her money."*

*I attend an Al-Anon program to help
me deal with her and live by the tenet,
"I didn't cause it, I can't control it,
and I can't cure it." I do my best to be
respectful to her, fly down to Florida
to visit her, invite her to my house and
call her twice a week. I seek the advice
of Rabbanim and a Rebbetzin with whom I am
close, and try to do the right thing always.*

*My question is, do I return the money
to her as she wants? My husband is against
this, because he is concerned that we will
be left supporting her if she is swindled. I
understand this; however, I am torn between
my responsibility to keep her financially
protected from herself, and the idea of
letting go, of not trying to control her. I*

don't want to be irresponsible, and believe
me, the easiest thing would be just to
return the money and be done with it. But
part of me feels that this is irresponsible,
even though it's what she wants. If you
could also offer me any chizuk or tools
to deal with her, I would appreciate it
greatly.

A s far as *chizuk* is concerned, I suggest you read *Understanding the Borderline Mother*. This book describes several main types of borderline mothers. The first is one who feels helpless (termed "waif"). The waif with BPD has difficulty in taking care of herself and her belongings, and invalidates her own competence. She feels victimized. She may either neglect her health or make frequent medical visits. She is extremely needy, and if she feels abandoned, may even threaten to end her life. She is alternately indulgent and negligent with her children. She may lose or destroy valuable things. She may have crying spells, depression, or panic attacks. She thinks that life is too hard.

A second type is the "hermit," who lives in fear. She may have fantasies that she or others will be harmed, and may attribute hostile intentions to others. She is possessive and over-controlling, reclusive and avoids groups. She is intensely jealous and acutely perceptive. She evokes guilt and anxiety in others.

A third type is the "queen." In order to win her admiration and love, her children must reflect her interests, tastes, and values. She expects the children to reflect her importance. She seeks attention and prominence. She demands total loyalty and discards those who betray her. Her hysterical reactions can terrify her children. She believes that rules do not apply to her. Her motto might well be, "I deserve more."

A fourth type, for lack of a better term, is the "witch," who is characterized by extreme rage. She can be very punitive, even sadistic. She can enlist others as allies against whoever is the target of her rage and may stir up conflict in groups. She is intrusive and domineering and may have a feeling of being evil. Her motto might be, "Life is war."

Although I've listed four types, there may be a mixture of symptoms. Each type may have some symptoms of other types.

It is important not to jump to the conclusion that any person with some of these behaviors has BPD. It is only when these behaviors are accentuated that they constitute BPD. In moderate forms, some of these behaviors may be within normal range. Do not diagnose anyone as BPD. Just as a lay person is incompetent to make a medical diagnosis, he/she is incompetent to make a psychiatric diagnosis. Consult a mental-health therapist for a diagnosis and for guidance on how to relate to the person with BPD.

To answer your specific question, while it is considered wrong to "rescue" her — i.e., to extricate a BPD patient from the difficulties she gets into because that just reinforces her idea that she can do what she pleases and someone will get her out of trouble — holding her money for her so that she does not squander it is not rescuing. If she is impulsive, she can spend irresponsibly and then expect her children to support her.

FAILING TO DAVEN

I have been very happily married for 13 years KA"H. My husband learned in kollel for the first few years. He is a good husband and father and he is basically a very erliche person. However, there is one puzzling and disturbing problem. He often forgets to daven. I know that it sounds strange, but I have grown accustomed to it. I try when I can to remind him to daven Minchah and/or Maariv, but if I don't, he usually forgets. He usually does daven Shacharis — but rarely with a minyan. It has always been a problem and many years ago I phoned a Gadol. He was so upset that he wanted to send someone to speak to my husband. Because my husband is proud, I

knew he would be horrified if he found
out I had discussed it with someone and
I knew he would never forgive me for it.
I have spoken to my husband about this
countless times, but of course he feels
uncomfortable and promises to work on it.
He tries but it doesn't last very long. He
has been diagnosed with ADD and he does
take medication for it. (Of course, I need
to remind him to take his medication, too)
He claims he's become more focused and more
organized with the medication but it doesn't
make much difference in this area. Although
this has always been a problem, I'm becoming
increasingly concerned because my children
are getting older and I have lately been
lying to cover up for him. I should mention
that he works many hours a day at a very
stressful job. He works late most nights,
though this is not an excuse.

Do you have any ideas or suggestions?

This is so much out of character for a person like your husband that I cannot consider it to be due to a lack of commitment to Yiddishkeit. It is much more likely to be due to his ADD, and although he is taking medication, the treatment may be inadequate. If this is so, talking to him will not help. I am sure that he is well aware of the importance of *davening*.

You may say to him, "I know that *davening* is important to you, and it is just not like you to neglect it. If I were to ask a *rav* about this, you would be very upset because you would feel terribly embarrassed. That means that you know it is wrong to omit *davening*.

"There must be something that is causing this.

"Although you are taking medication for ADD and it is helping, it is important to have a re-evaluation. For you, skipping *davening* must be due to the ADD, and you would feel so much better if you would not forget."

I suggest that you contact JAADD (Jewish Association for ADD), (718) 376-3079 and ask for a referral to a specialist for re-evaluation. See the Appendix for a partial list of referral agencies.

INSOMNIA IN YOUNG ADULTS

I'm a 19-year-old yeshivah bachur. I have experienced quite serious insomnia problems and have consulted a G.P. who specializes in homeopathy. He informed that I only need 5 hours sleep a night, and that I was going to bed too early. He did not give me any kind of physical test before telling me this. He said that if I feel tired after having 5 hours sleep, it is probably psychological, triggered by myself. I was wondering whether this sounds reasonable to you, or whether you can suggest another explanation.

It is generally thought that the average person needs 7-8 hours of sleep. However, there are many variations. If a person does not feel tired during the day and functions well with 5 hours of sleep, that may be normal for him. The problem is when a person feels tired during the day or has difficulty functioning, such as while studying or trying to concentrate.

Transient insomnia is usually due to a limited stress situation and usually corrects itself. If sleep difficulty lasts more than a month, it should be investigated.

There are many possible reasons for insomnia. Caffeine, either in coffee or in soft drinks, may cause insomnia and should be omitted. Although it may seem that alcohol induces sleep, it actually causes fragmented sleep. In addition, some over-the-counter medications may cause insomnia.

Anxiety, stress, and depression are frequent causes of insomnia.

However, recourse to tranquilizers or sleeping pills can be dangerous, because most of these can lead to addiction. If a psychological cause is found, it should be treated with psychotherapy. If depression is the cause, most antidepressants are not addictive.

When insomnia is more than just occasional, it is best evaluated in a sleep-disorder laboratory. Most major hospitals provide this service.

I have a problem with my 16-year-old son. He has great difficulty staying awake during the day, but comes alive at night. He has been unable to keep a chavrusah because he tends to doze off. We've tried having him go to sleep earlier, but he can't fall asleep until 3 or 4 a.m., and then cannot get up in time.

I am not aware of any emotional problems. Could it be that he wants to avoid people during the day, or has some other psychological problem? He can't go on like this.

This pattern is not too unusual. We know that there are "day" people and "night" people, but most are able to function normally. However, your sons' pattern is interfering with normal function.

Before jumping to the conclusion that he has a psychological problem, I think that he should be evaluated by a sleep-disorder specialist. They have seen cases of day/night reversals and may be able to suggest a way to correct the pattern.

Most major hospitals have a Sleep Disorder Clinic. Call to arrange an evaluation.

BEARD-PULLING

I have a friend in yeshivah who has a problem which is terribly disturbing to him.

He has a bad habit of pulling at his beard while he is learning, and has thereby caused a bald spot. This pulling only gets worse when he is tense or nervous or when he needs to concentrate more intensely.

He has tried almost everything to help himself stop, for example, taping up his fingers, holding other objects in his hand, etc., but to no avail.

Do you have any suggestions how he can stop this terrible habit and save the remainder of his beard?

This condition, known as trichotillomania, is not at all uncommon, affecting between four to eleven million Americans. It is an impulse-control disorder, which causes people to pull out hair from their scalp, beard, eyebrows, or eyelashes. Until 1989, this condition was not well known, and as a result people with trichotillomania may feel that they are the only ones with this problem and are ashamed of it.

Trichotillomania is more common in women, but also occurs in men. It usually begins in childhood or early adolescence, but can begin much later.

Research on trichotillomania is being conducted. At this point, there is no single treatment. A number of treatment approaches have been suggested, including medication, cognitive-behavior therapy, support groups, and some alternative therapies.

More information on this condition can be obtained by contacting one of the referral agencies in the Appendix.

IS RITALIN NECESSARY?

I was told that my 9-year-old son has ADD and the doctor recommended Ritalin. When my mother heard of this, she became very upset. "Don't you dare put that child on Ritalin! That's all that doctors know how to do — prescribe medication! According to doctors, all children should be on Ritalin." I'm at a loss what to do.

What did people do with these children before Ritalin? Is ADD a new condition?

There has indeed been some controversy about Ritalin, but I believe that is because it has often been prescribed without adequate evaluation by a competent child therapist. We are living in an age where people have come to expect a "quick-fix." Not every child who is fidgety or seems to have a short attention span has ADD. But parents and teachers who want to see dramatic improvement in a child's behavior may jump to the conclusion that he has ADD, and may ask their doctor to prescribe Ritalin. Only a competent child psychologist/psychiatrist can make that diagnosis.

In cases of bona-fide ADD, there is strong evidence that it is a neurological condition. Some skilled therapists have developed a behavioral method of treating ADD without medication. The important thing is that a child with ADD should be effectively treated, whether with or without medication. Allowing ADD to go untreated is unfair to the child. He may feel he is a failure, and such feelings are difficult to overcome later.

Your question about what people did before Ritalin is interesting. I am not sure that there is an actual increase of the incidence of ADD or if we have just become more aware of it. Life in the shtetl was far less demanding than life today, and people with limitations adjusted more easily to a simpler life.

Be that as it may, ADD should not be neglected. If a child's behavior is not due to ADD, the parents should seek proper counseling to help the child for whatever the problem may be.

ASPERGER'S SYNDROME

My eight-year-old son is having difficulty in school. He does not make friends. He is bright, but the teacher says that he seems to "be living in a world of his own." He is not rebellious, but seems to be unable to follow instructions, as if he did not understand what he was told to do.

At home, we felt that he was different from our other children, but we saw nothing that was alarming. One thing we noticed was that he would avoid eye contact, and sometimes react improperly to things, taking offense at something which was in no way meant to be offensive.

At the school's recommendation, we took him to a child psychologist, who thinks he has "Asperger's Syndrome." I've never heard of this. What is it and what can we do about it?

Although this condition was described by Dr. Asperger in 1944, psychiatry and psychology did not deal with it until fairly recently. Dr. Asperger describes a condition in which children with normal and even superior intelligence lack social skills. They have difficulty relating to other children because they lack the ability to properly recognize other people's behavior, and may be unable to start or maintain a conversation. Consequently, they turn their interests inward. It seems that they do desire friendship, but just don't know how to make it happen. This lasts into adult life and may interfere with occupation as well as relationships. They may be unable to empathize with others. It is felt that Asperger's is a neurological problem.

In the past, people with Asperger's were considered odd or loners, but inasmuch as they did not have a psychiatric label, it was not an obstacle to *shidduchim* for other family members. Today it may be, which is why the parents are often reluctant to be open about the problem.

Sometimes these children are very sensitive to stimuli, such as sounds and smells, that do not bother anyone else. They may use big words (e.g., "commence" instead of "begin"). They may develop an interest in something and become totally involved in this one thing, ignoring everything else. They may be clumsy. One mother described her son as "walking to the beat of a different drum."

These children have sometimes been diagnosed with ADD, OCD, or Tourette's Syndrome. Because this condition is rather vague, it is difficult to diagnose. Treatment is usually directed at trying to teach the child social skills. Some medications have been tried, but there is no specific medication for Asperger's.

Family and friends can learn all they can about Asperger's, which may have a variety of manifestations, and find out how to best relate to the person and family as if it were in the pre-diagnosis days. In other words, find the best way to relate to someone and his family even though he is a "loner," "odd," or "socially withdrawn." There is no particular gain in using a diagnostic label. Rather, try to relate most effectively to someone whose behavior is different than the norm. This way, you can provide whatever help you can without causing a problem that might be associated with a psychiatric diagnosis.

What is most important is that the child should not be considered as being willfully uncooperative. Do not force him to do things that he is able to do although it may seem as though he is unwilling to do them.

A diagnosis of Asperger's Syndrome should be made only by a competent child psychologist or psychiatrist. If this is indeed Asperger's, you can learn more about the condition in the book, *OASIS Guide to Asperger Syndrome*, by P.R. Bashe and B.L. Kirby.

WITHDRAWN SON

We are desperate. My son is 23.
Until about age 17, he was a good

*student. He was always shy, but not
unusually so. At about 17, he began having
trouble being in people's company. When
learning with a chavrusah, he would look
around to see if people were watching him.
Eventually, he could not keep a chavrusah
and became more and more withdrawn. We knew
something was wrong, but we could not get
him to see anyone for help. He would say,
"There's nothing wrong with me. Just leave
me alone." If we pushed the idea, he would
get angry.*

*Things have gone from bad to worse. He
stays in his room most of the time. He
doesn't talk to me at all, just ignores me.
He will say hello to my husband but that's
all. When his married sister visits, he may
say a few words to her. She cannot convince
him to get help. He doesn't eat with us.
Friday night he comes down to Kiddush, then
takes food up to his room. He hasn't been
in shul for two years.*

*Psychiatrists tell us that there is no
way to force him into treatment. I have
said to him that I know he is suffering
and that medication could help him feel
better, but he won't hear of it. We have
gone to tzaddikim for berachos and we give
tzedakah. How can we stand by and see our
child deteriorate before our eyes? He was a
good child and never gave us any trouble.
I wonder what it is that we did wrong to
bring this on. Please help.*

The worst feeling in the world is to be totally powerless,
especially to see a child deteriorate and to be unable to do
anything about it. Involuntary treatment is not desirable,
but if it is the only thing to do, one must try it. Years ago, a statement

by two physicians would allow a person to be taken to a hospital involuntarily, but that is no longer possible.

Today, the only way to get involuntary treatment is to go to court and have yourself appointed as legal guardian. This requires a procedure with a lawyer. You can then have him hospitalized. This is terribly unpleasant and he will, of course, resent you for it, but with progressive deterioration and no outlook for relief, it is the only thing you can do.

You are suffering enough without adding on guilt and assuming that it was faulty parenting that caused this. Many conditions like this are caused by an alteration in brain chemistry, whose cause we don't understand. Medication may help, but since he refuses medication, it cannot be forced on him unless you become his guardian, and then take care of him as you would an infant.

I wish I had something more positive to recommend. May Hashem hear your *tefillos* and give him a *refuah sheleimah*.

DEPRESSION MAY BE SEASONAL

For several years, I've been getting depressed before Rosh Hashanah, sometime a week before, sometimes a month before. It lasts until a few weeks after Sukkos. I've never gone for treatment because it only lasts about two months and I sweat it out.

I can understand why it happens before Rosh Hashanah, because the awesome period when one is being judged is very serious. I don't know, though, why it doesn't improve with Sukkos, which is such a happy Yom Tov. Maybe it's because everyone is celebrating joyously and I'm not "with it."

Anyway, is there anything I can do to avoid this depressive period?

The period of Rosh Hashanah–Yom Kippur is indeed awesome and is so consequential to our lives. We stand before the judgment of Hashem, and, as we say in our *tefillos*, no human being is without fault. The gravity of these days is certainly understandable.

However, I believe that *yiras shamayim* should not be a cause for depression. I have cited the *Tanya* which states that *lev nishbar,* (lit. "broken heart") is not *atzvus* (depression). The *seforim* cite the *Midrash* that on Rosh Hashanah we dress as for a festival, and, as it says in *Nehemiah*, 8:10, we should not be sad on Rosh Hashanah, being secure that on this Holy Day we will have a favorable judgment from Hashem.

In the past, it was believed that depression was due solely to psychological reasons. A person was depressed because of some incident in one's lifetime that was depressing. Psychotherapists searched for an emotional trauma during childhood, such as early parental deprivation, to explain the depression.

In more recent times, it has become evident that many cases of depression are due to chemical changes in the body rather than to psychological causes. I elaborate on this in my book, *Getting Up When You're Down*. In these cases, treatment consists primarily of prescribing the correct medication that will correct the chemical changes in the body.

We have become aware that some of these changes are seasonal, and they are referred to as Seasonal Affective Disorders. They occur at about the same time each year. Your depression may be related to the season rather than to the solemnity of the Holy Days. Because Rosh Hashanah varies, occurring earlier or later in the solar year, the depression may begin a week or a month before Rosh Hashanah.

I had a patient with this pattern. I prescribed an antidepressant beginning August 15 through the end of October, and this prevented the occurrence of the depression. I suggest you discuss this with your physician.

EARLY-ONSET ALZHEIMER'S DISEASE

I am the oldest daughter in a average-size frum family. B"H, my siblings and myself are all married and have done wonderful shidduchim. The issue at hand is my father, who is now 60 years old. The problem began approximately 10 years ago. My father began acting very tense and nervous. Together with some physical disabilities, my father's mental health began deteriorating. In conversation he always says the strangest things. Basically, his sanity seems to get worse every day. His behavior in public is very peculiar. This is increasing to the point that most of my siblings are embarrassed to be present with him in public. My mother is definitely a tzadekes for putting up with him. I think some Torah'dikah advice can be very beneficial to me and other people in my situation.

I'm sorry to hear of your distress.

Whenever a person shows any indication of mental deterioration, as with memory, judgment, or behavior, regardless of age, a through physical, neurological, and psychiatric evaluation must be done. There are causes of mental changes for which there is treatment, anywhere from brain tumor to depression. Sometimes the symptoms of severe depression can mimic Alzheimer's disease. It should not be automatically assumed that the changes in an elderly person are due to Alzheimer's disease, yet this illness should not be ruled out even it first surfaces at age 50.

The problem of managing the care of a person with severe mental deterioration is vexing. It is, of course, important to maintain *kibud av*, and any specific problems with regard to this should be discussed with a *posek*. If his behavior in public is inappropriate, then it may be necessary to reduce the time he spends in public. People with Alzheimer's disease have been taken to their children's and grandchildren's simchos for a short period of time and then returned home.

Although Alzheimer's disease is generally a condition of later life — over 65 — it can occur earlier. I recall a patient of 41 with this condition.

There is extensive research going on to try to identify the exact physiological causes for the brain changes, but while there is great hope of a breakthrough, there is no cure at present. Some medications are thought to slow the process of deterioration, and this should be discussed with your father's physician.

I recall the case of a 72-year-old man who showed typical signs of Alzheimer's disease. Careful examination revealed that because of a prostate condition, his sleep was repeatedly interrupted, and his symptoms were due to sleep deprivation. When his prostate condition was treated, his mentality returned to normal.

Jewish Family Service provides help with geriatric problems, and although your father is only 60, they can be helpful with him, because they have wide experience in cases like this. See the Appendix for a partial list of other agencies.

TORMENTED MOTHER — ANGUISHED CHILDREN

I am writing this letter with tears in my eyes on behalf of all my siblings, concerning our mother. Our mother has been suffering terribly from undiagnosed OCD [obsessive-compulsive disorder] for very many years; it manifests itself in religious matters, as well as in everyday life matters.

Besides that — or because of that — she also acts very queerly, such as talking

*to herself after finishing a telephone
conversation, or repeating things, as well
as asking others to repeat things, although
we know she heard, and she knows it pains
us.*

*We would like to know what our obligations
are as we want to preserve her kavod. Should
we leave it as is, or bring up the subject
with her, and ask her to go for therapy,
(although we feel she does not want to
be helped). This may be very painful for
her since she is very proud and extremely
sensitive, and has never brought up this
subject or gone for help.*

*We would truly appreciate if you could
guide us in this matter, since it has taken
an emotional toll on us.*

OCD is one of the most painful psychological conditions a person may have. It may give a person no peace, constantly producing doubts. The various behaviors in OCD are an attempt to relieve the distress, but the respite is only temporary.

As much as you and your siblings are suffering, I am certain that your mother's suffering is even greater. You will be doing her a great favor by trying to help her.

You and your siblings should get together and meet with her and tell her, "Mom, we see that you're in much distress, because you never feel sure of anything and are always doubting, maybe you did not do enough or maybe you didn't hear correctly. We checked into this, and this may be due to anxiety that can be safely relieved. We'd like to ask Dr__ [your family doctor] to prescribe something which can relieve your suffering. Why suffer unnecessarily?" She may reject this initially, saying "There's nothing wrong with me," but is quite likely to agree a bit later or tell you that she will call the doctor.

You should alert her doctor that she may be calling him. He should prescribe an antidepressant medication rather than a tranquilizer. Tranquilizers give just several hours relief, and if one uses them regularly, they may lose their effect, so that the person increases the dose, and this may lead to addiction. Antidepressants are not addictive. They are often effective in OCD, although it may take several weeks for the effect to be seen.

For unknown reasons, the incidence of OCD has increased. It is believed that OCD may be due to a chemical imbalance similar to depression. People who are religious have religion-oriented symptoms, and non-religious people have other symptoms, but it is the same disease. The scrupulosity of OCD should not be misinterpreted as *frumkeit*. One woman with OCD had constant doubts about possible remote contacts of *milchig* and *fleishige* dishtowels, and in spite of reassurance from her *rav*, threw out three sets of dishes. Another woman who could not feel certain that she was able to get rid of all *chametz*, did not allow any bread in her house all year round. These are clearly not reasonable *chumros*.

It is a torment to live in constant doubt. I hope your mother will accept your suggestion that can improve her quality of life.

FAMILY

IT WAS OUT OF MY CONROL

This past winter, my wife's brother married off his son in another city. Knowing how unpredictable airline travel may be, we booked an early-morning flight, expecting to arrive in plenty of time before the wedding. About two hours before flight time, a severe blizzard developed, and the airport was shut down for the rest of the day. Of course, we called and explained what had happened.

Things between me and my wife's family have never been smooth. They were furious that we missed the wedding, and called to tell us that we did not have to come for sheva berachos. I don't know what they expected. Was I to predict the weather and get there a day early?

My wife disregarded what they said and flew in for sheva berachos. I did not feel welcome. I thought their reaction was inappropriate, so I did not go.

*They are still holding this against me.
They are interpreting our absence at the
wedding as a hostile action on my part,
and claim that I prevented my wife from
attending. What can I do to convince them
that I was innocent, and that I do not
control the weather?*

I n spite of their angry reaction, it would have been wise if, like your wife, you had ignored their statement and gone to the *sheva berachos.*

Insofar as correcting their misinterpretation of your absence, that is probably not the route to go.

My father used to cite the *Midrash* stating that when Hashem told Moshe *Rabbeinu* to write in the account of creation, "*Na'ase adam* (Let us make man)," Moshe inquired, "Why use the plural 'us' and give people the opportunity to come to the wrong conclusion that there is more than one G-d?" Hashem answered, "You write '*Na'ase adam*.' If anyone wishes to come to the wrong conclusion, let him do so."

My father explained Hashem's answer to Moshe: "Whoever wishes to think properly will come to the correct conclusion regardless of what you write, and whoever has his heart set on a wrong idea will have it whether you write 'Let *us* make man' or '*I* will make man.'"

If the relationship between yourself and your wife's family is strained, trying to correct a misinterpretation is futile. If they wish to find fault with you, they will do so. The thing to do is to make every effort to improve the relationship. Whenever they have a *simchah*, you should attend even if you feel unwelcome, and even if they ignore you when you are there. I know that this may be unpleasant for you, but the right thing is to be a *mentsch*. The Talmud has the greatest praise for someone who does not react to a personal insult and behaves as though nothing happened.

Many family feuds were settled when one side decided not to keep the feud going, and was, as the Talmud says, *ma'avir al midosov*, willing to overlook a personal offense. This requires both restraint and effort, which is why the Talmud considers it so meritorious.

So, act as though nothing ever happened. Go to their *simchos*, call on appropriate occasions to say *mazal tov* and extend greetings, send *mishloach manos*, etc., and disregard it if they fail to reciprocate. Eventually, everyone will benefit.

DISCORD OVER INHERITANCE

I am a very bitter and disillusioned mother. My husband took our two sons into his business. When he died, an argument broke out between the two about how to divide the business. Eventually one bought out the other, but during the negotiations there was much strife and bitterness, each one feeling he was cheated. They communicated only through their lawyers. Attempts by the rabbi to reconcile them haven't worked.

My daughter is making a bar-mitzvah, and each one called and said that if she invites the other brother, he won't come. This is crazy! Let them not talk to each other if they don't want to, but not boycott a sister's simchah! My daughter is beside herself. How is she to explain to her children that her brothers hate each other? I think the only time they will both come to the same event is to my funeral. Is that why I raised a family? They are frum boys. What can I do to make them act like mentschen?

Unfortunately, this is not uncommon. At one time there were only a few people in the whole world. Cain could have taken half the world and Hevel the other half. Yet their relationship ended disastrously. The Torah is telling us how irrational strife between brothers can be.

You might call each son and tell him that you want him to be at your home at a specific date and time. Tell him that you are commanding him to be there *b'gzeras kibbud em* (by decree of respect for a mother). Tell him that his brother is going to be there and that they don't have to communicate, but you are demanding that they both be there. Inasmuch as they are *frum* men, they will obey.

When they come, tell them that whatever complaints they have about each other should not affect their sister, and certainly not you. Tell them that you a right to have all your children at your *simchah*, and that their squabbling does not give them the right to cause you pain. They do not have to sit near each other in *shul* or at the dinner, but that staying away will cause you pain and is a serious violation of *kibbud em*.

Close on a positive note. Tell them that by overlooking their personal feelings and coming to the *simchah* they will be fulfilling the precious mitzvah of *kibbud em*, for which Hashem promises them abundant *berachos*.

I WAS NOT MY MOTHER-IN-LAW'S CHOICE

My husband and I are happily married. He had been engaged to a second cousin, but broke off the shidduch. He says that he never wanted it in the first place, but his mother pressured him into it. However, he felt that he was not interested and broke it off. His mother has been angry with him over this. Since he married me, his mother has resented me. She acts as though if I had not come along, he would have gone back to his cousin, so I am the guilty one.

There have been several family affairs to which my mother-in-law invites this cousin. She goes out of her way to shower attention on her in my husband's presence, as if to say, "Look whom you could have had." There are many other cousins, even closer ones, whom she does not invite. I feel that she is doing this just to provoke my husband and me.

What should we do? Should we boycott family simchos?

I don't believe that family *simchos* should be boycotted. There are many other family members with whom there should be relationships, and these should not be thwarted by your mother-in-law's actions.

Your husband and you should have a frank talk with your mother-in-law. Point out to her that not only is she making it difficult for both of you, but also that she is not being kind to the cousin, who sees her former *chasan* married to another woman. You may point out that she does not invite the other cousins.

Your husband should respectfully tell his mother that he understands that she is angry with him, but that marrying someone in whom he was not interested would have made for a very unhappy marriage. He understands that she wishes to help this cousin, but an unhappy marriage would have been no help for her. He had to make the decision to sever the relationship. Anyway, it is all in the past, so why continue to harp on it?

If your mother-in-law persists in inviting her regularly, I think you should brace yourself and continue attend family affairs. You and your husband should be as cordial as possible to this cousin. She is undoubtedly hurting too. It is regrettable that your mother-in-law pressured him into the engagement, but that is not the cousin's fault.

This is one of those times where one must adjust to an uncomfortable situation.

"DISPOSABLE" RELATIONSHIPS DISRUPT LIVES

The article on "A Broken Home" and your commentary were indeed impressive. However, I wish you had put greater emphasis on the responsibility that parents who bring children into the world have to work harder at making the proper adjustments so that they could have real shalom bayis and give their children a wholesome home in which to grow up.

People are too quick to give up on the marriage relationship.

I re-read the commentary, and I don't see how I could have been more emphatic on that point. Parents do indeed have an awesome responsibility, and if they made a more concerted effort at *adjusting* to each other, they could have real *shalom bayis* rather than just a peaceful co-existence.

I believe that our culture has been brainwashed by some of the marvelous advances of technology. Just think of how many disposable items we have; e.g., disposable dishes and cutlery, disposable cups, disposable diapers, disposable contact lenses, and disposable cameras.

When I became a Bar Mitzvah, I received a Sheaffer fountain pen that I had for 20 years, and when I lost it, I felt a real sense of loss. Today, I never end the week with the same ballpoint pen with which I began the week. These are disposable. I remember carrying a radio to the repair shop. Today, there is no way to repair a radio or a tape recorder. If there is something wrong with it, people just throw it out and get a new one. We have developed a lifestyle of not trying to fix things that go wrong. We just get rid of it and get a new one.

Unfortunately, this kind of thinking has carried over to human relations. If things go wrong with a relationship, the knee-jerk reaction is to dispose of it and replace it with a new relationship.

We need to remember that people are not "things." If we took the teachings of *mussar* seriously, we would realize that every Jew is holy and must be treated accordingly. Indeed, marriage is referred to as *kiddushin*, which is holiness. Mature people should realize that the proper attitude in marriage is what you give to the relationship rather than what you can get from it.

Problems in marriage often result from people being frustrated by not getting what they want out of the relationship. One of the *berachos* which *Chazal* prescribed for the newlyweds is *"yotzer ha'adam,"* affirming that Hashem created man. The point is that animals are totally motivated by satisfying their own desires, and do not sacrifice their comfort for others (except for pets that adopt human traits or animal mothers that instinctively care for their young). The message to each spouse is "Be a *mentsch* and behave like a *mentsch* rather than just pursue self-gratification like an animal."

I have repeatedly said that young people are not adequately prepared for marriage. I address this in *The First Year of Marriage*, and at the risk of being accused of commercializing, I think this is essential reading for every *chassan* and *kallah*.

I think that young people should be taught much more about how to relate, and the preparation in the *chassan* and *kallah* classes falls short of this. With a better understanding of the *kedushah* of marriage and how to properly relate to a spouse, many problems could be forestalled, and many more marriages could be happy and enduring.

SELF-CENTERED PARENT

I read in your book, Dear Rabbi, Dear Doctor (page 312), your explanation of the term "narcissistic personality syndrome." The description fits my own father to the very last detail.

Unfortunately, my father's behavior wrought irreparable damage. One sibling had a mental breakdown, and has not yet recovered. Another sibling was not able to settle in his marriage. As for me, twice I experienced my thoughts racing out of control with negative messages that made me feel worthless. I was told that I was on the verge of a breakdown.

The advice you gave in your book is to show respect for the narcissistic person, and this will make him much milder. However, for close to twenty years my father belittled me, shouted at me for minor things, blamed me, made fun of me, and pressured me to give in to his unrealistic demands. He never gave me love or appreciation. He is tough and I have to argue endlessly in order to get my basic needs. And — I have to thank him heartily for whatever he does give me. He constantly insists that we should give him an abnormal kind of respect. I cannot bring myself to show this man any respect! Just to answer his never-ending questions without exploding takes a tremendous amount of strength.

Also, I am concerned that trying your advice will perhaps feed his sickness, and make him even more demanding.

I went for counseling but it did not improve the situation, I also asked a rav if the mitzvah of kibbud av applies to me, and he clearly said that it does not.

Now my questions: Is there anything that can help us? Should I escape the situation by ignoring him totally? And since that rav is not a professional, he gave his answer without diagnosing the problem. Can I rely on his psak — and just not care about kibbud av?

I reviewed the section in *Dear Rabbi, Dear Doctor*, and nowhere do I say that showing a narcissistic father respect will make him milder.

The issue of *kibbud av* is unrelated to whether respect would make any difference. Inasmuch as *kibbud av* is of such great importance, the question of whether one is exempt due to a parent's psychological condition can be ruled on only by a competent *posek* who understands the problem. For example, Rabbi David Cohen is the *posek* for Nefesh and he deals with such cases.

Going for counseling was wise, but cannot be expected to change your father's behavior. What counseling should do is strengthen you and help you build your self-esteem in spite of your father's belittling you. Understandably, constantly being criticized is crushing, yet if you know that those comments are not valid, you should be able, with proper help, to regain a sense of self-worth.

I recognize how difficult it is for you. If you feel that your health is in jeopardy, separation may be necessary. This should be discussed with both the *posek* and your therapist. The Appendix at the back of this volume contains a partial listing of referral agencies that can guide you to find the proper therapist and provide you with the names of several *poskim* who have broad experience in such cases.

HELPFUL AUNT IS REJECTED

I'm writing regarding a machlokes, a family dispute, because I want something to be worked out on behalf of both parties. I don't know what to do.

There is a deep rift in the family because of this situation between an aunt and niece.

My aunt (62), who is a tzaddekes, never married and has no parents or children. She was a teacher for 28 years and a school principal. She has had a very hard life; her fiancée died, and her brother is very sick. I would do anything to spare her any additional aggravation.

Twelve years ago her niece called when she was in desperate need of help after her first child was born. My aunt was retired, so she helped her. Since then, she has helped her with all of her children since birth. The niece is anorexic, has low self-esteem, and is very controlling with her six children, who are between the ages of 2 and 12. My aunt practically supported her emotionally and monetarily, in every aspect. She provided food, clothing, and toys. She assisted when they were sick, she paid for their after-school programs and vacations.

The mother went to work, her husband was seldom home, and they enjoyed all these benefits, rarely showing hakaras hatov.

My aunt is the most wonderful, warm, giving person and the children love her. A little over three months ago, the niece severed the relationship. She claims the children are too close to the aunt, who, she views, is usurping her role. She still finds fault in the kids and wants to totally control them. The children are devastated over this loss and so is my aunt.

Should a compromise be made? How can it be implemented? Is the mother right? The situation is very bad and sad.

I recall when I was in psychiatric training, I was discussing a case with a colleague, who interrupted me, saying, "Stop talking logic!" He was right. I was approaching an emotional problem with logic, but emotions may be totally unaffected by logical reasoning.

I am assuming that your information is not one-sided. If you have only heard your aunt's version of what happened, all your conclusions may be off the mark. If however you have verified that this is an accurate description of the situation, you may be right. The mother may feel jealous if she thinks that the children care more for the aunt than for her. There is also another possible reason.

The Chasam Sofer once expressed his surprise when he realized a person was hostile to him. "I can't understand it," the Chasam Sofer said, "I never did him any favors."

What the Chasam Sofer was saying is that some people who are the recipients of a person's benevolence may be unable to have *hakaras hatov* because they do not want to feel obligated or beholden to the benefactor. This psychological insight is clearly stated by *Tosafos* (*Avodah Zarah*, 5a). What the Chasam Sofer pointed out is that not only may they not feel and express gratitude, but may actually turn against the benefactor.

The great effort the aunt put out for her niece may unfortunately have resulted in this distortion, breeding resentment instead of gratitude. If that is the way the mother feels, she may seize on anything to justify rejecting her aunt. At this point, she is giving the reason that the children are too close to the aunt. There may even be some validity to this. If you argue against that, she will come up with another reason to justify her behavior toward her aunt.

The aunt is a mature adult and may be able to swallow the pain, but the children are young and could certainly benefit from the aunt's love.

Talking to the niece about this may put her on the defensive and she may just reinforce her stand. Any attempt would have to be done very gently by someone with psychological savvy so that she does not feel she is being criticized. If you can find such a person, she/he may try to approach her and work out some sort of compromise whereby the break would not be complete.

CARING FOR A SIBLING — AT WHAT COST?

My mother is exceptionally close to her younger sister, who developed a dreadful disease almost four years ago, but kept it secret until recently, when treatment stopped working and she began to deteriorate. My mother is now constantly with her at her bedside, neglecting her own family who also need her. She is also neglecting her own health, not eating or sleeping properly.

I dread to think what is going to happen to my mother if there is no miraculous cure. What can we do to impress on her that her family needs her?

W hen there is strong emotion, logical argument may not accomplish much. Nevertheless, if there is a rav whom your mother respects, he may be able to impress her.

Considering that unfortunately the situation may not be of long duration, sit back and let your mother do as she sees fit. Make sure your mother is eating and drinking adequately and in no risk of severe repercussions to her own health. As to how she will eventually adjust, let me cite something from the Torah (*II Samuel*, 12:15-23). King David had a child who was very sick. He fasted and prayed fervently and could not be consoled. When the child died, the palace personnel did not tell him, because they were worried about his reaction. To their surprise, when he discovered it, he bathed, changed his clothes, and ate. He explained, "As long as the child was alive, I prayed to Hashem for mercy. But now, I cannot retrieve him, so why should I fast? He will not come back to me, and eventually I will go to him."

It is important to allow your mother to do as much as she feels able to for this sister. Perhaps her own family's needs can be taken care of without her input at this time. Empathize with your mother and help her so that in the end she will not have any feelings of guilt or despair.

May Hashem grant your aunt a *refuah sheleimah*.

COMPARING MY LOT WITH THAT OF MY SIBLINGS

We come from an out-of-town community. My wife and I have only two children after close to 20 years of marriage and both have special needs. But that is not what I am writing about; they attend appropriate programs that are good for their needs. I am productive and have a career.

My problem is that I know that in the frum world someone in our situation is pitied because of the perception that success means having a large family with outstanding children who excel in learning. I feel that while we are friendly with many people they pity us even though they will not say anything, while in the secular world I would be considered a respected person since I have a career and the children's situation is not considered a shortcoming as it is in our circles.

With Pesach coming, the problem is magnified, since we are going to my parents. My siblings are more modern than we are, but they have larger families that provide more nachas, excel in yeshivah, etc. When everyone is at the table together, the contrast is obvious. I feel uncomfortable in this situation. I spend much time learning about bitachon and overcoming envy but the feelings are still there. Making the seder alone is not really an option, since my sons do enjoy being with the extended family and my wife has no family with whom to share Pesach.

Any ideas you can provide will be appreciated.

We cannot avoid being influenced by the values of our environment, although they may fall far short of what is just and proper. The standards people use to judge others are those that each society or subculture establishes, but are not true values and certainly not Torah values.

The first paragraph in the *Shulchan Aruch* states that a person should be firm in his Torah convictions and should not retreat if others mock him. Nor should a person feel less worthy if he does not achieve what society considers to be success.

You are doing what is best for your children to maximize their potential. If you are a devoted husband and father, fulfilling Torah obligations to the best of your ability, then you deserve to have self-respect. You need not compare yourself to others.

To be proud is not to be vain. Sometimes the feeling, "I am being pitied" is the result of the feeling, "I deserve to be pitied."

I think that there is truth in the statement, "No one can put me down except me, myself." You have every reason to be as proud of your family as your siblings are of theirs. You have to be able to continue on your course without making comparisons. There is no one at fault here and there is nothing that can be changed. Your family may feel badly that things have not worked out differently for you, but that is not the same as pitying you. I am reasonably sure that they are proud of the way you are caring for your children and that you are leading a productive and successful life. Maintain your self-respect and you will have an enjoyable Pesach with the extended family.

DAUGHTER HEADED TO A SECOND ABUSIVE MARRIAGE

My daughter emerged from a very abusive marriage. She has met a man whom she likes a great deal, but I can see that he is a very domineering type, and I'm afraid that she is jumping from the frying pan into the fire. He seems to be very controlling. I pointed this out to her, but she disagrees. I think that she is very lonely, and her need for companionship is blinding her to this character flaw.

I don't know what to do to prevent her from making a second disastrous marriage. I could take a stand and say that I am absolutely against her marrying him, and that I will refuse to go to the wedding. Is that the right thing to do?

W e don't know if you are correct in your evaluation of this person, but let us assume that you are. If your daughter really wants to marry him, your objection is not likely to stop her. She will probably marry him, and you will be out of the picture. If he is a controlling person, you will have saved him the job of alienating your daughter from you, because the break will already have taken place.

Actually, everyone leaving a failed marriage would be very wise to promptly avail themselves of counseling. There are many painful issues that should be discussed, and getting help in disentangling from the previous relationship can pave the way for a much better remarriage.

In your present situation, you might suggest to your daughter that she consult someone to discuss this relationship. You can point out to her that her painful experiences from the first marriage have undoubtedly left some emotional scars, and these can prevent a happy adjustment in remarriage. You will then not come across as an obstacle. If she accepts this suggestion, she will be much more capable of evaluating this new relationship.

Whatever happens, your daughter should feel that she can always turn to you, even if you disagree with her on any particular issue.

TORN BETWEEN TWO OBLIGATIONS

I'm in a dilemma. I'm the oldest of eight children. My mother battled depression for most of her life, but was somehow able to manage until the past few years, when she hardly gets out of bed.

I married six years ago and we have B"H three children. For the past two years, I've been making Shabbos for my parents and siblings (the three youngest are home, the others are either married or in yeshivah). I sometimes have to help the two youngest ones with their homework.

My husband has been great about it, but there is just that much time in a day, and he says that my spending all that time at my parents is taking away from the care I should be giving our own children. I know he is right, but if I don't do for my parents and siblings, I feel terribly guilty. What is the right thing to do?

It seems that you have several siblings who are married. Are they helping out as much as they can, or is the entire burden placed on you?

You may actually be spending more time with your parents than they require, but if you are motivated by guilt feelings, you may be unable to see this. It is of the utmost importance for you to figure out how much time you can reasonably give to your parents and your unmarried siblings. Once you have this figure, you must prioritize and take care of the most pressing matters in the allotted time. It is entirely possible that if your siblings see that you are not there to take care of all the necessary matters, they will fill the void. But whether or not they assume their share of the burden, your first obligation is to your husband and family. I reiterate — prioritize and do all you can do and not one iota more. You should consult a social worker and go over all the details of your parents' conditions and what their needs are. You may find that by attending to what their real needs are rather than to what you *think* they are, you will not be spending as much time there. If necessary, the social worker may be able to find additional ways in which some of their needs can be met.

PARENTS-IN-LAW

MOTHER-IN-LAW SPILLS THE BEANS

My mother-in-law is a very nice woman but she cannot keep a secret. After I was married I was shocked to hear our private matters, which we told only to our parents, being openly discussed by my husbands' siblings and nieces. My mother-in-law also tells us about her other children's private matters (for example: This one is into a shidduch with so-and-so, or that one is considering a new apartment, etc.) and she'll add, "But don't tell anyone, because they don't want me to talk about it." When my sister heard something private about me from a third cousin who heard it from my husband's sister, we decided we'd had enough. We stopped telling my mother-in-law anything until we were ready for it to go public. Sometimes I feel my mother-in-law might be hurt when we do not reveal things

*that people normally tell parents. Must I
take her feelings into account and let my
private matters become public knowledge
before we are ready to tell anyone?*

According to halachah, if you tell someone something with instruction not to reveal it to anyone, it is forbidden to do so.

You certainly have a right to privacy, and if your mother-in-law reveals things you wish to withhold from public knowledge, you do not have to share them with her. She may not even notice this. If she does bring it up, you may say, "Mom, there were things we told you in private that came back to us from others. We share with you information that we consider private and personal, because we feel so close to you and love you dearly. However, these matters are truly personal and were not intended to be told to anyone else. We'll be glad to share everything with you if we can be assured that it does not any further."

MY MOTHER-IN-LAW INTIMATES THAT I'M JUST NOT GOOD ENOUGH

---

*I am newlywed, actually for only four
months, but I'm beginning to have trouble.
My husband's mother says and does things to
put me down. I think I am a good balabusta,
but she intimates in many ways that I am
not good enough, and that she has to do
things for her son to compensate for my
deficiencies. When I repeat these hints
to my husband, instead of supporting me,
he defends his mother, and this drives me
crazy. How can I get him to see that unless*

he puts her in her place, this can ruin our marriage?

This is very early in your marriage, and I think that counseling from a Torah-true marriage counselor or a *rav* who is competent in marriage counseling can clarify the problem and prevent the development of serious friction.

I cannot speak for your particular situation, but I do wish to share with you a case that I had, in which competent counseling saved the marriage.

I have written about the problem of low self-esteem (*Life's Too Short* and *Angels Don't Leave Footprints*). Many people have *totally unwarranted* feelings of inadequacy and inferiority, and may resort to one or more ways to escape these distressing feelings.

Wilma is a woman whose unwarranted feelings of low self-esteem caused her to feel unlikable, and she desperately wanted to be liked. Wilma became a people-pleaser, doing things for others in the hope that this would gain her their affection. Naomi, who married Wilma's son, defended her own low self-esteem by being extremely self-sufficient. Naomi considered accepting help from anyone in any shape or form to be an indication of weakness, and this was intolerable to her.

You can imagine what happened when Wilma wanted to be helpful to Naomi, who could not tolerate being helped in any way. When Wilma sent the children a cake for Shabbos, Naomi said, "What is it with your mother? Does she think I can't bake a cake? What does she think I am, a helpless cripple or something?" Zalman tried to explain that his mother had no intention of insulting her, but Naomi could not accept logic. "Don't try to defend your mother!" she said. This caused a rift between Zalman and Naomi.

A brief period of counseling enabled Zalman and Naomi to understand Wilma's behavior. Naomi realized that by accepting things from her mother-in-law, she was actually helping *her*, and this made Naomi feel good. In addition, Naomi was enabled to see that while it is good to be self-sufficient, there was no need to be defensive when someone wanted to do something nice for her.

This may not apply to your situation, but it is very likely that with a better understanding of what is transpiring between you, your mother-in-law, and your husband, this issue can be smoothed out, with benefit to everyone.

MORBID EXPECTATIONS

My mother-in-law is a wonderful person, and we get along very well. There is something that has really started to annoy me lately, however. She is a very nervous person and has always displayed her over-concern about many things (such as driving at night, or my driving alone). She is anxious and worried over the slightest things and is constantly thinking up unlikely scenarios and imagining that they can happen if I don't do something to prevent them. Recently, it has gotten to the point that it bothers me more so than before, since B"H I now have children for her to overly nervous about as well. I am a responsible person, as I believe she knows, and am in no way the type that would let my toddler run around outside by himself, or leave my stroller outside or at the front of the store, which unfortunately I see too often. It often seems that she doesn't trust me, which obviously doesn't make me feel very good, but what's worse is that it seems as if she doesn't trust that Hashem is watching over us.

I am aware that people are very bothered by faults in others that they themselves have, and I admit that I, too, am struggling with this as well. I am by no means as nervous as she, but I have an overactive imagination and do tend to worry. I am

*working hard on this because I would hate to
live a life like that. I know that Hashem
runs the world and we are not in complete
control. I want to feel calm and not be an
overprotective mother. When I see how she
is, I feel so bad for her. I know that it is
a terrible feeling to always be so worried,
and I know only a fraction of what she must
be feeling. Is there any respectful way I
can mention this to her? I don't want to
ruin our relationship, but I also don't want
her to have to feel this way for the rest of
her life, and her suggestions and comments
are really starting to get on my nerves.*

S ome people have "morbid expectations." The reason for this is not clear. As far as what to do about it, I recommend saying *Perek* 112 of *Tehillim* daily, in which King David says that a person who is a *yorei shamayim* "will not fear any evil tidings; his heart is firm in trust in Hashem." Although this a statement of fact about a *yorei shamayim*, it can be said as a *tefillah*, i.e., "Please help me to have *bitachon*, so that I should not have fears of bad things happening."

We pray to Hashem for all our needs. *Bitachon* is certainly a great need, and we should pray for it.

You might share this with your mother-in-law, saying, "I know how you are always worried about us. Here is a *tefillah* that may relieve your stress." This is a very respectful and constructive way of saying it.

WHAT SHOULD I DO? MY MOTHER-IN-LAW IRKS ME

*I have a very sweet, special, mother-in-
law, an almanah, for whom I am constantly
struggling to have proper respect. Although*

I share a very warm relationship with
her, many times, unfortunately, I am
noticeably irked by her and have often made
underhanded, cruel comments.

Over the years, I have come to realize
— with the help of others from whom I
have asked advice — much of the root of
the problem. The underlying causes: my
own insecurity and jealousy. I fought the
feeling of having my home "taken over" even
though she never did, or meant to do, that.
I was also very self-conscious about my
imperfect housekeeping abilities, especially
as my family grew, bli ayin hara.

Not that she ever criticized me — on the
contrary, she complimented me to the high
heavens, which itself would irk me very much.
I was rubbed the wrong way by her formality
and what I perceived as her superiority.

At present, I can best define the problem
as not properly fulfilling the mitzvah of
v'ahavta l'reiacha kamocha — especially
someone to whom I owe so much.

I realize that, on the one hand, I am very
much a victim of normal human frailty. On
the other hand, I desperately must rectify
the aveiros I transgressed, which include
kol almanah lo sanun and lo sonu, etc.

Many years ago, on the advice of a rav,
I began learning shemiras halashon daily
(in addition to Hilchos Chofetz Chaim) to
help me work out this problem. I developed
a chart for myself which I read each time
she comes and mark afterwards. And, more
recently, I began learning a few lines of
Igeres Ha"Gra each day.

It has been a nisayon to treat her with
proper respect, to have the patience to make
her feel worthwhile and needed — especially
when I am under pressure.

Although I have improved much in this area, I have slipped far too often and hurt my bitterly lonely mother-in-law. I would appreciate any insight, mussar, and/or suggestions on how I can completely correct this problem.

From your description, it appears that there is no logical reason for the way you feel. As you point out, she was complimentary rather than critical, and you know that she did not intend to "take over" your home. If there is no *logical* reason for your feelings, the only conclusion is that there is a *non-logical* reason.

Intellect and emotion do not operate according to the same rules. Intellect operates according to logic, emotions do not.

For example, I may meet someone for the first time, and although he has not spoken a single word to me, I may feel some negativity toward him. This may be a psychological quirk. In some way, often trivial, he reminds me of someone I did not like. To the subconscious mind, any similarity between the two is reason enough to identify one with the other.

At some point in your life, there may have been a person who irritated you, and you may have had an intense dislike for that person, (let's call him/her "A"). You may think you have totally forgotten about that, but your subconscious mind did not forget. Many years later, another person comes along, (let's call him/her "B"), who in some way, even in a very minute and remote way, has some kind of similarity to the person you disliked. It may be a mannerism, a hair style, a facial expression, or anything else. While you know that person A is *not* person B, and you have no reason to dislike person A, your *subconscious* thinks otherwise. The fragmentary similarity of A to B is enough reason for your subconscious mind to generate negative feelings toward person A, *as if* he/she were person B.

It may well be that there is some subconscious reason for your feelings toward your mother-in-law. So, when you feel irked by your mother-in-law, it is not she who irks you, and you really have no logical reason to feel irked by her. But your subconscious mind makes you feel irked by her, because it does not operate according to logic.

If you understand this, you need not feel guilty, because you can say to yourself, "My mother-in-law really does not irk me. It's this residual emotion from the past that makes me feel this way." This can actually eventually eliminate the negative feelings toward her, and you will be able to feel true appreciation and *hakaras hatov*.

Some people may choose to receive therapy to overcome these feelings. I believe that what you are doing is very wise. There is much in our *sifrei mussar* about dealing with improper feelings. And, of course, *tefillah* is very important. It is related that the Chofetz Chaim would open the *aron kodesh* and pray tearfully that Hashem should take away his feelings of anger.

One method is to continue working on your positive *middos*, which, of course, every person should do. Just as light and darkness cannot coexist, neither can good *middos* and bad *middos* coexist. To the degree that we increase our good *middos*, we lessen the strength of the bad *middos*. As you increase your feelings of *chessed* and *ahavas Yisroel*, the negative feelings are lessened and may be totally eliminated.

HUSBAND DOMINATED BY HIS FATHER

I have been married for nearly two years and I love my husband very much, but I'm about ready to leave the marriage. Does that sound crazy?

My husband's father is a very domineering person, and my husband cowers before him. He's been that way since childhood. Anything his father says, he jumps to it. It makes no difference what we have planned or want. We make plans to go on a vacation, and his father vetoes it, to give just one example.

My husband says I should talk to his father because he can't stand up to him. I don't want to be the "bad guy" and be accused of being the boss and turning my husband against his family.

We just bought a car. When his father discovered that we had not consulted him regarding which car to buy, he refused to talk to my husband for a week. (Actually, I welcomed that, but my husband was a wreck.) My husband was actually ready to give the car back, and I said, "If the car goes, I go." I couldn't care less about the car, but I feel we have to stand up for ourselves.

My husband knows this situation is wrong, but says he can't do anything about it. He knows it hurts me and he doesn't want to hurt me, but he's helpless. I've even suggested moving 3000 miles away to save our marriage, but my husband says he can't do that. Besides, his father would control him from the moon. I'm living with a very unhappy man, and we fight constantly about this. We have a beautiful baby, and I don't want to break up the marriage, but it seems that I may not have a choice.

This is a problem that should be carefully discussed, either with a *rav* who is experienced in marriage counseling or with a marriage counselor. Nevertheless, I can mention several points that you should consider.

Marriage is often a delicate balancing act. On the one hand, there is the overwhelmingly important mitzvah of *kibud av*, and on the other hand, the same Torah that requires *kibud av* says, "Therefore a man shall leave his father and mother and devote himself to his wife" (*Bereishis*, 2:24), and halachah states that a wife's first loyalty is to her husband. It takes great skill to steer a safe course between these two principles.

Parents do not want their children's marriage to fail. I am sure that your father-in-law does not understand the stress he is putting on your marriage. He is simply relating to your husband the way he has for two decades, and quite likely, that may be how it traditionally was in his family. It has simply not occurred to him that there is any other way, and he may not realize that his son's marriage has created a new situation in which the rules are different.

You and your husband must first come to the conclusion that the two of you are a unit and not two separate individuals. You cannot get anyone else to respect this if you do not do so yourselves.

Don't criticize your father-in-law to your husband. That puts him on the defensive, even though basically he agrees with you.

There are indeed sacrifices that may be necessary to make for parents, but *the marriage cannot be sacrificed.*

Both of you actually want the same thing but don't know how to go about it. You should understand your husband's feelings and he should understand yours. After discussing it patiently and cool-headedly between yourselves, you should consult a *rav* to make sure that you do not violate *kibud av.* With the guidance of a counselor, you should both meet with your in-laws and assure them of your love and respect for them, and tell them that they may not be aware of the stress they are wreaking on your marriage. Point out to your in-laws that you know they want your happiness. (Decide beforehand who is going to speak for both of you, and make it clear that it *is* for both of you.) Whichever one is the speaker, you should give your husband much support. He's going to need it.

Let your in-laws know that you appreciate how they have raised their son, but now that he is married, the relationship changes, although the love, loyalty, and respect for them does not change. You will be happy to consult them, because they are more experienced and wiser, but ultimately you will be making your decisions as a couple, and you hope they will respect that.

I wish it were possible to do this without hurting them, but they may be hurt by realizing that they must relinquish the control they have had for the past two decades. Although they may not be pleased with this, parents generally do not forfeit relationships with their children. As you wrote, after refusing to talk with your husband over the car incident, your father-in-law resumed conversation after a week.

Realizing that they may be hurt by your joint stand, you should do everything possible to demonstrate your caring for them. It may take a while, but they will adjust to the reality that their son now has a family of his own.

Again, this is a delicate balancing act. You must preserve your marriage while observing *kibud av*. With patience and proper guidance, this can be achieved.

I BEG TO DIFFER

I was surprised at your response to the woman with the domineering father-in-law (FIL). You ignore the fact that the FIL is a dictatorial personality who seems to have destroyed his son's personality and is about to destroy their marriage. You advise the woman to sweetly, "Let your in-laws know that you appreciate how they have raised their son"! Can she say this honestly to a FIL who needs to crush all signs of independence and autonomy in his child and has caused them both untold anguish? Then you say, "Point out to your in-laws that you know they want your happiness." Really! Have you ever confronted a control freak and tried to point anything out? Do they listen to reason or logic? Do they care what anyone else thinks or feels?

Abusive parents do not have their children's best interests at heart. It is a terrible disservice to give the impression that kibud horim is an all-encompassing mitzvah that requires that children to accept abuse passively and allow their lives

> to be utterly destroyed. All too often the
> term kibud horim, like shalom bayis, is
> misused by abusers to satisfy their appetite
> for power. And this seems to be the case
> here. It's very naïve to think that mere
> "communication skills" will solve such
> problems.

Perhaps you should re-read the response. I pointed out quite clearly that one need not sacrifice one's marriage for parents. However, just where the parameters are for *kibud horim* is something a *posek* must decide and provide guidelines for proper action. Neither you nor I can make that decision. As you know, even if one sees one's father committing a flagrant sin, the halachah is that one should point it out to him in a way that is not offensive.

Insofar as your comment that controlling parents do not have their children's best interests at heart, that is simply incorrect. The real problem is that *they think they know* what is in their children's best interest. Furthermore, I suggest you read Rashi in *Shemos*, 22:1. Halachah does not recognize any exception to the love of a father for a son.

This woman's husband is a person of whom she thinks highly. Obviously, he grew up to be a decent person. The fact is that the son was raised to be a fine person. This does not exonerate the father's controlling, but neither should the parents be denied the credit for raising their son. In *Yevamos* (88b), the Talmud points out that even when one is punished for a sin, his good deeds should be mentioned.

The response began with the caveat that competent marriage counseling is essential. That would provide the husband with the opportunity to examine his relationship to his father, and guide him to do what is best, giving him the requisite support.

The suggestions I made are to be considered as "band-aids" to forestall the confrontation that would put the husband in the terrible position of having to make a choice between his father and his wife, without the counseling and support that would enable him to act prudently.

REJECTED OUT OF HAND

My daughter was an older girl when she married and we were not involved at all with her finding her husband. We met her choson for the first time at her vort, and did not see him again until the chasunah. After they were married, we found out that my daughter's husband had decided he wants nothing to do with my husband because of some motzei shem rah he heard when making inquiries about our daughter. I tried to ask him nicely if he could show some derech eretz to my husband but he refused, saying that he makes up his own mind. My husband never did anything to provoke this; our son-in-law simply decided, before he ever got to know my husband, that he doesn't want to know him, period. Their relationship never even got off the ground. When we visit our daughter, if her husband is there, he walks out, or ignores my husband totally, never greets him or makes any small talk whatsoever. If my husband calls to speak with our daughter and her husband answers, he'll say she's not there and just hang up. They have never visited us in our home although they have been married for several years. He doesn't act that way with me; he is friendly toward me, but I feel very cool toward him because an affront to my husband is an affront to me. There are no valid grounds for our son-in-law's behavior, because he only based his opinion on hearsay and he never gave my husband a chance. What can or should we do to make this relationship better?

If your son-in-law's behavior is rooted in emotional reasons, logical argument is not likely to make an impact. "Don't confuse me with the facts — my mind is made up," as the saying goes.

If your son-in-law is a Torah-observant person, and you do communicate with him, you might tell him that halachah involves not only the laws of Shabbos and the laws of *kashrus* and the like, but also *bein adam lachavero*, interpersonal relations. A person's impression that something is kosher or *tereifeh* does not justify a decision. He must take his observations to a *posek* for a ruling.

The halachos of *lashon hara* are every bit as complicated as the laws of *kashrus*. Before one acts on the basis of negative information, one must ask a *sh'eilah*.

If your son-in-law is adamant in rejecting this consideration, you may wish to talk to his *rav*, who may be able to convince him that he is not at liberty to make decisions such as this on his own. If halachah justifies his behavior, it must be respected. If he refuses to consider halachah, I regret that I cannot suggest anything.

I do not recommend that your daughter try to convince him, because that is unlikely to accomplish anything and may jeopardize their *shalom bayis*. However, it would be wise for her to receive some counseling, because she is in the difficult position of conflicting loyalties, and may need help in steering a course.

BUT WHAT DID WE DO WRONG?

I have always enjoyed the wisdom of your responses. This time I am faced with a crisis myself. We married off our fourth child about a year ago. We were very happy with the shidduch and the whole simchah was celebrated with much excitement.

Shortly after the wedding, my new daughter-in-law fell into bed for a few weeks, she totally lost her appetite and felt extremely weak. As a concerned mother I called to hear how she's feeling, what the doctor said … if she took blood tests … if perhaps there may be good news, etc. All the tests came back fine and slowly she regained her strength and started feeling better.

At that point, I was informed by my new daughter-in-law that my son had made her sick, and that **he** will be going for therapy. She also told me that my son will not be allowed to talk to me for the next three months because I had meddled too much in their affairs. I was so shocked and confused and embarrassed by what was happening that I kept quiet, hoping it would resolve on its own.

But the three months are almost 10 — and I have not heard from my children since. I have called them countless times, but all my calls and messages are ignored. When I once reached my son in kollel, he said, "It's either you or my wife, whom should I choose?" Of course, I said "Your wife." He put down the phone and that was the last time I spoke to him. We've been through happy occasions and difficult times over the past year and each time the couple was notified by siblings and messengers and begged to join or at least call, but all our cries went unheeded.

We've tried reaching my son through various professionals, but all came back empty-handed. He refuses to speak to anyone about this, and claims that whatever he's doing is right, for the sake of his shalom bayis. My son was always assiduous in honoring his parents and enjoyed close relationships with his siblings. But he is rather soft in nature, and obviously doesn't have the courage to stand up to her. I feel like my son was kidnaped from us. He is being *brainwashed by a therapist who was hired by and is being paid by her parents, and is willing to speak only to them. My poor son is oblivious to the trap he is in, and I fear that one day he will wake up from his dream and have to confront a very harsh reality.*

I worry about my son all the time. I do not want to destroy his shalom bayis, but I am sure he is miserable being cut off from his parents and family. I am quite sure that his emotional abuse does not only affect his relationship with his family, but with his wife as well.

I need advice on how to deal with this situation. Should I be aggressive and let my son know what's happening, at all costs, or should I wait it out, perhaps forever, and hope that time will heal matters.

In order to try and remedy a problem, one must have access to it. If you lock the door and don't allow the repairman to enter the house, there's no way the appliance can be fixed.

I have seen similar tragic situations, where a spouse tries to alienate the other spouse from his/her family. Very often this is a "control" issue. In a control relationship, one spouse exerts control, while the other allows himself/herself to be controlled. In some instances, one may accuse the other spouse's parents of serious misbehavior. Sometimes when the alienated parents ask, "What have we done that was wrong?" the only answer they get is, "You should know." Some alienated parents said that although they did not have the slightest idea why they were being alienated, they said, "Please forgive us for whatever we've done wrong," but to no avail.

A therapist can know only what the client tells him, and if, for example, the client says that his parents abused him, the therapist has no way of knowing whether this is true, and generally accepts the client's account. In some situations, the parents may in fact have been negative to their child but are unaware of this, and cannot understand why their child is reacting that way.

In one case, when the couple refused to let the parents see the grandchildren, the parents went to court and sued under the law providing for "grandparents' rights."

Because of professional confidentiality, your son's therapist cannot talk to you without his authorization. If you know who the therapist is, you may write him a letter with any information you want him to have, but he cannot respond to you.

There is no point in being aggressive, because it is only likely to make things worse. In one situation, alienated parents went to their daughter's home in the hope of trying to find out what was going on. The husband slammed the door on them and said that if they came again he would call the police.

It is impossible to remedy a situation when there is no contact. Where there is a desire to improve relationships, a family therapist can be helpful, but if one party does not wish to participate, there is nothing one can do. If you know of a *rav* or *Rosh Yeshivah* whom your son respects, you may ask him to contact your son, and perhaps he can find out what is happening.

As difficult and heart-breaking as the situation is at the moment, there is nothing for you to do except wait it out and offer your deeply felt prayers to the *Ribbono Shel Olam* that it be resolved quickly.

ALOOF DAUGHTER-IN-LAW

My son was married six months ago, and appears to be happy, but his wife, who works as a teacher, is very cold toward me. I can't understand why, because I've always been very nice to her. She hardly talks to me. If she is cold toward me, I don't want to push myself on her.

Her mother died when she was eight, and her father remarried when she was sixteen. His wife seems to be a very pleasant person.

I just found out that my daughter-in-law's mother had been mentally ill, and was

Inasmuch as your son seems to be happy, and she is holding a job, I don't think there is any reason to be concerned that she is depressed.

What is much more likely is that since her mother was probably depressed through much of her childhood, she may not have learned the ABC's of relating to a mother. By the time her father remarried, her character was already formed, and she may simply not know how to relate to you.

It is very much like being in a foreign country and not knowing the language. You cannot relate when you don't have the tools with which to relate.

Your daughter-in-law may very much desire to relate to you, but simply doesn't know how, so do not misinterpret her being "cold" to you as an indication of dislike. Now that you can understand why she is this way, try to be warm toward her. Invite her over, offer to help her with shopping, etc., without pushing yourself on her. You may tell her, "I'd love to do things with you, but I know you have your own schedule. Don't be afraid to say 'no' to me. I promise I won't be offended."

Her behavior is not going to change suddenly, but if you continue being empathic and warm toward her, she will eventually be able to relate to you.

MOTHER-IN-LAW IS SELF-CENTERED

*I am writing about an issue that has been
addressed on several occasions, if not by*

you than by many others — the issue of
mothers-in-law. I have three main issues
that I feel that I could use advice on.

The first issue is the issue of apathy. My
husband comes from a family of nine sons and
one daughter. My in-laws have the attitude
that once their sons are married they are on
their own, both financially and emotionally.
Although "financially" has bothered me on
several occasions, I B"H do not need their
support so it does not bother me as much
as emotional apathy. My mother-in-law shows
no true sign of caring about her sons or
their wives; once in a while she may show
something in a very unnatural way, obviously
doing it only for show. She will never call
us when someone is not feeling well, nor
when someone has moved, etc. When one of
my sisters-in law moved, I asked my mother-
in-law who was going to help them, and she
answered "Who helped me?"

Now I feel that if she would be totally
apathetic I would ignore her and live my own
life, but that is not the case. When others
will see or hear (sadly, my mother-in-law is
very concerned about what other people say)
then she needs us there. For example, when
the new kallah came to visit she wanted us to
come. This was understandable, but when I told
her that it would be impossible since I had
just started a new job and was exhausted and
my baby was not feeling well, she angrily told
my husband that she would never forget it if I
did not come. Now she is definitely not being
malicious since it is not her personality, but
what bothers me is that she does not think
before she talks or acts. She also does not
think about her children and is very busy with
herself. My other sisters-in-law feel the same
way and are also upset about this.

Interestingly enough, this does not bother my husband at all, even through my mother-in-law does show interest in her daughter's life and is there for her much more than for her sons. I guess he was raised this way. It bothers me terribly, especially since I come from a warm and supportive home. It feels funny to write this, but it also bothers me that it does not bother him; this makes me direct my anger and frustration at him. Now, because it does not bother him, he wants us to have a close relationship with his parents by going to visit often and calling them. This is hard for me because every time I interact with my mother-in-law these issues come up and upset me.

My second issue is that my mother-in-law and sister-in-law will often degrade my husband, mostly about his learning and level of ruchniyus, in front of me. Although things are not said in a mean way, nevertheless it hurts. For example, one afternoon my mother-in-law called up my husband and nudged him to go with her to visit someone. Now my husband as well as my father-in-law learn in kollel, so my mother-in-law definitely knows the schedule. My husband asked if his father would also be going. My mother-in-law answered in a shocked voice, "Of course not, he has a chavrusah, and how could he miss his learning session?" I was right there and it hurt me terribly that she would never disturb her husband, but felt it was o.k. to disturb my husband. Sometimes my sister-in-law will ask my husband to baby-sit her children because her husband needs to learn. While she will never call her husband in middle of seder, she always calls mine during his learning. Also, they will often send my husband to places that their husbands would never go, etc.

My final issue is that I feel that my
mother-in-law does not like me. Throughout
the years of my marriage I have tried to
be a good daughter-in-law; I call her; I
compliment her, her son, and her other
children all the time; I send pictures of
my baby and call her to give her nachas.
This all does not help. I still feel that
she does not appreciate me and what bothers
me even more is that she has no problem
telling me about what she does for the other
daughters-in-law. One of them is very fancy
and is good for her image and another one
lives overseas (I am not jealous and am
actually very close to the one overseas) but
it hurts me that I am the one who tries and
my efforts are not appreciated.

For example, one day three of us daughters-
in-law went to a mall and the daughter did
not come along. Right before we left I said
that we should call the daughter since she
would feel left out. We did, but she did
not answer and we left without her. She
was very hurt and so was my mother-in-law.
What bothered me was that I got the flack
from both my mother-in-law and sister-in-
law. That night we went to a bar mitzvah
and I was the only one not complimented
on my clothes. My sister-in-law ignored me
throughout the affair. The entire time I
wished that I could tell her that I was the
one who called her, but I not want her to be
upset at the others.

Someone said that maybe my mother-in-
law feels intimidated by me since I am (I
hate to write this, but it may make the
picture clearer) B"H very capable. I am
a professional with a large clientele and
at the same time I am a very organized
housewife. I also appear to be very

*confident. My mother-in-law is the opposite
of me in these ways. Although this might
be the case, when I spoke to my mother-in-
law once about capable daughters-in-law, she
said that she loves to see her sons marry
good girls and wants them to have everything
that she is not. Knowing my mother-in-law,
she was telling the truth, and her nature
is to fargin other people, so she probably
means what she said.*

I f your description of your mother-in-law is valid, that she "is busy with herself" and does not think about her children, then you must understand that a person who sees only him/herself does not have a realistic perception of anything or anyone else. It is a kind of psychological blindness, and expecting a person such as this to act differently if you bring it up to them is like trying to explain a rainbow to a sightless person. Circumstances in her life may have formed her personality that way. If you understand this, everything else she does falls into place.

If people develop personality disorders that alter their perception of reality, we may not be able to blame them for their behavior. Unless they get help to change, they do not see that there is anything wrong with them, and precisely because they see nothing wrong, they will not seek help. But even though they may not be at fault for the way they are, one does not have to be a constant victim of their behavior.

Halachah requires that one respect parents-in-law (*Yoreh Deah*, 240). She is the way she is, and you may try to limit your exposure to her, but you must address her respectfully.

To your husband, she is a mother, and a child desires a close relationship to one's parents. Because of his feelings for her, he may not be able to see her shortcomings, and it is important that you understand that. You may point out to him how she behaves toward you, but if he doesn't react the way you desire, remember that when emotions conflict with logic, emotions usually prevail. His desire for a closeness with his mother is not a reflection of his feelings toward you. He holds you in high regard, but still wishes a relationship with his mother.

If your mother-in-law degrades your husband, you should respectfully state that you do not wish to hear any unwarranted criticism of him.

Your relationship with your sister-in-law is different than the one with your mother-in-law. If your sister-in-law takes unfair advantage of your husband, you should tell her that this is unacceptable. Ideally, he should stand up for himself and not allow himself to be mistreated. But again, the family dynamic may have been such that he has always complied with his siblings' wishes. He would need counseling to change this attitude.

You are to be commended for trying to be a good daughter-in-law. You must be respectful, but it is not necessary that you allow anyone to walk over you. If she does not appreciate you, it may be because, if she is absorbed in herself, she cannot appreciate anyone.

THERAPIST BLAMES PARENTS

I have a daughter who was quite "leibedig" as a child, and seemed to need a little more gashmiyus than my other children. I always bent over backwards to make her happy, which was difficult, because my wife grew up in an abnormally strict and unloving environment, and she was really too critical and too "tight" in gashmiyus for this child's needs, but I fought and won at every turn for everything I thought this child needed. In fact, by the time she got to high school she seemed to have turned into a settled, wonderful person, and was liked and respected by all, teachers, peers, etc. She married a wonderful boy from a wonderful family, and our other children held up this couple in particular as a role model that they would choose to emulate when they marry and raise their own children.

Last winter this child fell into a severe depression (after years of marriage, and several children). The blame was laid at our doorstep, for having been too strict and unloving. I cannot tell you how I felt, aside from my grief for the sake of my child, how hurt I was because I had stood at her side all the way through and many times suffered greatly on her behalf fighting for what I felt she needed. Many times we asked "sh'eilos" when my spouse and I disagreed on how to deal with her, and we were always told to be generous, and my wife always followed the psak. Of course that can't make up for lack of love (my wife is just not a warm person, surely as a result of the way she herself was mishandled as a child) but I had always tried so hard to compensate, and here she had been doing beautifully for so many years!

At a certain point my daughter agreed to speak with my spouse and she "let her have it" for the way things were when she was growing up. My spouse, who felt terrible, accepted the mussar and begged to be forgiven. About a half-a-year after the original incident, things seemed okay and it looked like it would be history — and then, about a year after the original incident there was a relapse. For three months we did not receive even a phone call. Then my daughter and son-in-law began calling once a week, speaking only to me, and I sort of understood that I am not allowed to call them, neither do I see my precious grandchildren. They do not speak to my spouse at all.

I have many questions, but I have never asked any; I am afraid to utter a wrong syllable. I am very concerned for my daughter, who I sense is not happy, even

*though she does stay away from us. How can
a person feel happy if she cuts herself off
from her roots? Why do the mental health
professionals not bring up any positive
aspects or positive memories of childhood
and our family — we are NOT evil people, and
Baruch Hashem she has wonderful siblings,
kain ayin hara. Why don't the therapists
say, "You have to move on, make a break
with the past, it's over"? What about the
fact that kibbud av v'em is not dependent
on the perfection of the parents? How can a
person feel good about himself/herself when
he/she knows he/she can't do that mitzvah?
And most of all, WHY DON'T THE MENTAL
HEALTH PROFESSIONALS INTERVIEW US AND GET
BOTH SIDES OF THE STORY? There is so much
of which they are not aware that could be
helpful. Please, can you help this child?
I am so worried for her.*

Although the way parents relate to a child certainly has an impact on the child's feelings, I have spoken out on numerous occasions that impaling the parents is a serious mistake. Parents cannot be perfect, and except in cases of frank abuse, parents' intentions are generally for the good of the child.

One of the mysteries of how Hashem runs the world is that we attain our maximum wisdom in our senior years, whereas the most important decisions in our lives, such as marriage and parenting, are made at an age when our wisdom is meager. But that is how it is. Children should understand that their parents raised them in the best way they knew, although this may have been woefully lacking. Blaming the parents for the child's difficulties may result in alienation from the parents, and the child loses the support of those who love him/her the most.

Therapists have a confidential relationship with the client, and cannot talk to the parent without the client's permission. Nevertheless, since the client's account may be a distortion, a therapist may suggest to the client that he/she would like to meet with the parents, and, if desirable, in joint session. If the client refuses, the therapist cannot communicate with the parents.

There is a concept of "psychic reality," which means that whether or not something actually happened the way the client describes it, the client is reacting to it as he/she remembers it. A skilled therapist should be able to help the client deal with these feelings without confirming that the client's account represents reality. If this is done, there is no reason for the client to be turned against one's parents.

There are therapists who specialize in family therapy. You might suggest to your daughter that you would like to join her in family therapy sessions so that negative feelings can be eliminated.

SHOULD WE BE CONCERNED?

This is an issue that I have been thinking about for a long time. I think your comments could help me and many other mothers, fathers, and families.

What should we expect from our young married couples? I am very concerned about my son who has been married for seven years. He looks very happy and is learning. We all are very fond of his wife. They have B"H a beautiful child. My son has always been close to his siblings. However, since his marriage, he rarely calls or visits them. He and his wife spend many Shabbosim with his wife's parents and her married brothers and sisters. They visit us occasionally but he has little contact with his own brothers and sisters. I know he has always felt very close to them and they to him. They have invited him for Shabbos, but he never comes. They never even go to visit or call on the phone.

*We don't want to interfere with his
marriage, but we are concerned. Is this what
is to be expected when a son gets married?
Enjoy him before — because he will be
totally absorbed by his wife's family? Is it
just in-laws who insist that their sons come
to visit and who see their sons?*

*I am concerned because this is the first
sign of emotional abuse — separation from
family. I have no other reason to think
of abuse. We very much miss having him
involved (even a little). Sometimes I ask,
"Have you spoken to Shmuly (his brother)?"
It's always no.*

*Please advise me. Should I just ignore
this, as long as he seems happy? Are
there characteristics I can be aware of
in girls to try to make sure my younger
sons don't marry wives who will be so
obviously possessive — or in this what is
to be expected in any marriage? We are very
fond of my daughter-in-law, but what has
happened?*

Find an opportunity when you have time and privacy, such as taking the couple out to lunch. Say something like, "I'm wondering if there's something that we have done that makes either of you less than comfortable coming to us. I see that you two spend a lot of time with (wife's name) family and less with us. We miss you and we'd like to see more of you. We love you both very much, and I'm wondering if we may have inadvertently done something, or if there's something you feel uncomfortable with that we can correct."

Don't bring up the siblings issue, lest they feel they're being "ganged up on." If your son denies it, don't push the point, and don't put the blame on your daughter-in-law. He knows you are aware and that you care. If he denies there's a problem or that anything is wrong, just say,

"O.K., maybe it's just hard in general to have children around less when they get married. I'm glad nothing is wrong."

In absence of anything more concrete, don't conclude that there is abuse. You've opened a door for better communication, and that's all you can do now.

SON-IN-LAW IS SLIPPING IN YIDDISHKEIT

We have a pressing problem that has been bothering us for a long time.

Our daughter is married to a fine man with many special qualities. She is happily married B"H and has a beautiful family KA"H. However, her husband shows obvious signs of modern behavior that is not acceptable to us or to our daughter, who has absorbed and appreciates everything she has seen in our home. This behavior has resulted in a definite yeridah (lessening) in our son-in-law's ruchniyus. We have never mentioned this to him or to our daughter, because we are loathe to upset them or to cause any rift in their shalom bayis. We are truly worried about the upbringing of our grandchildren.

Please advise us how to tackle this problem discreetly and with sensitivity.

It is difficult to answer your question because the details are unclear. For example, it is possible that a man slips in Yiddishkeit and does not put on *tefillin*. It is also possible that one slips in Yiddishkeit because he used to wear a full beard and now has trimmed his beard so that it is short, but he is still in full compliance with halachah. Understandably, this could be a deviation from his family's practice and from the group to which he belonged, but there is a clear distinction between the two types of "slipping."

It is possible that even if one remains in full compliance with halachah, the change might be the beginning of a "slippery slope," and one will slide further down. This may not be predictable, certainly if we do not have all the facts. It would also be important to know whether the change in lifestyle is due to a change in *hashkafah* or is it possibly the result of an emotional problem that the person is undergoing.

Since you have never mentioned your cause for concern to him or to your daughter, it is unclear if she finds his behavior acceptable. Despite her appreciation for her upbringing, they may have decided to raise their children differently.

Based on what is really going on may affect the question of whether there is a responsibility to protect the grandchildren from the change in their father's behavior. Because of the sensitivity of the situation and its possible effect on *shalom bayis,* this is something that would have to be discussed with a *gadol.* If it would be decided that an intervention is necessary, one would have to find a way to do so without disrupting the *shalom bayis.*

SUGGESTING BABY NAMES

*I have read several times your opinion that the naming of a newborn is the right and responsibility of the baby's parents. I fully agree that the decision is up to the parents of the newborn. However, in discussing your opinion with others, some feel that the grandparents of the newborn do not even have the right to **suggest** a name that they would like to be considered for the baby. If there are no immediate names to be given, how are the parents* *of the baby supposed to know of potential names, people who do not yet have a name, great-grandparents, etc, if they are not suggested? Did you mean to be taken so literally?*

Grandparents may tell the children that there are family members who have not yet had children named after them, and ask if they would consider these names. But this is contingent on it being no more than a suggestion, and grandparents should not be offended if the children choose another name.

I know of a situation when a grandparent flew off the handle when his son told him what he had named the baby, and insisted that his son go to *Minchah* and add the name the grandfather wanted. The son did not want to appear to be a fool, so he went to a different shul for *Minchah* to give the added name. I don't know what the validity of this is. I am only familiar with adding a name for someone who is, *chas v'shalom*, sick. I know that some *gedolim* do not approve of adding a name even then, although it is a widely accepted practice.

There are also parents who wish to give a *"shem hakodesh"* rather than a Yiddish name, and it is difficult to fault them for that. Some feel that other children may mock a child who has a Yiddish name that sounds funny to them

While on the subject, I wonder if anyone can enlighten me as to when about "naming after" began. I don't recall anyone in Torah, *Neviim*, or *Kesuvim* being named Avraham, Yitzchak, or Yaakov. The first case we find, to the best of my knowledge, is in the descendants of Hillel, with repetition of the names Shimon and Gamliel. Among some of Sephardic heritage, it is an honor to name a child after a living grandparent. It would seem that the naming issue has been blown out of proportion. It should certainly not be permitted to be a reason for causing anguish.

SHALOM BAYIS

MUST I STAY IN AN ABUSIVE MARRIAGE?

I'm in an abusive marriage. I'm not going to bother you with the details. It's like all the other stories you've heard. I've tried to stay in the marriage for the children's sake, and also, I really don't have a way to support myself. But all that aside, I can't take this for the rest of my life, and so my question is, can an abuser change with therapy? I've heard that an abuser never changes. Is that true? If there is any hope for change, I'll try to stick it out.

One cannot make a general statement that all abusers cannot change. That said, unfortunately, the track record for change is not great. Part of this may be due to the paucity of therapists with expertise on treating the abuser, but primarily it is lack of motivation or lack of awareness on the part of the abusive person.

The reason some abusers do not change is because they are not aware that they are abusers! This may sound strange, but even a person who has been frankly abusive, physically and/or emotionally, may not think of his/her behavior as abusive. Even if the person admits to it and promises to discontinue abusive behavior, this promise may not be worth much because *he/she just doesn't realize that the behavior is abusive.* It is much like trying to get a blind person to see an object or a color. Regardless of how much you may try to convince him and even regardless of how much he may try, he just can't do it. Obviously, the victim of abuse needs counseling on how to proceed with his/her life.

Each case needs careful evaluation by a therapist competent in domestic abuse to assess whether the abuser is capable of change and if he/she is motivated. You may get a referral to a therapist by calling the Shalom Task Force, 1-888-883-2323 (see Appendix for a partial list of referral agencies).

ABUSIVE SON WISHES TO BEGIN *SHIDDUCHIM*

I have a son in his low twenties who is very interested in beginning to go out and eventually get married. The problem is his abusive and violent nature. Any family member becomes fair game. If he doesn't get his way whenever he wants to do something, he will launch into a vitriolic diatribe of a very abusive nature. Of course he can be charming, but that is just the problem. I am certain that when dating he will be on his best behavior and make all the right moves. The problem is once he settles down and marriage becomes more familiar he will launch into his familiar tirade when a situation presents itself. I know this, because it didn't take too long for him to go after our son-in-law who didn't do or say anything negative to him.

My wife and I don't know what to do. We fear that he will marry and ruin some good girl's life as well as his own. We wanted him to go to counseling but he refuses. Someone suggested possible classes. Is this a realistic path? Do you have any suggestions?

I believe you are right: unless he changes his behavior he may bring ruin to himself, a young woman, and to children.

It is my recollection that if a young man or woman has a problem which, if the other side were aware of, they would hesitate to accept the *shidduch,* anyone who knows this is obligated to warn the other party. Failure to do so is a violation of *lo taamod al dam rei'acha.* Parents are not exempted from this obligation. I suggest you verify this with a *posek.*

You should tell your son, "Son, we know you have a serious behavior problem that could ruin your marriage and hurt a young woman. You can overcome this with proper counseling. If you neglect to do so, we will be obligated by halachah to warn a potential *kallah* of your behavior. If she continues with the *shidduch,* that will be her decision.

"You can understand how painful it is for parents to do something which will jeopardize their child's *shidduch,* but we are convinced that unless your problem is resolved, you will be doing great harm to yourself and to a young woman. We will do this out of sincere concern for you."

If your son knows you are sincere, he may accept counseling. If your son rejects counseling, I think you are bound to do as above. (Again, check with a *posek.*)

PITCH IN FOR *SHALOM BAYIS*!

We've been married five years. My wife is a
tremendous person. She is very intellectual
She is a teacher, and reads many sefarim
and books to prepare her lessons. The
one problem is that she is not at all a
balabusta. She leaves the supper dishes
undone, and when I come to breakfast, the
fleishige dishes from last night's supper
are still on the table. I can see why this
is — her mother is exactly the same way.
In addition, she obviously enjoys reading
her books more than housework. I've talked
to her about this, but I've gotten nowhere.
It's very irritating to me to have a sloppy
kitchen. How can I convince her that it is
important to be a balabusta?

A young man came to Hagaon Harav Gifter with a similar problem. Harav Gifter came to his home, took a broom, and showed him how to sweep the floor. Your supper dishes would not be on the breakfast table if you put them in the sink and washed them.

As you've noted, this may be the way she has been accustomed to in her mother's home, but there is a way she might change this lifestyle.

First, as I said, do the dishes yourself. Second, go out of your way to show how you care for her and do things that please her. She is a bright and studious woman, so show her that you value and appreciate her intellectual strengths. It's always good to ask, "What can I do to make you happy?" Very often, her awareness that you are doing things to please her will result in her doing things that will please you.

JAM YESTERDAY, JAM TOMORROW

I have been married to my dear wife for over ten years now, yet some things never seem to change!

Early on in our marriage I noticed that my wife had a bad habit of failing to screw lids on securely after use. Thus, each time I would pick up a jar of jam or honey, etc., there was a real risk of the jar crashing to the floor. I gently pointed this out to her and explained the merits of tightening jar lids after use.

This advice clearly fell on deaf ears, as now, many years into our marriage, the situation remains unchanged.

Can you please explain why some people fail to recognize and act upon sound logical reasoning, even when it is presented to them in a friendly, non-confrontational manner? Also, am I to give up on ever expecting her to change her ways, or can you suggest a method of dealing with such situations that may achieve the desired results?

O.K., so this bothers you. But if you know that the caps are not on tight, why not just pick up the jar by holding onto the jar itself rather than by the cap?

I know of no way to make a person change a habit. For whatever reason she continues doing this, logical argument is not likely to be effective.

Obviously, this has been very annoying to you. I cannot make an authenticated statement, but I have seen some writings by *gedolim* that the amount of annoyance a person experiences in a lifetime is *bashert,* decreed from heaven, and that if one annoyance is eliminated, another will take its place.

If this annoyance is the only thing that bothers you in the marriage, there are thousands of husbands who would gladly accept such an annoyance. Unfortunately, some husbands and wives put up with far more severe annoyances than this.

I am not belittling this annoyance. However, in his preparatory *tefillah* Rabbi Elimelech of Lizensk prays "that we might see only the merits in others, and not their faults." Obviously, every attempt should be made to correct a fault, but if nothing works, husbands and wives should concentrate on the positive traits of their spouse's character and praise them for it. Ironically, praising the merits can be quite effective in lessening the magnitude of the faults.

DISCORDANT PARENTING VS. SINGLE PARENTING

At first, when I started reading the article "A Broken Home," my reaction was anger. Let me explain why. I am married to a true ben Torah, baruch Hashem, for many years with a nice-size family. I must admit that I had a very rough beginning and yes, if I had not been mature I definitely would have been divorced by now. I know my husband is a talmid chacham and also knew that he has shortcomings, just like me. Nevertheless I married him and worked hard with professional and non-professional help to get to where I stand today.

This is the reason why I'm bothered when I hear about couples getting divorced. Yes, it wasn't and isn't easy to always be nice and always be forgiving, but isn't it the reason we were created?

Then I read your commentary and I got to see it from a different perspective. Sometimes there are spouses who have very

*rotten middos and will not work to change
the marriage. They can be either abusive,
addicted, or immature, which will in fact,
make it impossible for the other spouse
to live together peacefully. In that
case a divorce would be recommended. As
you explained, a child growing up in a
home where there is no harmony will have
emotional problems and scars.*

*My question is then as follows. I have
a close acquaintance who has a horrible
marriage with a spouse who has rotten
middos and is at times emotionally abusive.
It is very clear that their children have
emotional problems, and some of them are
treading that same rotten path.*

*Wouldn't it be beneficial for the children
and spouse that the parents divorce? At
least then the children won't get to see and
learn these all the damaging traits. Yes,
they have been through marriage counseling
and even separation. But being the person
the abusive spouse is, nothing has changed!
Old habits have stayed the same and it gets
worse as the kids grow older and learn
to follow the destructive behaviors. It
is extremely painful to watch time go by
and see people suffer and suffer - being
prisoners in their own home.*

*Is there something I can do to help the
situation?*

The Talmud says that the *mizbe'ach* (The Altar in the *Beis Hamikdash*) weeps for a person who divorces his wife (*Gittin*, 90a). The common interpretation is that the *mizbe'ach* bewails the tragedy of a failed marriage. Another interesting interpretation is that the *mizbe'ach* is accustomed to the sacrifice of animals, and weeps when a human is sacrificed.

There can be a number of considerations that determine whether it is best for the couple to separate or to stay together in spite of their problems. This requires very serious attention by a *rav* competent in family issues or by a Torah-true competent marriage therapist. The complications of divorce are many, and all factors must be taken into account. Sometimes it is necessary to amputate a diseased limb, with full awareness of the hardship that this will cause, but the option of not amputating may result in loss of life.

In a case such as the one you mentioned, where there is frank abuse, it is not only the abused spouse who suffers, but, of course, the children. Children of an abusive marriage have a greater likelihood of becoming abusers or victims, depending upon with which parent they identify.

Your role in this case is to provide a listening ear and to suggest that your friend consult a therapist with expertise in abusive relationships. She needs to know what her options are and be guided to weigh the pros and cons of each option for herself and for the children.

LIVING FAR FROM FAMILY

We are in a real dilemma.

When we were married, my husband was to enter professional school in another city. We moved there, and although we never said so in so many words, my assumption was that after he graduated, we would return to our home city where our families live.

During the four years that we spent away, my husband developed roots in the community and made professional contacts. He now feels very secure in this community, and returning to our home town would be starting from scratch. Career-wise, he sees his future here, and I can certainly see his point.

However, I am much closer to my family than my husband is to his. I want my children to be close to their grandparents, *aunts, and uncles. The idea of visiting them just a few times a year is not to my liking. My husband understands my feelings, but is very insecure about making the move.*

We can't come to a decision. Can you suggest a way to resolve this?

This reminds me of the story of the rabbi who listened to the argument of one litigant and said, "You are 100% right." The other litigant presented an argument that was the diametric opposite, and the rabbi said, "You are 100% right." The rebbetzin, who overheard this, said, "They cannot both be 100% right." The rabbi said, "You are 100% right."

I don't know of any way to resolve a problem when the two opposing options are both 100% right. Either way you decide will disappoint someone. You may get some clarification by discussing the problem with a third party who can be objective. In such a situation, I suggest placing the issue before *daas Torah*.

Obviously, you are going to have to come to a decision, one way or the other. It is important that after you have acted on your decision, *do not second-guess!* Nothing can be achieved, except heartache, by saying, "If only we had done things my way." Looking back is a mistake.

Be careful not to let your decision become divisive. Even though one of you will not get your desire, do everything possible to have a positive attitude and be supportive of each other.

On the other hand, your decision is not written in stone! After an agreed-upon term, you and your husband can reassess the situation and decide if you are both happy with the way things are working out.

TEASING HURTS

I shouldn't really complain, but I have a problem. We've been married for three years.

*My husband is a wonderful person. He helps
around the house and is a talmid chacham.
Only one thing bothers me. He is a teaser.
He thinks teasing is a joke, but sometimes he
says things teasingly that really hurt me. On
a few occasions I've gone into the bedroom to
cry. But when I tell him that, he just shakes
it off and says he's only joking. Is there
anything I can do to stop this?*

Your husband may not understand that a "harmless" joke can be painful

You may tell your husband that there is usually nothing wrong with a friend giving someone a pat on the back, saying, "How are you doing, pal?" It is a socially accepted gesture. However, if this friend happens to have a severe sunburn, that friendly pat can be very painful. You may tell him that you know he does not mean to hurt you, but that because of your sensitivity, his "friendly" well-meaning teasing may hurt you deeply.

Since you know that your husband has no intention of hurting you, you might want to investigate why his teasing is so often painful to you. Sometimes our emotions are super-sensitive, very much like sunburned skin. There can be a variety of reasons for this. A child who was humiliated when kids made fun of her may retain a sensitivity, and a teasing comment that was meant as a joke may evoke the pain of an earlier experience.

You might react to "innocent" comments made by other people if they touch a raw nerve. Sunburn goes away by itself, but overly sensitive emotions usually do not. You may want to relieve yourself of this exquisite sensitivity by discussing it with a therapist.

WIFE FORGETS THE LIGHTS

*We've been married for seven years and we
have a wonderful relationship, but there's*

one thing that annoys me. My wife never turns off the light when she leaves a room. I can come down in the morning and find that several lights were on all night. I've pointed this out to her numerous times, but it did not change things. Do you have any suggestions?

Yes. My suggestion is that before you retire at night, turn off all the lights.

CAUGHT IN A TRAP

I hope that this is the correct forum for such a question. I know that there have been many discussions about the internet. I recently found out that my husband has been visiting inappropriate websites. My husband comes from a frum home. He recently started working to support our growing family, and learns quite a few hours a day. He is a very warm, loving, devoted husband and father. He is currently seeing a frum therapist to help him with this, as he knows it is assur (and that I will not tolerate it).

My questions are as follows: Should I be in touch with the therapist as well? Am I supposed to constantly ask him if he is being careful when he does go on the computer for business? And lastly, how do I restore some of the respect and trust that I had for my husband and no longer have because of this whole matter?

I n response to your question about being in touch with the therapist, the professional standards on the relationship between a therapist and client require absolute confidentiality. Unless the client gives specific permission, the therapist may not divulge anything that transpires in therapy. If you feel there is something that you wish to communicate to the therapist, it is best to write to him. There is concern that the client may assume that any conversation between the therapist and another person is a breach of confidentiality.

It is to your husband's credit that he recognizes that he has been caught in a trap from which he cannot extricate himself on his own. In addition to his sessions with the therapist, it would be beneficial if he installed a service that filters his internet access to only those sites he needs for his business.

It is to be hoped that your husband will overcome his problem. However, you cannot control him, and the desire to overcome it must be his own. Checking up on him or continually asking him is counterproductive.

When your husband succeeds in overcoming this problem, and assuming that he does what is necessary for proper *teshuvah*, he then deserves to be respected. When there is true *teshuvah*, the person is at a level which the Talmud considers superior to someone who had not sinned (*Berachos*, 34b).

FRIEND DEMEANS HUSBAND

I am, B"H, a wonderfully happy married 24-year old woman with children. I have a friend, the same age, married for 3-4 years, with a child. I cannot help but hear and feel that things are not quite as they should be between her and her husband. She has an extremely strong character, insists on always being right, and openly puts down her husband. Her own parents were divorced many years ago (her father has since

remarried, and has a happy, hemishe, normal
family, B"H) and because I know her for
that long, it upsets me terribly to see her
following in her mother's direction. I feel
I must do something but I am not trained or
experienced to deal with this, and I feel
that my comments will fall on deaf ears,
for though our friendship is strong, she is
so defensive and overpowering that there is
no way she will ever admit to herself that
there is a problem.

How do I get her to realize that she must
change? Should I get involved at all?

I f you feel that there is no way she will ever admit that there is
a problem, then there is no point in bringing it up to her. Nor
can you tell the husband that he should not let her act this way
toward him.

However, if the husband should express his displeasure with the
way she relates to him, then he should be advised to bring his problem to someone with established competence in marriage counseling.
If your observation is correct, there is no point in suggesting that
they both see a marriage counselor, since she doesn't see that there is
a problem. If he feels there is a problem, he should consult someone
himself for guidance on how to act or react. With proper counseling,
he may be able to act in a way that will cause her to act differently.

If the husband says nothing, there is nothing you can do.

ENVIOUS OF FRIEND'S MARRIAGE

I am a 32-year-old woman from a yeshivish
family. My father is a businessman who has
daily shiurim and takes his Torah very

*seriously. When it was my time for a shidduch,
I wanted a fine ben Torah who would be a
businessman like my father or a professional.
Although I admired full-time learners, I
didn't feel that would be my lifestyle.*

*My father thought otherwise, and I was
introduced to a young man who wanted to
be a long-time learner. He had wonderful
middos and came across as very considerate.
My father urged me to marry him, and I did.
We have B"H four children. My husband is a
wonderful person, kind, considerate, a devoted
father, just what any woman would want.*

*So what's my problem? My friend, with whom
I was very close through high-school and
seminary, did marry a ben Torah who is a
professional, and their income and standard of
living are much higher than ours. They can go
on cruises and afford many things we cannot.*

*I know I shouldn't feel this way, but I
can't help feeling that if my father had
respected my wishes, I could have had that
lifestyle. I know I shouldn't be envious,
but I am. I fargin my friend her luxuries,
but I wish I also had them. I feel guilty
for feeling like this. It isn't fair to my
husband, who is really an ideal person and
totally devoted to Torah. What can I do to
rid myself of the thought that I could have
done better? I don't like to feel this way,
but I can't help it.*

I t's a mistake to compare ourselves to others, but if we do, we
should follow the phrase, *"bashamyim mimaal v'al haaretz
mitachas,"* which has been interpreted to mean that in spiritual
things, always look above you at who is higher and greater spiritually
than you are, and when it comes to earthly, material things, look at
those who are beneath you and have less than you do.

You have the great *zechus* of having a husband who is a true *ben Torah* with fine *middos*. Throughout history, there have not been many people who had *Torah ugedulah bemakom echad*, both wealth and great Torah scholarship. It seems that we have to make a choice, and every person is free to choose.

In *Pirkei Avos* we are told to calculate the gain of a mitzvah against its cost. Whatever cost there is in doing a mitzvah is far, far outweighed by its enormous merit. Of course, you have no way of knowing whether you would really have had a more luxurious lifestyle had you married a professional person. But let us assume that you have sacrificed some luxuries to have a husband who is a serious *talmid chacham*. While there is no denying that luxuries may be enjoyable, just how long does the pleasure of an enjoyable experience last? The delight of a tasty delicacy is gone soon after you've eaten it, and this is true for all earthly pleasures. By contrast, the *simchah shel mitzvah* lasts much, much longer.

In spite of this realization, it may still be difficult to overcome feelings. Ramchal in *Mesillas Yesharim* and *Tanya* both state that our actions impact on our feelings. Intellectually, you know how fortunate you are to have your husband, but your intellectual knowledge does not affect your feelings. Do what *Mesillas Yesharim* and *Tanya* recommend. *Act* according to what you know to be right. Every day, say an extra *tefillah* of *hodaah*, gratitude to Hashem for what He has given you. Your repeated acts of expressing gratitude will overcome your feelings that you might have done better.

You can receive additional help by discussing your feelings with one of the *gedolei Torah*.

HUSBAND DOES NOT ENJOY LEARNING

I am, Baruch Hashem, very happily married. I have a wonderful, kind, and loving husband who will do anything for me.

However, I am very bothered by the fact that my husband does not enjoy learning Torah. He's simply not made for it (if that's possible.) He lacks tochen, depth, and isn't even fluent in his berachos or other basic things. This truly breaks my heart.

Frequently my husband is in full-time kollel. He feels no satisfaction with himself although he doesn't share his feelings with me.

Unfortunately, I drop hints to my husband showing him that I am not happy with his learning abilities. He is not to blame; rather, he was born without a clever head.

How am I supposed to respect him when I don't feel he deserves it?

What s'char do I get if my husband is not a learner?

It is known that the woman has the power to persuade her husband to learn Torah. How can I do this?

I must add that I am Baruch Hashem considered a very clever girl and I always begged Hashem to find me a talmid chochom as a husband.

How do I tackle my marriage?

It is important to know that learning Torah is a great mitzvah even if a person feels he does not understand it well. The Chasam Sofer had a student who felt that he simply could not grasp Talmud. The Chasam Sofer assigned other students to help him, he persisted in learning, and actually became a great Torah scholar.

Inasmuch as your husband goes to *kollel*, even though he does not feel satisfied, and is willing to do anything for you, you have adequate reason to respect him. Rabbi Yitzchak Silverstein of Bnei Brak quotes R' Chaim Vital as saying that if a husband does not treat his wife properly, his mitzvos are discounted. People with fine *middos* deserve to be respected.

Many people who do not readily grasp something write themselves off as "not having a head for it." You may apprise your husband of this, and tell him that he may have unjustifiably given up on himself. If he has a problem with learning, he should discuss this with one of the *Roshei Yeshivah* who have had experience with such problems. You may tell him that you are aware that he is unhappy with himself, and that there is no reason to suffer unnecessarily when the situation could be helped.

There are many aspects of Torah that are more easily understandable, such as *sifrei mussar*. These are important for women to learn as well as for men. Try to have a regular *shiur* with your husband in *Mesillas Yesharim* or *Nesivos Shalom*.

Pirkei Avos says that there are 48 *middos* that are necessary for the acquisition of Torah. The *zechus* of learning these *sefarim* and developing his *middos* may actually enable your husband to grasp other aspects of Torah and feel better about himself.

Simchah is vital for good functioning of the mind and understanding of Torah. Try to make your home a cheerful environment. The *Chinuch* says that our behavior impacts on our feelings, and *Mesillas Yesharim* also stresses that one should act *b'simchah* even if one does not feel it, because the actions will bring on *simchah*. A cheerful attitude can increase one's motivation and understanding.

Some men who do not adjust to full-time learning may go to work and be *koveah ittim l'Torah*. They deserve to be respected and appreciated no less than those who are full-time scholars. Both Yissachar and Zevulun are meritorious.

FRESHEN UP!

This is a subject that I have agonized over for many years. Who should and how most effectively do we teach our young men to take a shower daily, use deodorant, brush their teeth, etc.

People must have different senses of smell. This is a very sensitive topic — I find it very difficult to mention to my husband. Why doesn't he realize that he is not presenting himself well? So many men shower only once a week, for Shabbos. It is so hard for a wife to broach this subject sensitively? How can I explain to my grown sons? Should the Rebbe in yeshivah be telling the bachurim that this is the part of the "dress" of a talmid chacham? Just as we shouldn't wear a suit with a stain, so should we be and smell fresh and clean.

B odily cleanliness is absolutely essential. The Talmud states that when Hillel left the *Beis Midrash*, his disciples asked him where he was going. "To do a mitzvah," Hillel said. "What kind of mitzvah?" they asked. "I'm going to the bathhouse," Hillel said. "Why is that a mitzvah?" they asked. Hillel answered, "The statues [images] of the emperor are washed and cleaned regularly. How much more so I, who was created in the image of Hashem, must keep myself clean" (*Vayikra Rabbah*, 34).

There is also an issue of *chillul Hashem* if a *talmid chacham* appears in any way less than meticulously clean. The Talmud says that a *talmid chacham* who has a stain on his clothes deserves the death penalty (*Shabbos*, 114a). This is an extremely harsh judgment, because his lack of cleanliness is a dishonor to the Torah.

It is, therefore, halachically mandatory that a person keep himself clean and avoid being offensive. Of course this should be emphasized by Torah teachers.

MUST MARRIAGE COUNSELOR BE FRUM?

My question relates to my marriage. I have been married now for six years and have two children, baruch Hashem. During the course of the past year, the quality of our marital relationship has greatly declined. I have only fond memories of the warm love and mutual respect that we both once shared. It is very distressing. I know this is based on certain problems that could have been foreseen during the dating period but the point of my letter is to focus on the present and not to rehash the past. I am living now so I want to focus on the best solution to my problem today. I feel that we would benefit from marital counseling or therapy of some sort. Is it preferable to see a frum marriage counselor? I feel that this is better because my frumkeit is the foundation of my life. However, if I do research and discover that either there are no frum therapists in my vicinity or there are better non-frum therapists in my area which should I choose? Lastly, do you feel that people should work on their marriage at any and all costs or should they not sacrifice their happiness to such a great degree? I would really appreciate your wise insight on these matters.

I t is, of course, important to do everything possible to save a marriage that can be pleasant and harmonious. This can often be accomplished through marriage counseling.

The question has often come up about what to do if one does not have access to a *frum* therapist. In many communities, one or more of the rabbis has developed a relationship with a non-*frum* or non-Jewish therapist, wherein it is understood that for any issue pertaining to Yiddishkeit, the rabbi must be consulted. A therapist who does not practice Yiddishkeit may not understand some things that are of great importance to the client. A working relationship between the rabbi and therapist can resolve this problem.

While it is true that there can be issues that are indeed problems within the marriage, it is not unusual for either spouse to have personal issues that are causing distress, but instead of recognizing them as personal issues, he or she blames his or her dissatisfaction on the marriage. It is always easier (and quite natural) to be unaware of one's own shortcomings and very cognizant of others'.

If the first several years of the marriage were pleasant, there is reason to believe that there is much good in the relationship. While some changes in both spouses may be necessary, resolution of problems should not call for any sacrifice of happiness.

LEVERAGE IN A *GET* PROBLEM

In your book on spousal abuse, The Shame Borne in Silence, you are very critical of a husband who exercises control by refusing to give a get. You fail to mention that the wife uses the weapon of refusing to allow him to see the children, which is every bit as bad.

You are absolutely right. If, for whatever reason, a marriage does not work out, there should be no "weapons" at all. A failed marriage should not end up as a war.

It is a severe enough shock for the children to deal with the parents' separation. But if the husband and wife can be reasonable *mentschen* and avoid rancor and battle in the divorce, it greatly diminishes the negative effect on the children.

A man and woman who bring children into the world have an awesome responsibility. If both spouses relinquish their self-centeredness and focus on what is best for the family, many marriage problems can be resolved. But if there is no resolution, the parents owe it to their children to minimize the effect of the separation on them.

It is unconscionable that children should be made to suffer because either or both parents want things his/her way. If the two cannot come to an understanding, they should accept the guidance of a competent *rav*/marriage counselor. If it turns out to be a battle, one of the two may "win," but the children always lose.

Of course, if both husband and wife were really reasonable *mentschen*, perhaps the marriage would have worked out better in the first place.

DISAPPOINTED IN HUSBAND'S YIDDISHKEIT

I have been married for 11 years and B"H I have five wonderful children. My greatest desire was to marry a true ben torah, a masmid, and yirai shomayim. Unfortunately, my husband is none of the above.

You can imagine my devastation in the first months of our marriage, as I realized what I had fallen into. I even contemplated getting divorced but in the end chose to work it out. With time my patience and loving manner won him over and over the years he has become much more of a "mentsch," although he's far from perfect.

I was pressured into doing this shidduch and therefore, I keep wondering if this is my real "bashert." Had I not been coerced, I certainly would have looked further. I know that everything is min hashamayim, but even a forced shidduch?

> *Can children grow up "emotionally healthy"*
> *with only one parent "doing it right"? While*
> *the other parent does not "squash" the*
> *children, he has no relationship with them,*
> *he merely "exists" in their lives.*

The concept of *bashert* is not clear. For example, although one may not marry during the *sefira* period, one may make an engagement, lest someone else precedes him and engages the woman (*Orach Chaim,* 493). Now, if *bashert* means that a person always marries the woman destined for him, how could someone else pre-empt him? Furthermore, we have no way of knowing how the marriage to the *bashert* is brought about. Conceivably, one may not have wished to marry the *bashert,* and *hashgacha* arranged that he should. Even a "forced shidduch" can therefore be *min hashomayim.*

You say that your husband has made great progress but that "he's far from perfect." If you have been married for only 11 years, he is still young and can continue his spiritual growth. You might talk with a *rav* to help him grow further.

Obviously, it is not ideal if one parent "merely exists" in the children's lives. You might consider counseling to help him enhance his relationship with the children. It is normal for a father to desire a relationship with his children, and if this is lacking, there may be some things that are blocking this relationship. Counseling may be able to remove these barriers.

COMMUNICATION PROBLEMS

> *I am a newlywed and my personality is about*
> *to ruin my life. I've always been very*
> *sensitive and my mother knows it well.*
> *My childhood experience, I'd rather not*
> *mention. I hoped to get married and forget*
> *the past, but it seems to follow me, to*

the point where going to shul and having an avriech so much as glance in my direction makes me believe he's mocking me. This brings me to misery. In the past my mother kept warning me to talk more, but eventually she left me alone.

Now I can't come home to my naturally happy, good-hearted and devoted wife, like this, so I stay outdoors but eventually, I must come home. And I come home to a most welcoming, beautifully-set dinner table and all I do is to keep silent. If my wife initiates conversation I end up either giving her mussar or criticizing her. This is what I grew up with and my misery just overpowers all the sefarim about shalom bayis. There are weeks when I don't talk to her. My mother keeps nudging me, asking if I talk to her, if she is happy.

Lately I am aware of the changes in my wife. She is no longer so attentive to me, and she has stopped coaxing me to reveal what's bothering me, which makes me angry at her. She has become very withdrawn. I am afraid it's the "silence before the storm." What should I do?

I t will help put your wife's mind at ease if you tell her, "You are wonderful, and I care for you a great deal. My problem in not being able to communicate is something that has been bugging me since childhood, and it is probably related to some early experiences. I thought I'd be able to put all those things behind me when we were married, but they seem to hang on. You've been very patient with me, but inasmuch as I'm not getting any better, I'm going to consult someone to help me get over this." I'm sure she will be very supportive of you.

Some people attribute problems in communicating or being overly sensitive to traumatic experiences. This may be so, but just as often it is not a single trauma but rather being exposed to an environment, either within the family or external to it, that may cause a person to become withdrawn or to keep silent.

Your critical response to your wife is a defense mechanism. You know that you should be more communicative, and when you feel you are unable to, the defense mechanism is to lash out at the other person. Point this out to your wife and let her know that you are aware that your criticisms of her are defensive and unjustified. When you overcome your reticence, you will not need such defenses. Until then, exert restraint rather than criticize. You may say to her, "Please don't withhold conversation. I need to hear you, and eventually I'll be able to respond appropriately."

This is not a "do-it-yourself" job. This has been going on for years. You should enlist the help of a therapist, but realize that even with therapy it is going to take some time before you feel comfortable in communicating.

HUSBAND STAYS OUT LATE

I have been married for almost two years and B"H have good shalom bayis. There is one thing that is very hard for me. My husband goes out with his single friends from time to time and ends up coming home very late, between 2 a.m. and 3 a.m. When he comes home I try to explain to him that he is married and has an obligation to his home and he must be home much earlier. I try to impress upon him how much I want him home. What more can I do to impress this upon him?

Inasmuch as you have good *shalom bayis,* if your husband's coming home late is only an occasional occurrence, and there is no reason to suspect any improper activity (such as gambling), it is probably not worth making an issue about it. However, if it is more frequent or it is really distressing to you, you might suggest to him that you bring your disagreement about this to the attention of a *rav* or counselor to determine whether your request is unreasonable. Hopefully, he will listen to their opinion.

DEGRADING NICKNAME

My mother degrades my family in public, she doesn't take care of us properly, she doesn't cook suppers, buy us clothing that we like, etc. To top it off, my mother made up a nickname for me that I don't like. Whenever a friend of mine calls my house and asks for me by my real name, my mother says, "That's not her name, her name is … (nickname)." Do I have an obligation of kibud em to call myself by the nickname even though my mother gains nothing from it and I am embarrassed by it?

Halachic questions, such as about *kibud em*, should be directed toward a *posek*. However, inasmuch as calling someone by a nickname to which one objects is against halachah (*Bava Metzia*, 58b), it is inconceivable that you are required to answer to it.

HUSBAND SAYS WIFE PROVOKES HIS ABUSE

My wife's family is accusing me of being abusive, and they threw your book, The Shame Borne in Silence, at me.

> *I admit that at times I shouted at her and said very sharp things, but why didn't you write anything about the wife provoking the husband to the point where he can't help reacting? She does things that she knows will irritate me. Am I expected to just sit there quietly and take it all? Doing things she knows I don't like is also abusive.*
>
> *Doesn't Rambam say that a wife should treat her husband like a king?*

I t is wrong for spouses to provoke and irritate one another. However, I cannot accept that you can't help reacting. If your wife provokes you, that is wrong, but it does not justify speaking to or treating her in an abusive manner. Verbal abuse is also abuse.

Rambam indeed says that a wife should relate to her husband with great respect. However, students of the Rambam know that his work must be studied carefully, noting not only what he says but also how he says it.

In *Ishus,* 15:19, Rambam says that the respect of the husband for the wife should be greater than for himself. He should not cause her to fear him, and should speak to her in a soft manner. He should not be tense nor in rage.

Following this, Rambam says that the wife should greatly respect the husband and obey him, treating him royally. Note that Rambam states the halachah that a husband should respect the wife *before* the halachah that she must respect him. This means that it is the husband's duty to *initiate* respect. Furthermore, although it is certainly regrettable if the wife provokes him, Rambam does not qualify his ruling that the husband should not express rage. When the Talmud says that rage is equivalent to *avodah zara,* it does not exempt rage in a response to provocation.

Just as we are obligated to observe Shabbos under all circumstances, and one cannot say, "I couldn't help it" (with the exception of *pikuach nefesh*), neither can one violate the *middos* that a person is required to have and claim, "I couldn't help it."

I hope that you and your wife will have a calm discussion, with the help of a third party if necessary, and agree to be mutually considerate and respectful.

HUSBAND'S YIDDISHKEIT SLIPPING

I am desperate.

I have been married for 14 years, and we have three children. My husband is a fine talmid chacham. He always conducted himself as a talmid chacham should. He had a shiur morning and evening, always davened with minyan, etc.

About a year-and-a-half ago, he began to slip. He would often get up late and daven at home. Gradually he dropped his shiurum. When I brought this to his attention, he said that his Yiddishkeit is none of my business. When I try to talk to him about it, he says that if I nag him, it will only get worse. He will not listen to his father either.

I stopped talking to him about it but it got worse anyway. He doesn't get up until 11 a.m. and davening takes 10 minutes. He is self-employed so he doesn't have to be at work early. We hardly communicate any more.

I told him to talk to his rav, because something is wrong, but he won't hear of it. He certainly will not consider a psychologist. What can I do? I don't think I can go on like this.

A radical change such as this, which is so out of character, may be due to a depression, and this should be evaluated by a psychiatrist, because his behavior is self-destructive, and as you have seen, is progressively worsening.

In such situations, an "intervention" may be necessary. This consists of several people who care about your husband getting together with him in one session. In addition to yourself, there should be his father, any siblings, his *chavrusah*, and his *rav*. You all come together at a time when you know he is at home. Each person expresses his/her concern, stating that they realize that something has happened that is out of character for him, and that he must be in distress, and that he can be helped to return to his old self.

In order to do this intervention you should consult a psychologist, who should first meet with all the people who will participate in the intervention and rehearse what they are going to say and how to react to him. The psychologist should also be at the intervention. A well-conducted intervention can be very effective. It will show your husband that there are a number of people who care for him, who recognize that he needs help. This often overcomes the resistance.

The psychologist can recommend a psychiatrist. If the psychiatric intervention determines that it is not a psychological problem, the *rav*, who participated in the intervention, will then be in a position to work with him.

You can get a referral to a psychologist by calling ECHO (845) 425-9750, or RELIEF (718) 431-9501 (see Appendix).

FRIEND NEEDS COUNSELING

I have a friend who, I feel, needs to go to a marriage counselor but I'm afraid to say anything to her about it. The reason I feel this way is because I know for a fact that she does not get any help from her husband in taking care of the house and their two

children. Even before she had her second
child she kept telling me that she feels
like a single mother and that she hoped her
husband would realize that she needs his
help when the second child would be born.
On rare occasions he has "helped" with the
kids. And by "helped" I mean that he has
watched the kids very reluctantly for a
little while so that she could clean up a
bit. Almost every night he hangs out with
his friends till 1 or 2 in the morning and
then when he can't get up the next morning
to go to work, it's all her fault because
she didn't wake him on time. She couldn't
even kimpurt normally after her second child
was born because as soon as she came home
from the hospital this had to be done, that
had to be done. I can go on and on with
the different examples of how childish and
demanding he is. There were so many times
where I had wanted to say something about
counseling, yet I can't because I don't know
how she will take it. She might feel that
I'm mixing into her personal life and I do
value her friendship. But I can't watch her
torture herself.

I n my book on addiction among high-achievers, I cite an article by a doctor who was admitted to a hospital five times for alcoholism. Each time, his doctor friends wrote a false diagnosis in order to cover up his alcoholism and "protect" him from the consequences of being diagnosed as alcoholic. He almost died as a result of this, and he says, "My friends nearly killed me with their kindness."

It is a mitzvah to reprove someone if he or she is doing wrong. Understandably, a person may resent being criticized, but the Torah requires one to do this, just to be careful not to do it in a way that is embarrassing (*Vayikra*, 19:17). The risk of losing a friendship does not exempt one from this mitzvah.

Your friend needs help in how to relate to her husband. According to your description, they are both suffering. She is not getting the consideration she deserves, and he is living a self-destructive lifestyle, although he is not aware of it. For her to just absorb this is detrimental to both her and him, and eventually to the children.

With proper counseling, she can learn how to act in a way that will eventually improve the situation for everyone. The husband will probably not want to go to counseling, because he sees himself as being perfect and blames her for everything. This is typical.

It is important that she seek competent counseling for herself.

In my trade, we refer to this as "co-dependence." This is a term frequently used in alcoholism, where the alcoholic "plays the fiddle" and the co-dependent "dances to the tune." This same phenomenon occurs even in absence of alcoholism. If your friend can set aside the references to alcohol, she may find helpful advice in *Codependent No More*, by Melody Beatty.

I believe you should tell your friend what you've observed. Even if she should initially resent it, she will ultimately be very grateful to you.

SHANAH RISHONAH IS OVER

I have been married for B"H 3½ years to a wonderful man who treats me Kan ayn horah very well. However, I feel like I've been married forever. After shanah rishonah was over, the flowers stopped being bought every Friday, the birthdays and anniversaries were all of a sudden forgotten. When I remind my husband about an anniversary or birthday, the response I get is, "Big deal." Then if I make a "big deal" out of not celebrating, he does me the big favor and "celebrates" by wishing me a happy birthday or anniversary. Why do some husbands think that they're done

*and over with the flowers and celebrating
once the first year is over? Don't get
me wrong and think that I'm spoiled. I've
always loved flowers and always bought them
even before I was married, it just makes me
feel more special when my husband buys them,
knowing how happy and appreciated it makes
me feel when he does. Why does he feel that
a co-worker's wedding is more important
than going out by ourselves on my birthday
without our two little children tagging
along? Again, I'm not a kvetchy housewife,
I just want my husband to understand that
I feel that going out once in a while and
that celebrating is important to me and to
our relationship.*

There is much about reality that I would like to change, but I must accept reality and try to adjust as best I can.

Your husband's behavior is not at all unusual. We are repeatedly told to consider Torah as being new each day (Rashi, *Devarim*, 11:13), and we make the *berachah*, *"Nosein Hatorah"* in the present rather than in the past tense, so that we should consider the Torah as something new that we receive each day. That is the way it *should* be, but not too many people achieve this level, to feel the enthusiasm and excitement of Torah as though it were totally new.

Most family photo albums have many pictures of the oldest child. We have the camera ready to photograph every new (and even some old) move the child makes. There are not as many pictures of the second child and still fewer of the third child. The seventh child often appears only in pictures of the whole family. That does not mean that the parents love the seventh child any less than the first. That's just the reality of human nature and the busy lives we lead.

I believe that you know that your husband's feelings for you now are no less than in the first year of marriage, and I'm sure that in fact they are much stronger and will continue to grow. However, the manifestation that occurred early in the marriage tends to wane. The same is also true of special days, such as birthdays and anniversaries.

This is one of the ways that men differ from women. Some things that are important to women may not be as important to men.

You might say to him, "I know you care for me deeply, and I'm very happy with you. But, it's so true what the Talmud says, that women are more emotional than men, and things that may not be a big deal for you are significant to me. It makes me happy to receive flowers for Shabbos, and to have birthdays and anniversaries remembered, and I know you really want to do everything to make me happy."

It's also important that you remember *his* birthday and celebrate it. I think he will get the message.

To all men and women who read this column, try to rise above this aspect of human nature. Keep buying flowers for Shabbos, remember special days, and make every year a *shanah rishonah* in this regard.

DIFFERING VALUES

I have been married for a year. My wife is wonderful woman, the daughter of a very frum family. My in-laws are great people, and they are wonderful to me. They are fairly wealthy, and they measure everything by money. They give us more than we need. Their way of showing love is to give things.

My family was different, of very modest means. I grew up feeling that you need money for the necessities of life, not for luxuries. Money was never a symbol of love, so this bothers me. When I say this to my wife, it upsets her, because she thinks I am criticizing her family and rejecting their gifts. How do I get her to understand that material things are not the most important things in life?

Many young men would wish that they had your problem.

I remember a patient in the hospital for the chronically mentally ill. He was extremely obese. On visiting day, his mother would bring him a basket of food and watch with much pleasure as he gorged himself. It was very painful to see that this was the only communication of love between the two.

Different people show love in different ways. Your in-laws obviously mean to show you love, and if this is their manner of doing so, it should be appreciated.

It is possible that your wife may interpret your words as meaning that you consider yourself more spiritual than, and hence superior to, your in-laws. It is possible that you may come across as wanting to win the battle of attitudes. That will repel her.

A much better way is to have sessions of learning *mussar* together. The message of what is really important in life will come across eventually and she will absorb it without feeling that you are being critical of or condescending to her family.

HUSBAND IS POOR PUBLIC SPEAKER

Thank you so much for this column. This is the only place I can think of to turn to with my dilemma. My husband is a brilliant yungerman learning in Lakewood. Not only is he brilliant in his Torah learning but he is very knowledgeable and talented in many other areas as well. He can build walls, decks, bookcases, and just about anything. He can put in new bathrooms and kitchens with plumbing and electricity. He has a very nice, clear voice and can daven and lein beautifully. On Rosh Hashanah he blows the shofar and on Purim he leins the Megillah. He is caring and very giving and anything I ever ask him to do for me is done immediately with a smile. All in all he is really a wonderful person and I am extremely grateful to have him for a husband. There is, however, one major issue that keeps coming up and that bothers me to no end. He is slightly socially awkward. I say "slightly" because it's not something one would notice at first glance. I didn't realize it until we were married for a couple of months. What's strange is that he doesn't realize it at all. He actually loves social gatherings and events. He thinks that he has many friends and that he can talk to anyone. And he can and he does — but people often don't understand what he is trying to say. He often leaves out details and so people are left guessing — Who? What? When? Where?

He also tends to talk about himself and our children a lot. For example, my uncle once asked him what time night seder is over. He told him the time but then added, "but of course when I go home I continue learning for a couple more hours."

The time when all this reaches a peak and bothers me the most is when it comes to family simchos and speeches. My husband, as they say, is easy prey. He seems to think that he is a most amazing speaker. Therefore, whenever he is asked to speak, he agrees. And because it's always hard to find people to speak, he is always asked. The problem is that he is a terrible speaker. He may have a clear, loud voice but his speeches are very boring and tend to go on and on and on. Either he'll just say a long dvar Torah or, when he does have nice things to say about the chassan or kallah and the

*family, he speaks in such an awkward way
that I just feel like running out of the
room from embarrassment. I would be able to
handle it if it just happened once a year
or so. But with a large extended family,
he is asked to speak quite frequently and
he always says yes. We just finished a week
of aufruf, chasunah, and sheva berachos
for his brother. My husband spoke several
times during the week. I feel so humiliated
in front of everyone. I just can't stand
it anymore. The fact that his siblings sit
through the speech continually making fun of
him doesn't really help either. What should
I do? I once tried hinting that when people
constantly see the same person at the podium
they get bored so maybe he shouldn't speak
at every occasion. But he seems to think he
is needed and wanted.*

This is an opportune time to cite what some of the commentaries say about the Torah expression, *ezer kenegdo*. Literally, it would mean that the wife should be "opposed" to her husband, which is, of course, absurd. What it does mean is that in order for a wife to be a true *ezer*, a helpmate, she may occasionally have to take a position of *kenegdo*, being critical of him.

This seems to be so in your case. Your husband is ideal in almost every way, but has this single shortcoming. If his speaking results in his siblings making fun of him, and others thinking his speech is boring, you are not doing him a favor by ignoring it.

Your husband knows your appreciation of him is genuine. Tell him that you feel that in this instance you must be the *ezer kenegdo* on his behalf. You may point out to him that this one area, his speaking, is out of synch with his wonderful *middos* and character strengths, and therefore, you want to bring it up to the level of his character assets. You may tell him that he will benefit greatly by a course in public speaking.

There are courses in public speaking for *rabbanim,* and there is no reason he should oppose taking such a course. He will feel that your interest is genuine, and you will be doing him a great favor.

If by some chance he refuses, or he takes the course but his speaking is still not pleasing to you — you must make a concerted effort not to let it bother you. In the broad scheme of things he is everything a husband should be — appreciate what you have. The embarrassment you feel should be mitigated by your blessings.

WHY DO I CONTINUOUSLY BERATE MY HUSBAND?

I am in a serious dilemma and I fear that it may end tragically chas vesholom. Please advise me how to handle my situation.

I am a bright, capable woman from a very talented family, with exceptional, loving, and intelligent parents. They raised us with devotion and patience, and showered us with knowledge and positive encouragement. I have a well-paid job that keeps me stimulated. Baruch Hashem, I excel at what I do — be it cooking, cleaning, or at my job.

My husband is of average intelligence, but not stupid. His parents have no emotional connection with their children. A large part of his chinuch involved rigid rules and criticism. Understandably, his self-esteem is very low. He has little knowledge and I find his way of thinking very naïve, and yet he wants me to accept his views. His lack of capability frustrates me, especially when we are in the company of my (overpowering) siblings. To make things worst, he was diagnosed with a fertility problem a year after our chasunah. The problem is so severe that the doctors give him minimal chances of ever fathering a child. It is needless to mention how insecure he feels.

He is an extremely nice person. He is loyal, understanding, patient, and basically his middos are excellent. He goes out of his way to try to please me.

The funny thing is that I am overly sensitive in our relationship. When he displays a hint of disapproval, or does not show me enough that he cares, I lose control. All my disappointed feelings surface and I attack him without mercy. Unfortunately, my attacks happen too often. He always listens, accepts, and apologizes. He never fails to improve, no matter whatever I demand. But I suspect that my shouting comes from my overall disappointment with my marriage and therefore he never seems to please me.

After such an attack, I feel terribly guilty, to the extent that I cry bitter tears. Then I apologize and shower him with compliments in an attempt to repair the damage. But I am disgusted with myself, for I know I wronged him terribly. Mainly I am very concerned that his emotional health should stay intact.

Is something wrong with me for losing control so often? Is there a way to build a successful relationship? Is my husband in danger of developing emotional problems?

Your strong positive feelings for each other are the basis for an excellent marriage. It is important that the problems be addressed.

Your husband's sensitivity toward you, his fine *middos*, loyalty, understanding, and his desire to please you are invaluable ingredients to a marriage. His desire that you accept his views may be a manifestation of low self-esteem. A person with good self-esteem is not threatened when his views are disputed. He does not always have to be right and can accept criticism, whereas a person with low self-esteem becomes defensive. If his self-esteem can be improved, it may reveal strengths and talents of which he is unaware. He may be much more capable than he appears to be.

By the same token, you indicate that you lose control whenever he shows even a hint of disapproval or does not show you how much he cares. Your statements, "He never fails to improve no matter whatever I demand," and "He always listens, accepts, and apologizes" indicate that he cares very much for you, yet you feel insecure about the extent of his caring. I suspect that you, too, are bothered by low self-esteem, which causes you to doubt whether you deserve his affection. A person who does not feel worthy of being loved may never be satisfied, regardless of how much affection he/she is shown. That may be why you are so sensitive. It is also very likely that the fertility issue is causing painful and unwarranted feelings of inadequacy and perhaps guilt, resulting in your loss of control.

As I've pointed out in my books (*Angels Don't Leave Footprints, Life's Too Short,* and *Ten Steps to Being Your Best*), low self-esteem is the result of *unwarranted* feelings of inferiority, unworthiness, and inadequacy. These can be overcome when a person develops a valid self-image, instead of the negative self-image one grew up with.

Books on improving self-esteem may be helpful, but therapy to acquire a better self-awareness may be necessary. This kind of therapy is not directed toward finding what's wrong with you, but to the contrary, to help you discover what's *right* with you.

I think that if you and your husband are both able to elevate your self-esteem, your marriage can be very happy.

OPTING OUT OF MARRIAGE

I am 24, and the daughter of a very frum family. I don't remember my father, who died when I was two. My mother remarried, and her

*husband was very abusive to her and to me.
Living with him was a horror, and I swore
that I would never get married. I developed
both a fear and a hatred of men, which has
never left me.*

*My brothers and other family members are
pushing me to date and get married. They say
it is the proper thing for a Jewish woman
to do. I can't see it. Why should I make
a man miserable? I have a good job and I'm
comfortable. Why rock the boat?*

When Hashem said, "It is not good for a person to be alone," he was indeed referring to Adam, but this applies to women as well. The desire for companionship and the maternal instincts are your natural components, and to frustrate them may result in unhappiness. There are many women who, unfortunately have not met their *basherte*, and they are indeed suffering.

True, there are some women who have chosen a career over family life. The Scriptural mitzvah to marry and have children is not incumbent upon a woman, and she is free to choose to remain single, although she is encouraged to have a family. However, in your case it is not really a choice. Rather, you have been frightened away from marriage because of exposure to an abusive man. Although you know that most men are caring and not abusive, your emotion outweighs your logical thinking.

I suggest that you consult a therapist to overcome your fear and hatred of men. If you then choose a career over family life, it will be a matter of choice rather than of being forced into solitude by fear.

TO "BROK" OR NOT TO "BROK," THAT IS THE QUESTION

---

*With Pesach approaching, I'd like your
advice.*

> *My family eats gebroks, but my husband's family does not. It's no problem for me at his home, because I can live without knaidlach. But last year, at my parents' home, we had to make a separate table for the two of us.*
>
> *It just felt strange. Is there any solution to this problem? I don't think it's fair that my whole family should have to give up knaidlach and other gebroks to accommodate my husband.*

I cannot give you a solution. This question should be submitted to *daas Torah*, to determine what is the right thing to do.

I hope a solution can be found. It is important to realize that family unity is so important that the very first mitzvah given to our ancestors as they were liberated from the enslavement in Egypt was the *korban Pesach*. This *korban* was to be shared with the family (*Shemos*, 12:3). In fact, the *korban Pesach* may not be divided and eaten in two separate houses (ibid., 12:46). It is a family mitzvah, stressing the importance of family unity, and two separate tables do not express unity.

I'm sure that everyone will respect the opinion of *daas Torah*.

AM I ONLY SECOND FIDDLE?

> *We've been married for three years. From the onset, I've felt that my wife's primary loyalty is to her family rather than to me. There are times when our needs conflict, and I can see that her consideration for them comes first. I cannot tolerate being second fiddle. We have a child and another on the way, and I do not want our marriage to fail. What do you suggest?*

This is too important and too complex an issue to be dealt with adequately in a newspaper column, and I suggest that you consult a Torah-true marriage counselor. However, I would like to highlight several points to bear in mind.

This is not an infrequent problem, which can go both ways. Either a husband or a wife may exhibit what is seen as a preference for his/her family.

We come into the world as helpless little children, and we can survive only by virtue of our trust in our parents, on whom we depend. As we mature, this dependency should be replaced by a feeling of personal strength. However, along the way, many things may occur that keep a person dependent on one's parents for security. For these people, separation from parents may result in severe anxiety.

When a person marries, the relationship should be such that one develops adequate security in the spouse, so that one is not threatened by letting go of the dependence on parents.

Remember that for about twenty years, your wife's security was in her parents. In three years, she my not have been able to build enough security in her relationship to you to be able to let go.

But it is not only a question of time. You must be able to provide adequate security for her so that she will not be anxious in letting go of her dependence on her parents. Financial security is, of course, important, but it is not everything. She needs to feel that you are there for her. In some marriages, a spouse is motivated more by what he/she can *get* from the marriage rather than what he/she can *give* to it.

In addition, it may be that your wife's parents have emotional and/or physical needs of their own that your wife fulfills for them. She may believe that they need her more than you do, and feels that she has an obligation to be there for them.

It is possible that your wife feels like the second fiddle in your relationship with *your* family? She should feel that she is most important to you just as you want to feel that you are most important to her.

Every person has needs of one's own. I know of a case where the wife said, "I'm sorry, but I just don't have enough respect for my husband. If he would get up every day to go to *minyan* and have a daily *shiur*, it would be different. But I have to wake him several times to get him up." In this case, even if the husband provided an adequate income, it would not be enough. It is important to understand a wife's emotional needs and to provide for them in order for her to feel adequately secure in her husband to be able to let go of the dependence on her parents. Of course, this is equally true when the husband has difficulty letting go of his dependence on his parents.

It is also important for a spouse to understand that one cannot write a permanent contract with parents. All parents pray that their children should survive them.

Every effort should be made to do whatever is necessary to strengthen the marriage bond so that husband and wife feel secure in each other. These are some of the issues that should be dealt with in marriage counseling.

ESCALATING DIVORCE RATES

I'm alarmed. In the past year, two of the weddings I've attended ended up in divorce after only a few months. It used to be that divorce among the frum community was rare, but today there are many divorces. What's happening to us?

We are not immune to environmental influences. *Tehillim* 106:35 says, "They mingled with nations and they learned [emulated] their behavior." In the United States, about 51% of marriages terminate in divorce! Unfortunately, this attitude toward marriage has affected us.

It is obvious that Torah teaches us that the way we relate to even inanimate objects can affect our interpersonal relations. We cover the *challos* Friday night so that the *challah* should not be humiliated when we give the *berachah* for wine preference over the *hamotzi*.

Moshe was told not to smite the water or the sand because they had protected him. Obviously, neither the *challah*, water, nor sand has feelings. Yet the Torah requires that they be respected, because our sensitivity toward *things* may influence our sensitivity toward *people*.

We live in an age of "disposables." I received a Sheaffer pen for my Bar Mitzvah and had it for than twenty years. When I lost it, I felt the loss. Today, I use "throw-away" ballpoint pens. I rarely have one that lasts a week.

I recall taking a radio to be repaired. Today this is impossible. If a radio or tape recorder breaks, you discard it and get another one. We have disposable dishes, cutlery, tablecloths, diapers, silvery *Kiddush* cups, contact lenses, cameras, and what-not. We have developed an attitude that we don't fix things when they go wrong, but discard them and get another. Unfortunately, this attitude has carried over to interpersonal relations. If something goes wrong with a marriage, why bother to fix it? Terminate it and get another one.

But people are not objects. Terminating a relationship has a deep effect on people, and if there are children, the effect on them can be very serious.

The Torah expects us to respect the sensitivity even of things, and certainly objects of *kedushah* command great respect. We must realize that marriage is *kedushin*, and must be treated as such.

Because we live in an environment where human relationships are treated lightly, it is incumbent upon us to study Torah *middos* and incorporate them into our lives.

It is also very important that we do not follow the prevailing cultural attitude, according to which people expect primarily to "get" from a marriage rather than "give" to it. Animals know only how to take, not to give. Twice in the *sheva berachos* we say *"yotzer haadam"* to remind *chasan–kallah* that they must be true *mentschen,* which means to be able to give of oneself.

Today's world is dominated by self-gratification. We must take great caution that we do not get *shlepped* along. It is vital that young men and young women learn much more about what marriage is and the obligations and responsibilities that it entails. Only then will marriage have the respect and durability it deserves.

Appendix

PARTIAL LISTING OF
REFERRAL AGENCIES

ECHO —(845) 425-9750

RELIEF — (718) 431-9501

BIKUR CHOLIM — CHECK YOUR LOCAL PHONE BOOK

ALCOHOLICS ANONYMOUS — CHECK YOUR LOCAL
   PHONE BOOK

MASK — (718) 758-0400

SHALOM TASK FORCE — (718) 337-3700

JAADD — JEWISH ASSOCIATION FOR ATTENTION
   DEFICIT DISORDER — (718) 435-0101

NEFESH — (201) 530-0010

OHEL — (718) 851-6300

COUNTERFORCE — (718) 854-7730

JEWISH BOARD OF FAMILY AND CHILDREN'S SERVICE
   — (718) 435-5700

YITTI LEIBEL HELP LINE —   (718) HELP NOW